Return to Calvary

Effie Katharine Dix Ford

iUniverse, Inc.
New York Bloomington

Return to Calvary

iUniverse books may be ordered through booksellers or by contacting:

iUniverse
1663 Liberty Drive
Bloomington, IN 47403
www.iuniverse.com
1-800-Authors (1-800-288-4677)

ISBN: 978-1-4502-4258-5 (sc)
ISBN: 978-1-4502-4259-2 (dj)
ISBN: 978-1-4502-4260-8 (ebook)

Printed in the United States of America

iUniverse rev. date: 07/28/2010

The following is a collection of short stories and poems written by my grandmother, while residing in Baltimore, Maryland more than six decades from the time she was a little girl in "the friendliest place in the world; Calvary," a suburb of Crisfield, Maryland.

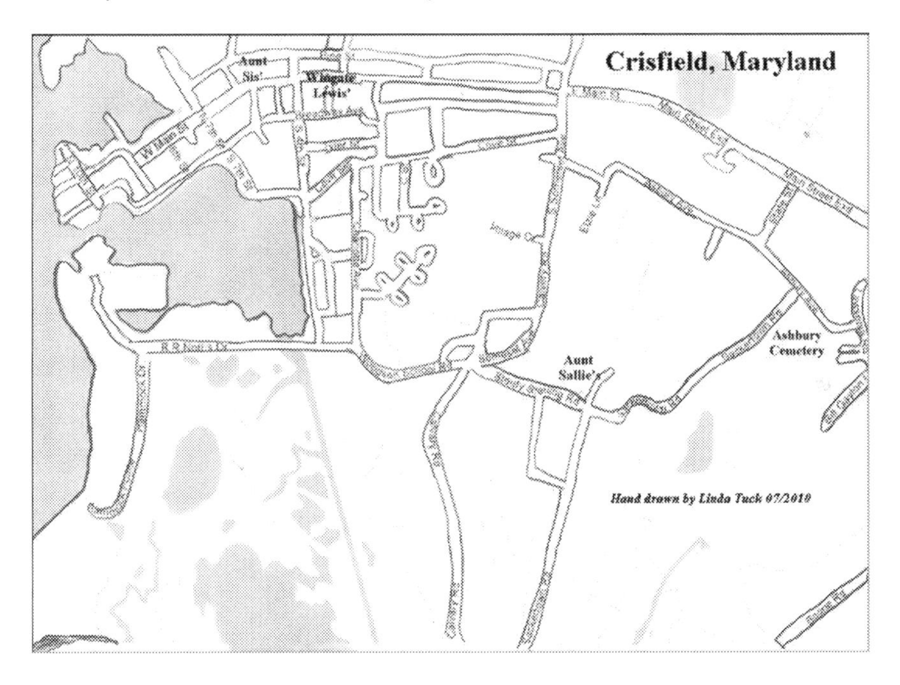

Her father ran a seafood packing business out of Crisfield in the early 1900s, the "Dix, Sterling and Company". It supported four families for over 35 years, my great grandfather, William Dix, his brother, Sam Dix, Stouten Sterling Senior (Aunt Sallie's first husband) and Junior. These stories are of the people and milestones that occurred during her childhood. They tell of a "time gone but not forgotten".

Dedicated to the memory of my grandmother, Effie Katharine Dix Ford 1903 – 1981

Many years ago in the early 1980s I started recording our family's history. This year (2010) marks a century has passed since Effie and Thelma played in Calvary. Our family no longer owns the house in Calvary. We have only our memories of it and the happy times once spent there. This book is for those who too want to remember Effie and visit Calvary, if only, as Effie might recite from one of her favorite passages, *"Here in these pages until they crumble to dust away."*

My hope is they will last forever…

Table of Contents

OH, SO BLUE

A dictionary is an interesting and inspiring book. There is poetry in it. Some words are defined so beautifully.

Remembrance, blue and bluebell are three. Once I had an English teacher who told our class that if asked to write an essay on any subject, first look up the meaning in the dictionary, and it would give you a beginning. If it was Beauty, look up beauty. Friendship, loyalty any subject at all.

So, Remembrance -N.: a remembering or being remembered; the power to remember; the extent or time over which one can remember; a souvenir; a keepsake.

These thoughts in this little story come over a bridge of six and a half decades of remembrance.

Blue - bloo. adj of the color of the clear sky or the deep sea; out of the blue, as from the sky; unexpected. bluely. Adv. Blueness-N.

Blue-bell - bloo bell N.: Any of various plants with blue bell shaped flowers.

Blue- bonnet -bloo-bon-it N. the Cornflower; a blue flowered lupine.

I have heard of blue-bonnets. I wonder how they look. The shade of blue; is it pale, medium or bright? They grow in Texas, but that is far away from our fair free state. (The politicians talk this way about Maryland.) I hope someday to see blue-bonnets. The dictionary sounds intriguing about them.

Our blue-bell is the bluest blue you can imagine and the last of April they come. They bloom twice, in April and again in June; in May they rest.

The April ones are small; but in June, they are big, with long stems and larger bells. They are in enormous clumps that cover the field. Oh, so blue, God gave them color so generously.

We have another little pale blue flower, that must not be slighted, called blue-box. It is very delicate both stem and flower and its petal are square. These grow profusely all summer long.

Somewhere I have read there are few blue flowers in nature. Not so, there seems to be to be many. These tiny blue-box have an ethereal appearance, as if they were not really meant to be. Every summer they come so perhaps they are like some people; they look delicate but are very strong.

Blue-box is not in the dictionary. Perhaps it was one Aunt Sallie named. She named many of nameless wild flowers. The square petals really made them look like a tiny blue-box.

Aunt Sallie really had a fine imagination and I reaped a lovely harvest from my daily association and love for her. I was the one who really knew her. I'm sure far better than her own three children. Her two boys went away to college at age 13 and 15, and never returned home to live again, only for vacations. Priscilla, her daughter, knew her best, but she was a person sufficient unto herself.

Everything happens for the best.
It is an ill wind that blows nobody good.

Two sayings Calvary people were fond of saying. The second one doesn't even sound like good English. Oh well!

Sometime such terrible things have to happen to make these sayings even remotely believable and yet, much later it would truly seem so.

Like my Uncle Sam dying and the family business falling, made it happen that I spent such happy years in Calvary.

My little boy dying at eleven could never have to fight in a war and be killed, crippled or worse. He would have been just the age for wars that were in the near future.

Of course, I would have been happy on the other side of the woods, but not the enchanted happiness that awaited me with Aunt Sallie and Priscilla added to my parents and brothers.

I'm sure when we went to Aunt Sallie's, my father fully expected to go back to our home, just as soon as he recouped the losses of his business. Neither he nor my mother felt they were relinquishing their home. It was just a temporary change. Alas, the bank rented our home; and before the spring came again, our home was burned to ashes. How sad we all felt. We three had been born there. My father's mother and father lived there at one time.

So, at first, it is hard to believe that everything happens for the best. I think I do really believe this old saying, which I do not recall being one of Benjamin Franklin's, The Bible, perhaps? Maybe just people of Calvary to give their hearts ease.

It was the last week in February and a Saturday that a gift of spring was given to us. As I finished my oatmeal, my mother said, "It is a beautiful day.

Let me see." She walked over to the window and looked at the thermometer nailed outside. "It's hard to believe, but it says 69 degrees, and only yesterday it read 32 degrees."

I put on my coat and my crocheted hat that Priscilla had made for me. "I'm going to look for a blue-bell. I wish Thelma was here."

"Effie, it is too early for ...." I heard but I was already out of the door, running to the field beyond the pear orchard.

I couldn't get there fast enough. As I ran along the bank, I noticed someone had been burning the underbrush and small pines.

The next thing I knew I was laying in the field, a four inch or more cut down the side of my leg, close to the bone. It was bleeding, but not too much. I wasn't afraid of blood anyway.

I was knocked breathless for a few seconds; but looking back, I knew what had happened. I had fallen over a sharp pointed burned small pine tree. Oh, how terrible my leg looked, purple, red, pink, green, yellow, it was one of the ugliest things I had ever seen in my life. I drew in my breath. Oh, oh, my mother, she will faint. She must never see it, never, until it was all well anyway!

When things were too bad, my mother left them. Thunderstorms with sharp lightning, fires, accidents affecting those she loved.

I tied my clean handkerchief around my leg and pulled up my torn black stocking, and walked into the field. No, there was nothing, no blue there; just last summer's dried weeds. It was too early for bluebells April was snows away.

The important thing to me was not how much it hurt. In fact, I put that out of my mind. The paramount thought was my mother must not see it.

Maybe it could be called a one-dimensional cut. It was as close as could be to my leg bone. One side was the bone, but it was deep. A small pine has a sturdy root and that burned point was sharp as a knife, and I was running when I fell over it.

Being Saturday, we three children all had baths. My mother's aim was Wednesday and Saturdays in the winter time. After my bath, I put on a clean piece of cloth and made it stay with two rubber bands.

A week went by and it didn't look very much better. It did make my leg stiff, but I washed it carefully every few days and put a piece of clean white cloth on. There were plenty of washed and ironed white rags in a kitchen drawer.

Weeks went by, in March, we had lots of snow. In April came some pretty days and the last week I went to the blue-bell field again, and there they bloomed, blue, oh, so blue. They were small, but I loved them and gathered some happily.

Walking back, I decided to give the first bunch to Miss Henrietta, who loved them, as she loved all the children of Calvary.

Miss Henrietta was Mr. Wash Tull's oldest daughter. He had two. She was one of the nicest people ever put on this earth. She was my Sunday school teacher and friend to every child. One summer she gave us all music lessons. Free, just because she wanted us to learn to play. Every family who didn't have a piano, had an organ, not electric, oh no, these came much later.

We all went to her house one day a week together, then the next week we went each at a separate time. She used a lot of her summer for us.

She had the largest house in Calvary and it had an enormous living room. Of course, there was beautiful furniture in this room, but I saw only the Steinway grand piano. It had a carved lacy wooden music rack, carved legs and the bench matched with carved wooden roses, buds and vines. I was spellbound. The polished mahogany was so beautiful and to this very day, I long for one just like it.

I knocked on the kitchen door and Molly, their cook, opened it.

"Miss Effie, I didn't know bluebells were in bloom yet. I'm sure they are for Miss Henrietta, but she has gone to town. I'll put them on the supper table and tell her you brought them."

"Thanks, Miss Molly." I went down the back porch steps and skipped around to the front concrete pavement. The only one in Calvary, around to the front walk and out to the road.

June came and one pretty day I knew the time had come. They were there now bib, blue and waiting.

As I turned to go along the path, I heard someone call.

"Wait, Effie, I know where you are going, and I want to go with you." It was Miss Henrietta.

We walked along and she said, "I knew you were going to gather bluebells. We will pick some pear blossoms too."

"Oh, do you think we should. They do make pears."

"Yes, but who eats them all. There is always too many."

Yes, June and bluebells were in their glory long stems and big bells. Oh, so blue they were.

The pear blossoms so white, with a tiny pale pink center. Their fragrance was divine.

"I'm so glad summer is here." Miss Henrietta was breaking blossoms and dodging bees. "Someday soon we will get some children and go on a picnic."

"A woods picnic. They're my favorite kind."

"Oh, they're mine too."

"We'll get Thelma, Nancy, Edith, and…."

"Shall we have boys?"

"Oh, yes, and you can do the inviting."

We walked away, our arms full of blossoms and our hands full of bluebells.

Happy summertime!

A year or two later Miss Henrietta was married, and when she had a baby girl Thelma and I went to see her, with flowers and fudge that Priscilla had made.

When we left, Thelma said, "Miss Henrietta that is the prettiest little baby I have ever seen. Miss Henrietta, I hope when she gets big she will be as nice as you."

"Well, thank you, Thelma. I hope she will be nicer than her mother for that is the way it should be."

"She couldn't be nicer than you, and that is a fact, no matter how hard she tried."

Miss Henrietta smiled as we said goodbye.

"Goodbye girls and come again."

So if, as my mother firmly believed, good people go to heaven, Miss Henrietta is there.

Surely, kindness to children is a golden key and Miss Henrietta always carried it in her pocket.

The next day Thelma and I were in the woods and sitting down among the pines to talk. I said, "Thelma, would you like to see my cut leg?"

"Your cut leg?"

"Yes, I did it in February; I fell down, running along the bank to see if the bluebells had bloomed."

"Effie, in February?"

"It was a sunny day and warm."

"Isn't it well yet?"

"Almost. I've never told anybody or let anyone see it. My mother would have fainted. It looked so terrible."

"I'd like to see it, but I don't want to faint."

"Oh, you won't faint."

I pulled down my stocking. It didn't need a bandage now, but it still looked very red and ugly.

"Lord!"

"Oh, Thelma, you took the Lord's name in vain."

"I couldn't help it. How did you live through it? I would have told my mother. I would have been scared."

"Yes, but your mother wouldn't have fainted."

"No.... why does your mother faint?"

"I don't know. I'm always afraid she is going to die when she does," I said miserably.

"One time I told her, I didn't believe in the devil and she got so pale, I thought I had killed her."

"Lord, help you. You had better be careful what you say. You do have burdens to bear."

This was something she had heard grownups say. Thelma looked at my leg again.

"Yes, but it is almost well now," I said.

"No—Effie—no—at least not yet. It looks bad, even to me. Wait till you start wearing socks. It's getting warmer every day."

"You said bluebells are in bloom. Let's go."

"Anyway," I continued, "that was years ago, when I was only seven when I told my mother about not believing in the devil. Mother believes if we are good we go to heaven, and if we are bad, we go to- you know - the devil."

"Well, so does mine, but I don't let it bother me, you think too much."

"All the preachers say so every Sunday, but I just don't believe it. If God is love, how could there be a devil? Anybody who made bluebells and violets and roses and sky and sunshine would not make the devil."

"I don't know Effie, I don't believe in him myself, but I'm going to be as good as I can be to be sure I don't go to hell and find out." Thelma continued, "That's why every kid in Calvary is good. They're afraid to be bad. After hearing two sermons every Sunday telling them if they are bad they will go there."

Miss Henrietta had said to me when we were talking about the picnic. "I believe in Calvary live the nicest children in the world."

"Thelma says they are good because they are afraid to be bad. The devil, you know."

"Oh."

"I don't believe in the devil myself, but I do believe in God."

"Of course you do."

I loved her gentle voice.

If one day in June, you should go on a picnic in the woods beyond the pear orchard, and coming back you cross a field for a short cut home, look down. If everything you see is blue, blue, blue, and there is a fragrance in the air like freshly home baked yeast bread, sit down and gather a big bunch of bluebells. Thousands of bells, blue, resembling hyacinths, but not really for bluebell bells are closed and no hyacinth is their special shade of blue, dark, but bright. Once in a while there will be a light blue been on one, in a longer while, a pure white blue bell, strange.

I asked Aunt Sallie about this and she said, "Effie, let's not dissect the flower. Just enjoy its blue." I didn't know the meaning of the word dissect at that time but I said, "I just wonder why God did that."

I am quite certain the bluebells bloom in the same field and the now children of Calvary have found them. The pear orchard will have bloomed out long ago. Fruit trees just have so many years of life.

I like to think the bluebells go on forever.

THE END

MISS MILLIE'S MOONFLOWERS

CHILDREN'S DAY
A sound of clear young voices
A burst of happy song
A rush of eager footfalls
The marching of a throng

A troop of flower like faces
That brightens all the way.
Till no one needs to whisper
Why; this is Children Day!

Within the solemn temple
And down the quiet aisles
The children bring their banners
And flash their merry smiles,

And hovering above them
I think the angels stay
And make the church like heaven
Upon the Children's Day.
Margaret E. Sangster

MOONFLOWER . N. a pure white flower of the morning glory family, blooming only briefly in the moonlight, large paper thin flowers, sometimes four to five inches across. Beautiful and fragrant. large leaf foliage. – Webster

Let me tell you about the 4th of July, when I was a little girl. Our family did one of two things. My mother made two big layer cakes one chocolate, the other with white icing and coconut. She also fried chicken and made small biscuits.

Early on the morning of the Fourth, we would go down to my father's seafood packing house. This was about three miles out in the water from Calvary, though it was built on the shore, a big rambling place that we loved.

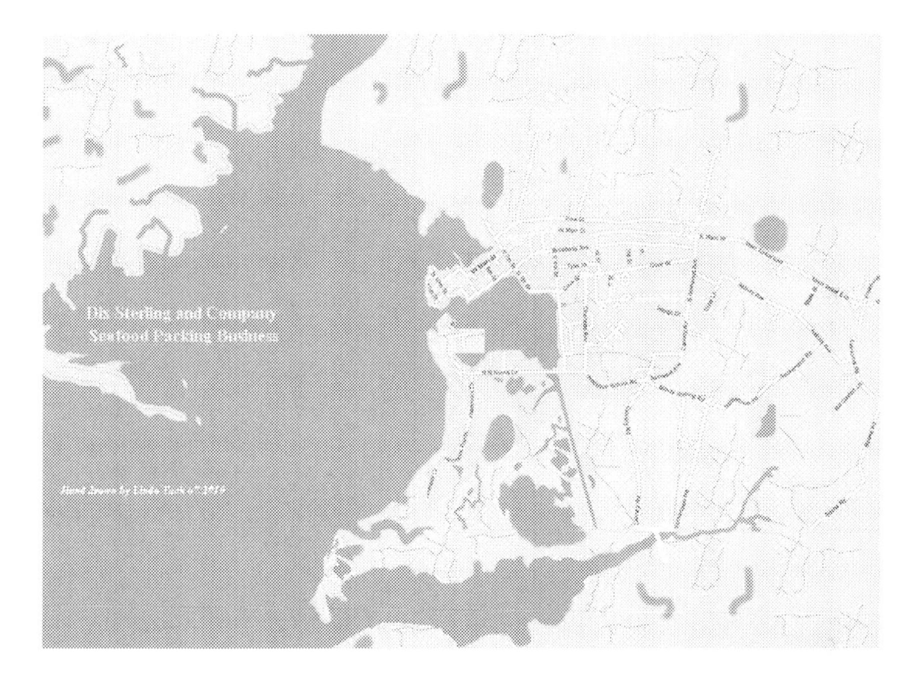

I am not positive but from references it sounds like the business was located near Old House Cove

Here we would stay all day, picnicking and bathing. We went in one of our father's large sailboats.

As soon as we got there, we would unpack our things. Then our father would take my two brothers into Crisfield in the sailboat to get—guess what—a two-gallon freezer of ice cream.

Every 4th of July that we didn't do the other thing, we did this. We always carried a few friends with us and our colored girl Lola to help out and to have fun with us. Lola was almost sixteen at this time, but she seemed like another child to us.

We would pick periwinkles off the marsh grass, and sit and say, "Periwinkle, periwinkle come out of your hole. We'll give you five dollars and a barrel of gold."

The droning of our voices would finally make him come out, or he just wanted to anyway. Periwinkles are a small snail, in a very pretty shell. No one liked to do this anymore than Lola. We just loved having her along.

One year, there was a very bad unexpected storm. High tides and high winds. Though all the children enjoyed it immensely, my mother and Lola were very, very frightened. Lola kept saying, "Oh, will we ever get home. Will I ever see my mother's face again? Oh, Oh, Oh."

"Now, Lola, of course the storm will get over. Of course, we'll all get home," soothed my mother. "Here, take this blanket, and wrap it around you and Effie. Now, we will have more ice cream and finish the fried chicken."

We loved doing this, and it was a wonderful way to celebrate the Fourth of July, but there was one big thing that we gave up when we did this. We missed the Fourth of July parade in town in the afternoon, and we also missed the band concert in the evening.

The other thing that we did to celebrate the Fourth of July was to spend the day with my grandmother and grandfather in town. My father took the day off from his business and we would leave home early. My mother did not make cakes or fry chicken. All this was ready at Grandmothers.

My father always ordered the ice cream to be delivered to my grandfather's home when we celebrated this way. The parade and the ice cream were the highlights of the day. We just had to walk up to the corner to see the parade. It came, gloriously and patriotically, on- and- on- and- on, no breaks in it at all, until the very end passed by.

Every year, leading the parade was a man named Harry Bloxom. He rode a tall high stepping brown horse, and he was dressed in a full dress suit with silk top hat and white gloves. I don't know where he was the rest of the year, but on the Fourth of July he was there in Crisfield to lead the parade. He was a person, whose talent was showmanship, gave a lot of pleasure to the average spectator.

One year the parade was bigger and better than ever before, Mr. Bloxom's horse seemed to step higher and his high silk hat seemed to tower. There were more bands and organizations, the Boy Scouts, the Campfire Girls, Veterans of the Civil War, both the blue and the gray.

There was quite a group of these in the early nineteen hundreds. The Spanish American War Veterans were a vigorous crowd, still young men. All the men's lodges of the town, the Masons, the Red Men, the Knights of Pythias, all of the church groups and all the clubs of the town. Almost everyone who had a baby was pushing a baby carriage in the parade. Afterwards it was to be decided, who had the prettiest baby less than one year. The older children were on decorated bikes (wheels), both boy and girls with tiny flags tied to the spokes. There was also going to be a prize for the best decorated bike. Lastly the Shetland ponies came, or rather, the two of the town, pulling wicker wagons filled with children.

My father, though a member of all the lodges at this time and some of the clubs, preferred to be with his family and was a spectator today. He was holding my hand, when a gentleman came up to him and said, "Billie, we don't seem to have such a turnout to view the parade today. I wonder why?"

My father looked up and down Main Street and pondered the noticeably small crowd.

"I think, Mr. Horsey, we have almost the whole town in the parade." And it was so, a wonderful parade. All of those adjectives that are used today would apply; stupendous, colossal, gigantic, and all in living color, too. There were, only a few, that were discerning enough to see that almost the whole town was marching that Fourth of July.

The end of the parade was in sight now. A few more boys on bikes and the parade would be over. The music had been loud and thrilling and of a true patriotic quality. We could still hear it going far up Main Street as we walked back to our grandfather's house. Ta-ta, ta-ta, they are playing "The Stars and Stripes Forever." That probably hadn't been written then but in retrospect, that was the very way it sounded.

It was such a beautifully happy time. The wars were over. Too bad two of the Civil War Veterans had only one arm, and a Spanish American veteran a wooden leg. Sad, but it was all in the past. The future was bright and beckoning.

The Fourth of July parade was now a whole year away, but the band concert was at seven o'clock, and at Grandfather's was supper, cake and ice cream and games of croquet, too. The day was still young.

The ice cream had not been delivered yet, and my Father was concerned about this, for he said Mr. Sy Hayman had promised that it would be at Wingate Lewis' house by two o'clock and he was a man of his word.

"Perhaps, Mr. Dix," said my mother, "he was waiting for the parade to be over. Maybe he took his children. He should be here soon."

We played croquet, my brothers, my grandfather and other relatives, game after game while waiting, looking up the street every few minutes for Mr. Hayman's wagon. He didn't come and the day was drawing to a close. Supper was fried chicken, hot biscuits and vegetables which only the grownups paid any attention to eating. The only one we liked was corn on the cob.

My grandmother said briskly. "I'll make lemonade to go with the cakes."

You see, this was before the days of everyone having a telephone. There were very few of them in town. Of course, doctors had them, and some business places, but home telephones were few and far between. So although, next door to my grandfather's there was a telephone, as Mr. Sammy Lawson was one of the town's undertakers, there was no phone at Mr. Sy Hayman's house to call him so we just waited, and waited.

The day had been a happy one, as all our Fourth of July's were. We children could never decide which celebration we liked the best. The one at my father's place, with the bathing and picnicking or the one at my grandfather's, with the parade and band concert. We just couldn't decide. We never did. Both were perfect, and why not? We had no cares. We just had to be good, and we would be happy. Our mother told us so.

Even the ice cream not being delivered, could not really spoil our Fourth. It was a big disappointment, of course, but lemonade is very good and three different kinds of cake! Well, we loved cake. One of them had brown sugar icing with black walnuts, ummm—good.

At about nine o'clock, it was almost dark, and my father said, "Annie, honey, we had better be going homeward. Our little children must be tired."

So we kissed our grandparents and said goodnight to all. The distance wasn't too far, but before the end, my father picked me up and I leaned sleepily against has shoulder.

We never locked a door, just closed them and walked away. My father said, just sit here on the steps and I'll go inside and light the lamps. In a second, he called, "Annie, honey, here is a surprise for all."

He had walked around the house and there on the side steps was the big two gallon freezer of ice cream, covered with a burlap bag.

Mr. Hayman had delivered the ice cream, but to the wrong place, a mistake had been made. We were surely not hungry, but who has to be to eat ice cream? It wasn't an everyday food then. It was like oranges at Christmas.

"This is a lot of ice cream," said my mother using a large spoon to fill pretty glass dishes.

"Yes, too bad it is so late or we could share some with our neighbors," my father said.

"Father, Miss Millie and Mr. Dave haven't gone to sleep. They sit up late every night to watch their moonflowers open in the moonlight."

"Annie, if you fill a bowl, Effie and I will carry some to them. They would enjoy it."

My mother filled a large bowl and put a napkin over the top and I skipped along in the moonlit dark, beside my father, not sleepy now, but happy for Miss Millie and Mr. Dave, two of my favorite people.

They were sitting out in their yard, in their cedar chairs that Mr. Dave had made himself where they had a good view of their screened porch, with the moonflowers covering the entire front.

As we came into the yard, Miss Millie said, "Mr. Dix and Effie, what a nice surprise. You came to enjoy our moonflowers with us."

"They are beautiful, but we came to bring you some of our Fourth of July ice-cream," and he told them the story of our disappointment.

"Thank you, Mr. Dix, Effie. Would you like some moonflowers? You can float them in a bowl of water."

"Oh, Miss Millie, you mean you would break some off?"

"Of course, child, there's plenty. Gather up your skirt, and you can carry them that way, without bruising them." I did, and she dropped the lovely white blooms into it softly.

"Goodnight."

"Goodnight Mr. Dix and thank you for thinking of us."

"It was my little girl, who knew you would still be awake," and he put his arm around me fondly, "Come child, I know you are very tired."

"Thank you for the moonflowers, Miss Millie. Goodnight, Mr. Dave."

As we walked home in the white moonlight, I said, "I wish Miss Millie and Mr. Dave were white, instead of being colored people father."

"Why, sweet, they are fine people. They go to church every Sunday. They are honest, upright, kind. They have the respect of all who know them."

"Yes, but….."

"You're tired. Let's hurry home to mother."

"Will you tell me about King Midas tonight?"

"Not tonight, sweet. I don't care too much for that story. Why do you like it?"

"Because I would like to turn some things into gold, so I could buy presents for everybody. It would have been alright, if he hadn't touched his little girl. That's the part you don't like," I teased.

"You're right. Here we are."

We were all very tired. It had been a long day. My mother and brothers were ready for bed.

"Father, I wish I could keep these flowers forever. They are so beautiful."

My brother Charles said sleepily, "You could press them in a book. People do that with wedding flowers and funeral flowers, and once at Aunt Sarah's I saw—."

"Charles, it is time for bed, Willie, bedtime. We've had a lovely day, a nice Fourth, goodnight boys," and she kissed each and gave them a goodnight smile.

"Father, could I…?"

"Yes, darling."

"Could I keep Miss Millie's moonflowers, forever? Can I put them in a book?"

"You can, love, but they will change with time. You will have their shape but not their beauty."

"I would like to put them in our best big Bible, the one with the gold clasp. They will be safe there."

"All right, I will get it for you."

"My father went into the parlour and brought out the large bible. He put it on the table.

"Daddy, this is a precious book. That's why I want them in the Bible. They are precious to me. Miss Millie never did break any before for anybody."

My father picked up a writing tablet and tore some pages out. He put a Moonflower on each sheet and put another over it. There were nine. He pinched their short stems close and laid them flat.

"The paper is to protect our pages from any moisture." He put them carefully in different sections of the bible.

"There's a beautiful ending to a nice day. It's time our little girl closed her eyes in slumber."

"Our bible is so beautiful," I patted it sleepily.

"Yes, this Bible is handsome enough to grace a pulpit."

"Now, Mr. Dix," my mother always called my father Mr. Dix. It was the Victorian way. "The Church has a very nice one, plain beading, but suitably adequate."

My father was well known for his generosity, but my mother's low, Mr. Dix, was sometimes enough to make him pause and think things over a little.

The little story that is growing, growing, is as you know now, about the Fourth of July, nine moonflowers and Children's Day.

I am going to tell you on paper just how it was, and why the Methodist churches gave it up is hard to understand.

There are still children, daisies, roses and lilies. I can see how it could never have been in the city, as it was in a small town. The abundant wild daisies and roses are not there. Florist flowers could never have made the Children's Day that I knew.

This little piece of my childhood, I want to give you. I hope that there will be a small chunk of yours, precious enough to give someone, someday. Now, let me tell you about children's Day. Alas, there isn't such a day anymore, perhaps it was too beautiful to last, like the peaceful years, that is was a part of for so long.

Every year, just after the school year was over, on the first Sunday, it would be announced in Church that on Monday, June I, Children's Day pieces would be given out, and all the children of the Church were asked to be present at two o'clock in the afternoon. Participation must have been 99%. No one was unqualified. All the children came.

Some were given recitation to learn and the ones who could sing were given solos to sing on the big day, two weeks from yesterday. Others were a part of groups to sing, or perhaps be in a drill. This consisted of singing, speaking short verses, and a lovely kind of marching.

First the group would stand in a long line across the back of the pulpit. Then the two in the exact middle would walk together to the front, then the next two and so on, then turn and walk in a circle around the sides, and form the straight line again and sing a song.

Everyone was dressed in white, with white slippers. No patent leather today. There were pink, blue, or white sashes and bows, but the dress was white. Thelma's was net over pale pink satin, but still it looked more white than pink. In some drills all carried large bouquets of flowers, mostly pink and white roses. Beautifully put together with a short cascade of ivy and clematis vine.

After the first part on the drill, this would be repeated with two pausing at the front and reciting a four line verse about summer or flowers or bits of bible poetry, before they marched around to the back again. Then, there were garlands. It would be hard to find anything more beautiful than a garland. These were made on the form of a half-hoop, covered with green tissue paper, and then covered with vines, daises, roses and clematis. Clematis vine has white flowers, with a delightful fragrance.

For the finals the garlands would be used, holding them for the girls with the bouquets in their arm to walk through, while singing. It was unforgettably lovely.

Our line, the drill that I was in, had the little verses to say, when we came up to the front. This time there was something tangible to hold. Mine and my partner's was a cup. This little girl's name was Erma Lawson, and she had black hair and dark eyes in contrast to my blondness.

Everything though of everything to make Children's Day more beautifully perfect. Today, my hair was not straight, but curly, with a big bow on top. My father used to say to my mother that he hardly recognized me with curls and they were curls. I suffered two days to have them. He liked my plaits best, but with everyone having curls, my mother saw that I had some.

My little prop, as it would be called today, was a cup. I had a verse to say about water from the bible. Sometime I will look up the exact one.

My mother said, I could use the pretty fragile one on the mantle in the parlour, pink and lavender with good leaf decorations. Alas and alack too, when we reached the Church on THE day, I had to confess, that I had forgotten my cup.

Tragedy, I begin to cry. Erma's mother was just coming in, and said,

"Annie May, what is the matter with Effie?" Erma had her beautiful pink luster cup in her hand.

"Oh, is that all, honey," Erma's mother said, "just run over to our house and get one. The china closet is full of them."

I ran, it was just a short distance, but when I got there I was out of breath. I stopped on the porch to breathe, opened the door, saw a cup on the kitchen table, picked it up and ran back to the Church. The cup was heavy white china, called ironstone. No decoration, but to me, salvation. I had a cup.

When it came time for our part, I had to hold the cup in one hand; and then hold it up in the air with the other hand, it was so heavy.

My mother said later that she was mortified. I didn't know what the word meant, but understood clearly that she was displeased. She realized too late that I was too young to remember important things, and this only happened one time.

Perhaps I should have described the decorations for Children's Day, first, but this story doesn't have to be perfect in its structure. It is not a long ago school assignment. It is a story for a little girl on her birthday.

Of course, it was the Church in the picture, Asbury.

Children's Day was always upstairs in the sanctuary, though we didn't call it that. We just called it Church. The Sunday school room was on the first floor, not used at all today, a beautiful place, with a grand piano.

Going up to the Church, there was a curved stairway on each side of some rich, dark wood. Carpet on the stairs was a deep blue, but showing a brightness.

The stair railing was the first beauty that met one's gaze; roses, daisies, ivy had been twined and twisted in a lovely way all the way up. White satin ribbon was wound softly among the flowers, with loops at the top and bottom.

Then one entered the Church, the fragrance met us as we walked up the blue carpeted aisle. Every pew (I had never heard that word, so I'll say every bench) at the end was decorated to match the stair railing, flowers, trailing vines and satin ribbon.

We came within six benches of the front. Here we were met with a barrier ribbon. Inside of this were the children's places where they would sit until they were ready to speak or sing, or whatever part they were to have in the day. THEIR-DAY.

At each end of the pulpit there were about six benches to face the preacher, side view, so to speak. These benches were called the A-Men corners, and on other Sundays here sat the older people of the congregation, who couldn't hear or see as well as when they were young. Today these benches were profusely and beautifully decorated. Here also, sat participants, eager little faces, waiting, some feet in their white slippers hardly reaching the floor. For a day, childhood reigned supreme.

Back of the pulpit was the choir. This today was breathtakingly lovely. Beauty ran rampant. Every bit of wood had been covered with flowers, pink and white honeysuckle for a background. There was one man of the church, quite elderly too, who took this work to do every year. If you could have seen this you could never have forgotten the way he used daisies, rosebuds and ivy together in a formal pattern, to make loveliness.

Daisies grew in abundance in June in all fields. Every yard had roses, pink and white honeysuckle was a gift from God. Once some children brought enormous bunches of Brown-Eyed Susan, being helpful, but although everyone loved the flower, they were not to be used on Children's Day. There was no note of discordance anywhere. There was only harmony and beauty.

All of this decorating was done late Saturday evening and at night, before the DAY.

The dedicated adults, who lived near the Church went over and sprinkled them lightly to keep the flowers fresh. The Chancel railing, which encircled the pulpit, was today a dream of flowers, vines and twining white ribbon. The ivy and clematis vine touched the blue carpet.

Oh, breathe deeply now. It's the perfume of the clematis and honeysuckle, summertime and roses. The breeze coming in the flung open high windows, stirring the flowers, make poetry of motion.

The services, both afternoon and evening, closed in the same way. Someone in the Choir, after the opening prayer had been said, stood up and said. "I think when I read that sweet story of old, When Jesus was here among men, how he called little children as lambs to his fold." All the verses were sung.

At the close or both services, the Choir and the whole congregation sang, "God be with you till we meet again." The afternoon was mostly for the small children and not so small. The evening for the older ones, speeches, solos, songs and drills. "Just a little pansy, but its cheery face smiles upon the passer, with a winsome grace," was said perhaps by a child of ten or twelve. She would have a basket of pansies on her arm.

"Only a flower, blossoming fair, sent out its fragrance, filling the air," was a solo song.

A drill, "So scatter your flowers, your smiles and your song. To cheer those around you, while passing along," and they would scatter rose petals as they marched around, during the last verse.

At night the Church was so beautiful. The stars in the ceiling twinkled and the clouds seemed to move, and there was that sapphire haze, as I told you about in the "Filigree Button". It seemed to float, underneath the pale blue of the painted sky.

Water drops bejeweled the flowers under the lights or the magnificent chandeliers.

I gazed at the two large marble urns, just outside the Chancel railing on each side, filled with pink and blue hydrangeas, so perfect. They are a flower of beauty. Vines, daises and roses had been added. I would say there was a preponderance of daisies, as all the children eagerly brought them.

Oh, I wish you could have been little with us, me and Thelma. It's not a real wish, for then I couldn't have you for my little girl, it's just a fantasy wish, so you could have seen it all and spoke your piece. If you had been my little girl at this time, I would probably have endeavored to acquire you a dress like hers when she said her long piece, so beautiful in satin, net, seed pearls and love....more about Thelma's piece later.

My father was always very proud of me, saying my recitation so well, clear and loud, as I had been told to do, but all the children were not so fortunate. Pauline Tyler started to say hers and said, "The pretty flowers sang in the trees, oh, no. I mean the pretty birds." The laughter was so subdued, as to be practically absent. There was no clapping of hands on Children's Day, just approbation for all. It was felt. It didn't have to be manifested.

Yes, this year Thelma's mother had said that she had to have a longer piece, as I was having longer ones, now being nine or ten and she wasn't having Thelma outdone. She said everyone knew I was smart for there was Aunt Sallie and Miss Priscilla, a school teacher, but who would know if she was, if she didn't prove it.

Thelma said, "I can t learn a long piece. It will kill me. I will decline away, oh the anguish of it all." We heard people talking like this due to hard work, bad health, an unhappy love affair, or some other dramatic reason. But her mother was adamant. Thelma had to have a long recitation. It was about a Preacher coming to dinner.

My cousin Priscilla read it, when Thelma and I came home from practice the first day that year. She didn't think it was quite suitable for Children's Day. Miss Dollie found it in a magazine, and pasted it on a piece of cardboard, and sent it to Thelma, saying it was the recitation her mother wanted her to say, and it wouldn't be necessary to give her one. So....

Thelma really had to work hard to learn it. She began with temerity, but stuck to it with tenacity. It was about as long as *Which Shall It Be.* This cut into our playtime, but learn it she did, with gestures. These were much stressed at the time. Elocution was brought into play, with correct timing for periods, commas and such.

Thelma did fine. She had a more fancy dress than ever before, light pink embroidered satin under white chiffon. An overskirt of seed pearl embroidered net, with a white satin sash with silk forget-me-nots, such a dream. She was resplendent, her winsome freckles pale today, but with a look of resolution in her eyes.

The Preacher even had something to say about it, right after she finished, so her mother's wish was fulfilled, and ever after Thelma was in drills or songs. She sat down happily on the front A-Men corner with me, and said, "Thank the Lord, that's over. Never again will speak a piece," and she never did.

Everyone who came to our church marveled at the lavish, traditional use of ten-inch wide white satin ribbon. We all knew that this Mr. Larry Lawson, Dry Goods and Heterogeneous Items donated this fresh every year as his contribution to Children's Day. He was a kind and generous man of fine disposition and courtly bearing who inherited wealth, as well as a flourishing business. Everyone said there would be stars in his crown.

It was a time of extravagant sayings, "Streets of Gold," "Snow White Robes," etc, etc.

We grew and grew. We were in the evening part now, but no amount of time would every erase the memory of Children's Day in the afternoon. Never could we forget, at one afternoon session, three butterflies shared the service with us. A white one, a yellow and a brown speckled one. Thelma had something to say about this, "Well, we can be glad they're not bees. I've got enough trouble today to remember my piece, without a bee getting me."

Two weeks or at least 10 days before Children's Day, my mother had my new clothes and white slippers. The new dress of fine organdie was sheer and beautifully trimmed with Valenciennes lace and many tucks and a tiny button. The ribbon for my hair and sash were ready.

Miss Millie stopped by, as my mother was getting me to try on everything, and she said, "Miss Annie, she reminds me of my moonflowers, all white, and..."

"Precious," my mother said softly.

"Yes, the years go fast," Miss Millie turned away, as she spoke.

Suddenly my mother said, "Effie, now that you are all dressed, speak your piece for Miss Millie."

"I don't think I know my piece yet."

"Well, say last year's dear." I thought a second.

Last year's had been a three verse one, and I wasn't sure.

"I know Thelma's last year's piece."

"No, dear, yours."

"I do know year before last, though."

"That will be fine, honey."

So I made my bow and said, "Happy June has come again with roses, sweet and gay. It brings the time, we dearly love. We call it, Children's Day."

"Miss Millie."

"Yes, honey?"

"As soon as I get home on Children's Day, I will come right over and say this year's for you."

"Please do that, honey. Me and Mr. Dave will feel honored."

I said after Miss Millie went home, "I wish Miss Millie had a little girl."

"She did; she's in heaven."

"Oh, I wish she wasn't!"

"Effie!" My mother was really shocked.

"No, I don't wish she wasn't there if she is dead, but I want her to play with me. I have only brothers, and Thelma lives far away."

"Effie, she only lives across the woods, I will take you tomorrow morning to see her. Come here. Let me re-plait your hair, before your father gets home."

Why was the *way between* so wide then? If this had been today, Miss Millie could walk proudly into our Church, with Mr. Dave at her side, and hear me try hard to speak my piece, clear and loud, with proper pauses for … and….. I wish she could have. True to my promise, and while still dressed in my best, I went over to Miss Millie's on the DAY.

Who knows, maybe I spoke it better for them than from the flower petal strewn pulpit. When I had finished both clapped their hands and Miss Millie said softly, "Effie, that was nice, but will you do us one more favor?"

"Oh, yes, Miss Millie."

"Say the little one you spoke when you were trying on your dress the other day." That was my first one and my favorite, so I bowed low and said very clearly. "Happy June has come again —."

During my last year in High School, my father with a small group of men, became interested in establishing a Meeting Place, near the downtown harbor, for the men who were on boats over Sunday, moored at the dock, or in nearby waters.

They didn't have anything to do or anyplace to go. They were not interested in dressing and going to the services at the fine churches of the town.

When it was known that there was a place, near the downtown wharfs, where one could go in work clothes to listen to someone read the Bible and sing hymns, the men gladly took advantage of this.

One Sunday afternoon, my father said, "Annie honey, I think I would like to let the mission (as it came to be called) use our best Bible."

"It will dress the room up and give it beauty and dignity," he said.

My mother looked at my father. "Mr. Dix, I don't think you should let them borrow our best bible."

"Why, Annie Honey, why?"

"Because," and she smiled, "I think it would make you happier to give it to them. It would make a nice gift. But first let's look through it and take out the…."

"There is only confederate money in it," said my father happily, "and that is worthless."

I came in and saw the Bible. "Oh, you have our best Bible out."

They told me of their decision.

Suddenly my father began turning the pages. "Effie do you remember the Fourth of July that we spent at your grandparent's, and the ice-cream didn't come, and…."

I put my hand on the Bible. Oh, how lovely the golden filigree clasp was. A tiny metallic sound as I turned the bible toward me.

"Miss Millie's moonflowers!"

"Careful. They will be fragile."

We lifted the papers with care and took them out. I counted them. Nine. I spread them out on the table, and lifted one sheet after another and gazed. My father had said I would have their shape, but not their beauty.

Beauty was there, but a changed beauty. Miss Millie's moonflowers had turned to gold. Beautiful, pale, but still gold. Not brown as most pressed flowers are, but a pure, pale, living golden color.

"Father, it is as if King Midas has touched them."

"Now, sweet, my unfavorite story. No, darling, it is a quirk of chemistry that the year's of time has wrought."

I touched one gently. They were thin, as the thinnest paper, almost as air itself. I tried to lift one. It broke into pieces. I touched another and it separated into bits. They were too fragile to survive another moment of time.

So, Miss Millie's moonflowers crumbled to dust away, and became a memory. The Mission grew and today, as then, every Sunday afternoon, the door is open. The men come in quietly, with their hats in their hands.

Someone reads from the bible, they sing hymns, and someone, very like my father tells them the old, old story, that God is Love.

Miss Millie was, of course, Mrs. Dave Bailey. It was the way to call ladies married or single. No one said Mrs., certainly not children.

Hydrangeas - These flowers have opposite leaves and corymbose clusters of unusually showy white or tinted flowers, pink, blue and lavender. -Webster

Corymbose - The outer pedals are longer than those nearer the axis. Well, anyway-beautiful. - Webster

Lectern - I believe that holds the Bible in the center of the pulpit. For Children's Day this was, of course, moved away. The Preacher stood inside the chancel railing, to pray. This was not his day.

THE END

MY MOTHER'S JEWELS

When he cometh, when he cometh.
To make up his jewels.
All his jewels, precious jewels.
His loved and his own.
Like the stars of the morning.
His bright crown adorning.
They will shine in their beauty.
Bright gems for his crown.
Rev. W, G. Gushing

This little piece of a hymn has nothing to do with this little story. I have always liked it, and as I like to think that I do just as I please, I have put it here.

No, this story is not about God's children, as hymn says. It is not about my mother calling her three children her jewels. This she did not do, nor have I ever called mine, jewels.

No, it is about nine pieces of jewelry that she wore to enhance the beauty of a dress or blouse, called shirt-waist, then. They were all expensive, for no one wore anything but real jewels from a jewelry store. Costume jewelry was not in. Not even made or sold. I never saw any.

Mother had nine pieces of gold and lovely sparkle. The dictionary defines jewel as a valuable ornament, often set with gems, a precious stone, any person or thing, very dear to one. Amethyst is spelled like this, and jeweler or jewelry can be spelled with one or two. Likewise, jewelry can be spelled as such or with an extra e, jewelery.

First, the earrings, small diamond, but cut with many facets, and held in by many gold prongs, keeping them safe. They never got loose though she wore them from twelve years until the summer that she was seventy four.

About once a month she took them off and washed them with a small brush and Ivory soap. Sometimes she would let me screw them back in for her.

I didn't want holes in my ears. "Didn't it hurt awful bad?"

"No, a doctor did it. He rubbed my ear until it was numb and I didn't feel the needle at all. My ears did feel a little sore for a few days."

There were gypsies who came around and would pierce ears very cheaply, but my Uncle Charlie and my father too, said. "No, she will be taken to the Doctor."

I couldn't wear earrings right away. For a week, I had a piece of wax string through the holes.

I said, thoughtfully. "Perhaps you thought it didn't hurt, because you wanted to wear earrings."

She looked at me. "Perhaps, you know how badly you have wanted some particular thing when Thelma …."

"Yes," I interrupted. "but the things I wanted didn't hurt. It was only an aching feeling, sort of. I don't like to hear about ear holes. Tell me about the emeralds."

"Oh, the emeralds, they were a birthday present May 11, 1888. In the morning at breakfast, I was given the single one and at supper the double one. Remember how one set was just a little above the other," she said dreamily, "a perfect springtime gift, sparkling green." I could feel tears coming, soon after it happened. She held me close. "Oh no, it was so long ago. It's just that one cannot forget such beauty."

I said sadly. "It was only last summer."

"Even so, we will have them forever. Sometimes I think memories are the very best thing in life. Like our pear tree in blossom, our lilac hedge last spring's hundreds of beautiful things in our minds."

Your filigree buttons on your gray coat that you loved, and even if our Church was destroyed, we could never forget the blue ceiling and the clouds and golden stars."

"Did they really twinkle, Mother?"

"No, darling, that is your imagination, and not only yours, others believe. They really do."

"They really don't."

"No, to be truthful, the artist was a genius and made a three dimensional effect. We can never forget the misty blue and the tiny stars."

"What is three dimensional?"

"Well, it is," she began again, "it is -, your father will explain that to you. It really is not my field."

"I can make a cake, your father can't, but he can explain a three dimensional effect and I can't."

"When?"

"We will say Sunday. The stereopticon is an example though. Remember how the flowers look and the kittens drinking their milk from the saucer, and the trees, and the snow."

"Is that three dimensional?"

"Yes and very real."

Until we moved from our own home, which was a counterpart of Louisa Alcott's, if you have ever seen a picture of that, I didn't really have any little girls to play with. The house that had little girls was at the end of a long road. Mildred of the birthday party had sisters, Bernice, Mabel and Lily.

Thelma was on the other side of the woods and I was too young to go so far alone.

What I liked to do was to play, *Lady*.

"Can I play *Lady* tomorrow?"

"Yes, but only use my second best plum trimmed hat and my second best fur piece. You can use any dress but my two very best, you know which they are, but hold the dress up, don't step on it."

"Oh, I wouldn't."

So I went to sleep happily. Tomorrow I would play *Lady*."

First, get my tea party ready. Get my table out, my dishes and set it under the pear tree. Put my best doll in her carriage and cover her with the pink satin cover.

I got ready in the parlour chamber. That was the best bedroom over the parlour. Here in the closet were my mother's things and my best ones. I cared nothing for them today.

I was all ready now and looking at myself in the mirror over the bureau, when my mother called.

"Effie, don't use any of my hat pins. You might get hurt and you know two of my prettiest ones have been lost."

"I won't." I called back. "It fits tight enough not to fall off."

As I stood at the mirror, my eyes fell on my mother's jewel box. I opened it. At that second, a sunbeam fell across the contents which made mother's two emerald rings flash and gleam, and sent rays out that made me a little dizzy. My mother had often let me wear all of her jewels, but only in the bedroom.

I quickly slipped one on each middle finger and I was ready. After I got down the steps, holding my dress, I sat down on the last one and changed the rings to one middle finger. I liked how they looked that way. My fingers were small and they did not fit at all tightly, but how pretty they looked.

I trailed over the grass, talking to imaginary visiting ladies, asking about their children and their health.

Finally I had played *Lady* to the end. I went back upstairs to put all the things away. The bed looked so inviting. I pulled the lacy spread back a little and soon I was fast asleep.

"Effie, Supper," my mother called, waking me from my sleep.

"Your father and I are going to a banquet tonight and Basy is coming to stay with you all, hurry."

Basy coming? We loved Basy. She had taken care of us all our lives, since Bud Charles was a baby, a long, long time. He was almost twelve now.

My mother came downstairs all dressed in her best, with a puzzled look on her face. "I can't understand it. My emeralds were not in my jewelry box."

She was wearing her amethyst ring.

She kissed all three of us good night and went out first. As soon as my father closed the door, I flung myself in Basy's lap, my arms around her neck and cried loudly, "I know where the emeralds are."

"Where, honey, where?"

"Lost!"

"Lost?"

"Yes, as soon as I got tired of playing *Lady* I put everything away, but not the rings. They were not on my finger."

"Oh, Effie, your mother will be heartbroken."

"I know," I cried more loudly.

"Tomorrow," said Bud Charles, "I will rake every inch of this damn yard, front and back."

"Oh, Charles!"

"I'm sorry Basy, but I can't bear to hear Ef cry like that."

"And I'll help," Buddie Widdie said. "I'll borrow Uncle Sam's rake and help."

There was silence.

Mr. Jim's is closer," I observed between sobs. "I'll be looking too. All the time you're raking." I drew a shuddering breath, "I'll look and look."

"And heaven hope they'll be found," Basy's voice was low and gave us a good feeling.

"Now, let's forget about lost things for a little while and I'll go make you all some cocoa and you can have some gingersnaps," Basy said.

No one really did forget, but she fixed it and we all sat down at the kitchen table, sadly waiting for bedtime.

"In the morning after breakfast, you must tell your mother, Effie."

"Yes, I didn't want to make her unhappy before going to the party."

"No, you did right. You are a thoughtful little child."

"What will she do to Ef, do you suppose, for losing them?"

"I know. She will cry and be sad and I will have to cry some more." Basy put her arm around my miserable little body.

"Charles, tear that July page off the calendar, this is the third of August."

As he tore it off he left the 10 of 1910, and had to tear again.

"Your mother must have been very busy not to notice."

"She has been making jelly all week, apple."

Next day, my father said, "Annie, honey, didn't you tell the child that when she played *Lady* not to wear your jewels?"

My mother thought, deeply, "No, I never did. At no time did it cross my mind that she would do that, Mr. Dix."

"How unfortunate, for the dear child does obey very well."

"Yes, and I will not have her made unhappy. We will never mention it. It is past and must be forgotten, as it is already forgiven."

And she never did, after the first few days when we were all searching so hard.

The amethyst ring was her only ring now beside her wedding ring.

My brothers had gone to play after all of their raking and we sat down on the front porch steps in the shade and mother told me how her Uncle Charlie had loved her so much and he was so happy to buy her nice gifts for birthdays and at Christmas, and even Valentine's Day.

He didn't live to be an old man. He died of a rare disease, which caused him much suffering and apparently she was a great solace to him. He was not a real Uncle, but Aunt Sis' (Narcissa) second husband, and a fine southern gentleman. He came from Virginia.

I put my arms around her neck and we cried a little together.

She never did mention me losing the rings. She did not nag, and she never told anyone, not her sisters, her mother or father. It was our family, my parents, my brothers, and Basy that made a circle of remembrance.

It would have been easy for some mothers to say, bitterly, "Effie lost my emeralds, playing *Lady*."

"Yes," my father conceded, "it will be a forgotten memory. They are quite often happy ones."

Not the next day, but the one after, my father began taking up a section of the boardwalk. I believe there were six.

"Yes, we will look carefully and replace as we look." he said.

Everyone or most everyone had a boardwalk. Ours was made of three broad smooth boards. These were nailed to a crosspiece at each end, then another length of boards and so on and on to the end of the yard.

I could pull my red wagon, and my doll carriage and my pull toys. Yes, a boardwalk was fun. I could just stroll and enjoy the flowers planted here and there along the whole length.

Buddie Widdie and Bud Charles were re-raking the yard, but they came over to look as each section was turned over. Yes, my father was doing so, as he said for perhaps the rings had fallen through a crack.

This was before cement walks got out into the suburbs. They were only urban for years. That word I didn't know back then or suburban either.

We all searched. No emerald rings, just funny insects, odd worms, scary snails with stripes, tiny frogs. I wondered about their mothers.

Where oh where had they slipped off?

Yes, my mother had sometimes worn both on one finger, and it had looked like a ring with three jewels. I suppose my subconscious little mind made me do this too. If not, I may have lost just one.

When she wore the emeralds she did not wear the amethyst or her bracelet, which was, and still is a thing of beauty. This bracelet was not like the other ladies wore. A gold circle, a little etching of flowers and a snap closing that was it - for theirs.

Hers was a pliable gold little spring between the flowers and covered with odd shaped pieces of gold, cut in the Egyptian style with pearls and rubles, very tiny, all around the circle. One thought vaguely of hot sun and sand and blue sky. It closed with a chain that ended in small circles. My mother said at the end of the chains there were tiny gold balls, but listening to so many long sermons she had played with them until one after the other fell off and rolled away over the big Church floor.

All of my mother's jewels, except the watch and chain and the fleur-de-lis pin had been gifts from her Uncle Charlie in her girlhood.

My father had given her the watch and chain for their first anniversary. My mother's little watch looked very small beside my father's large one. They both opened with a little spring. My mother's was engraved with tiny flowers on both sides. It was on a long chain to go around her neck, and to tuck into her belt. Somehow she pinned the chain up with a fleur-de-lis pin on the side of her dress.

It seemed a little awkward to me to look at it that way to tell the time but it did look very pretty and it was the style of the time.

Besides the fleur-de-lis pin, which was plain gold with a beaded edge, my mother had another pin with a double row of filigree gold and to simulate the bow where it was tired rested a sapphire that gave forth gleams in the light or sun.

This was pinned exactly in the middle of her collar. High lace collar held up by little stays with a rucking of chiffon at the top. Pretty, but looking to me uncomfortable, but for style one suffers gladly. Mrs. this and Mrs. that and all the other ladies, said so…. it had to be.

Once, when we were Sunday visiting my Grampa Wingate, I was sitting by him in the yard swing. He lifted my hand and touched the finger next to my little one.

"That finger looks bare. It needs a ring. What kind do you like best? Think?"

"Oh, I don't have to think, green, like the grass, like the leaves."

"Oh, emeralds."

I looked up and met my mother's brown eyes. She put one finger to her lips, then two.

"Oh, no, Grandfather. I like none. It feels free. If I don't have one, I don't have to think about it. They are pretty though."

"And that finger to going to have one. I am going to talk to Santa Clause."

"Oh, him," I laughed.

"Grandfather, you can give the money that the ring would cost to the poor children."

"Poor children?" He thought for a second.

"I don't know any."

"I do, Mr. John Williams, who is in the Navy has some."

"Well, Christmas is coming, and I'll tell my Katharine to fix a basket and you can ask your Aunt Sallie to let Bill stop by for it December 23rd. It will be ready." However, grandfather didn't have to buy me a ring, for my Cousin Priscilla did.

A fad swept our town. I think the whole country, maybe even the world.

Every little girl, who had anything had a turquoise ring. In my mind they could not be compared to the color and sparkle of emeralds, but pretty in their own beautiful shade of blue way. It was said that they all came from Mexico. Where, oh where was that?

Anyway, when these things happened, I was sure to have mine, for Priscilla loved to spend her check and not only on herself. She was generous. School teacher's checks were supposed to be quite large, a good paying job. Today she had bought shoes, a hat, this and that and I standing by, knowing that whatever I wanted I could have, before we stopped buying. Now, what did I want, it seemed I had everything.

"This is my last place," she said as we left Mr. Irvin Melbourne's big store. "Now we will go to the jewelers."

The jewelers, the word had an unhappy connection for me.

"I am going to get you a turquoise ring for your birthday."

"Oh, Priscilla, a ring? A turquoise?"

We went in Mr. Harry Tilghman's, the best jeweler. There were two.

"What can I show you, Miss Priscilla?"

"I would like to see your turquoise rings. It's for Effie."

"Yes, indeed. Here is a tray of beauties. One set, two sets, three."

Priscilla picked up the prettiest one, which was not one or two or even three. This ring was unique. A little circlet of gold where the set would have been and inside of the circle of tiny gold leaves was a heap or teeny-weeny turquoises, with many gold prongs holding them in.

"Yes, that is pretty how it makes a pile or stones, and made so well."

"Do you like this one best, Effie?"

"Oh, yes," If I had to have a ring, it might as well be ....

Mr. Tilgham picked up another with three sets. "This is a best seller, too. This one is $14.00 and the one you are holding is $25.00."

Priscilla never counted the cost, but he explained, "The circlet is twenty-two carat gold. That accounts for the higher price. The other one is 14 carat gold."

"We will take the $25.00 one. Effie, do you want to wear it or take it home in the little velvet box?"

"Oh, in the box, I want to show it to mother that way, then I will wear it."

As we walked down the street, I said, "Priscilla, if you were me, would you keep it for Sunday, or wear it every day and Sunday too?"

"Every day and Sunday too, that way you will get full value."

"That was a lot of money, Priscilla."

"Yes, but only money."

I knew better. It was love, too.

"Thanks Priscilla." She was not the kind one said I love you to, just thanks, but the love and true sincerely could be felt.

Yes, Christmas always comes. How beautifully it comes. All the songs in the air. People going home with their treasures. Maybe snow.

I was looking today through the antique shops for the unusual. The lady had a sprig of holly on her blouse, I remember.

"Here, dear," I think she said. Dear because I was older than she was.

"Would you like to look at this tray of rings. They are our loveliest," and she gave a little laugh, "and our most expensive."

She put them on the glass counter. I would say about two dozen, rubies, sapphires, diamonds, and pearls and there among the beauty were the two emerald rings the one set and the double.

"The emeralds," I breathed.

"Yes, the loveliest. Try them one."

I slipped one on. Then the other, then I held my hand up and away to see the sparkle, as gold touched gold. I could clearly hear my own little girl "Lady" voice over almost six decades of time.

The cool forest was before my eyes, the brown pine needles soft to my feet.

The little mimic make believe grown up voice, saying, "Let us go into the cool forest. It is so very warm today."

And I answering in my make believe *Lady* voice. "Yes, lets."

"Dear, don't you like any of those?"

"Oh, yes. They are very beautiful. I will be in tomorrow."

Oh to be home, to think. Why oh why did that little piece of a summer day lock itself in my memory, for over sixty years of time?

Bud Charles had said the next day as he was busily raking, "Ef, are you sure you just stayed in the yard? You didn't cross the street to Mr. Jim's or go in the cool fairy tale forest?" The cool forest was the name I used for the woods on one side of our house.

I had said, crossly, "No, Buddie, No, No. I had to stay in the yard. I only had one hand. I had to hold my dress with the other one." I was cross and tired and hot. We had all looked so long and hard.

Little unbelievable things have always happened to me, all my life, and yes, as incredible as what was now so real. These unbelievable things, I do not mention. It is better so. Some things are just so "your own", too personal to share.

No wonder I wanted to go into the deep cool forest. Over my blue and white checked dress, I had three of my mother's full petticoats on. Her dark blue brocaded taffeta with high neck and long sleeves. Her best fur piece was around my neck and a heavy dark blue velvet hat adorned with three ostrich plumes was on my head. It was no wonder I went into the cool woods.

Oh, to be home, to sit and think.

I am sure that the rings are this day under the cushiony brown straw, going deeper and deeper with every year's rains and snow. A new brown carpet of needles is spread each year.

Yes, the forest still stands.

No, I do not blame things on other things. If I did I would say it was the sunbeam falling across the open jewel box.

It is not even a temptation to blame you little sunbeam, you are innocent.

No, I will not say it was the summer sunbeam, for it was I, who lifted the cover of the jewel box.

THE END

VISITING CHRISTMAS TREES

Again, the apple tree was showing signs of springtime. Its wood looked alive, and little balls of crumpled green were just ready to burst into leaves, upon its bows, promising blossoms a few weeks.

We sat upon the wash bench, under the tree, Thelma, my best playmate, and I. And this was the way the conversation went.

Thelma, "I'm tired of it all. Playing house, making graves and wreaths, and burying biddies, jumping ditches, climbing trees, making doll baby clothes." and she kicked her little iron cook stove that we had brought out to play with. "I hate that little old thing. It won't cook, smoke, smoke, smoke," and she kicked it again, and its little lids scattered on the grass. "And this box of doll clothes, and all the dolls, I'm going to give them to the missionary people. I'm tired of all. I'm going to give them all away..."

"All?" I questioned.

"Well, maybe I'll keep one doll, and just the clothes that Aunt Allie made me. That will be enough for me," she said loftily. "The little children in China need them worse than I do."

"The stove too?" I asked.

"Well, maybe not," she said, gathering up the lids, and setting the stove upon its legs. "It is fun, to try to make it cook, and I did get it for Christmas but," with a dramatic gesture, "not today."

"Effie, don't you ever have an idea in your head? What is the matter with you?"

She knew what I was going to say, before I said it, and I knew she knew just what I was going to say. We were that kind of playmates. "We could visit Christmas trees," I said.

Thelma looked happy again.

"Yes, we could. How many do you think are still up?"

"Well, I know Miss Agatha Riggin's is and Miss Sallie Matt's, and Alice Losher's, though I don't know about going..."

"Who else, do you think?"

"Maybe the Truhart's upstairs one."

"Effie," she breathed, "would we dare go there?"

"Yes, I would."

"But we never have in all our born days have gone there."

"Well, you want to do something different, so let's."

Our special was of talking about doing things. This conversation happened every year, at this time.

Down in the most southern part of Maryland, the weather is unique. Anyone, who has ever lived there, will confirm this.

As a rule, the summers are very hot, though once, in several years, there will be one, with what the people call "cold spells". I remember a few Fourth of July's that were really cold. No one wanted to freeze even to celebrate the holiday, so no swimming. Then, it would get so hot, that it was hard to believe how it had been on the Fourth.

After summer, when we had gone back to school, came the most marvelous weather of all, Indian summer. This could last until Christmas and sometimes did. But, after Christmas, the weather got colder and colder. This lasted, some years, until the middle or last of April; March and April being especially cold.

Now, sometime, in this period, from December the twenty-fifth to April, maybe the fifteenth, there would be a kind of weather, called "warm spells".

These days were perfectly delightful but had an ominous undertone of disaster about them. The old ones said they were "weather seeders" and would make everyone sick; but how everyone, old and young enjoyed these days. The children were sure spring had come, and farmers were out at their fields, and thinking of plowing. Young mothers got baby carriages out and walked their babies about the streets in the sunshine. Housewives would think of spring house cleaning, but knowing of the fleetness of the "warm spell", would resist the urge, and sigh deeply and brush the carpet more briskly, until house cleaning time really came.

The weather of our little town was the reason that today we could go visiting Christmas trees.

You see, the houses were heated with stoves, all of them. Well, one wasn't. That one house was in Calvary (our small community), only one that had a furnace. This was Mr. Washington Ward's house. He had been very successful in the seafood business, and had an enormous white house, a library, with a globe, a grand piano, and two lovely daughters, but this little story does not need those people. I will say here they were extremely nice, and very generous with their telephone, everyone using it to call doctors, etc., etc.

After Christmas in most homes, the fire was not kept going in the parlour, especially if the house had sitting rooms, also. So, in some houses the Christmas tree was left up until spring house cleaning.

One time I remember, a little child died, and the parlour of that house was needed, so quickly the tree was untrimmed, and carried out. Thelma and I watched, and she stood there sobbing and said,

"Why didn't God take old Ten Truhart, and let Margie stay?"

I couldn't see, for tears myself, but said, "Thelma, Margie will be an angel, and old Mr. Ten would go to...."

"Come on, let's go home. I think Mama wants me."

Don't think that it was a sign of dubious housekeeping or anything that the Christmas trees were kept up so long. It was just plain common sense. There had been a fire in the parlour every day for two weeks, so that the family could enjoy Christmas, and the tree, among beautiful things that furnished the room, but now it was over.

The kitchen stove was refueled hourly, and the sitting room fire was going, so who needed the parlour? It was extra expense, and then why take the tree down, working in the cold room, endangering one's health, maybe even catching pneumonia, a terrible risk, in the days of my childhood for everyone.

"Where shall we go first?" I said, skipping along.

"Let's go to Miss Sallie Matt's. It's the closest."

So, we knocked on the kitchen door, and Miss Sallie opened it.

She really was a Mrs. and only called Miss Sallie Matt to designate her from the other Sallies in the neighborhood, including my Aunt Sallie.

Her husband was Mr. Matt Lord, short of course, for Matthew. Why we called married ladies Miss, I don't know, but everyone did this: Miss Dollie, Miss Hattie, Miss Mary, etc., etc.

"Well," said Miss Sallie, "Effie and Thelma."

"Miss Sallie," said Thelma, "can we look at your Christmas tree?"

"Yes, indeedy, you can. Come right in. You know where it is, and the parlour door is open."

We entered the sitting room. Rob, Miss Sallie's boy, was sitting in his little rocker putting his dishes lovingly into his little cupboard. Rob, I had heard my mother say, was Miss Sallie Matt's cross. He was now almost forty years old, and had the mind of a small child. He gleefully smiled at us and held out a small tea cup to me, and reached for another one for Thelma.

"Yes, Rob, Effie and Thelma can have a tea party with you. Mother will get the cookies. You look at the tree girls, and if you have time, Rob would like to play tea party."

"We'd love to," I said, "wouldn't we, Thelma?"

"Course we will. Miss Sallie, you do make the best cookies. How do you do it?"

We walked down the long hall that led to the parlour, and went in. It was almost dark as the green window shades were down. Miss Sallie called.

"Put up the shades, girls."

The winter sun hit the Christmas tree, and we gazed in delight.

"It's just like it was lit up," Thelma said. "Boy, is that pretty? I hate to think of it being taken down."

"Thelma, it is April," I said. The tea party was ready for us, and Rob was so blissfully happy.

"Miss Sallie," said Thelma, "that is the prettiest Christmas tree that I have ever seen.

Thanks for letting us see it. We put the curtains down. Goodbye."

"Goodbye girls and thanks."

"Imagine," Thelma said, "thanking us for eating those good cookies and all."

"It was because of her cross," I said. "We made Rob happy for a little while, so we made Miss Sallie happy too. We should go play with him more often, Thelma."

"We will. From this day forward, we will do that. It will be a star in our crown."

"And fun too." I said. "The hot chocolate was good, too."

Next, we stopped at Miss Alice Losher's. She really was a Miss. Her parents were dead, and she lived alone. We didn't have to knock, as she was out in the yard. Miss Alice was very pretty, with her brown hair fixed in the Gibson girl fashion of the early nineteen hundreds.

"Miss Alice," Thelma said, "we're visiting Christmas trees today. Can we see yours?"

"Well, yes, but you are two of the funniest kids. The place is full of children, but only you two ever come to see the tree, after Christmas."

"Yes, we just love to do it." I said, "I don't think the other children think of it," I said, "but we do."

"You both go right in and look to your heart's content. It's good you came today for tomorrow, she comes down, and house cleaning begins. Spring is here and I intend to have everything spic and span to greet it."

We entered the parlour, and gazed at the tree. To us, it was every bit as beautiful as it had been at Christmas.

Suddenly I had a feeling, vague and disturbing. I was deep in thought, when Thelma jerked my arm.

"Effie, come on. We've got two more trees to visit."

As we reached the kitchen, Miss Alice came in quickly and began bustling about with cups and saucers.

Thelma looked at me, and said. "Miss Alice, we'll have to say goodbye, as we have to go to Miss Agatha's and …"

"Couldn't you have some cake and hot chocolate? It's a chilly day for all that sunshine."

"Oh, no Maam not today." I had my hand on the door knob, when she said,

"Wait, girls. No one every leaves my home, without a word of prayer. Let's kneel right here in the warm kitchen."

Every year, we forget! We knew there was something that we should remember, about our Christmas tree visiting, but now, as always, we were aware of it too late.

"You take this chair, Effie, and you this one, Thelma."

Miss Alice fell on her knees, before the kitchen rocker and prayed, "Dear Lord, take loving care of these two girls. Make them kind and to want to minister to the needs of others, and lead them not into the dens of iniquity. Amen."

We got up quickly and said goodbye. When we were out on the road again Thelma said,

"We forgot again. Do you think she knew we were going to the Truhart's?"

"How could she?"

"Well, she knows they keep their upstairs tree up."

"But Thelma, the Truhart's is not a den of iniquity. He's only a drunkard, and Mrs. Truhart is a lady. I've heard my mother say so,"

We reached the Truhart home, which was down a lane, a nice old big house, with porches and large oaks in the yard, and a garden at one side. We knocked timidly and the door opened at once. Mrs. Truhart looked a little puzzled, as we were not frequent visitors not being allowed to play with the Truhart children, and we had never been to see their tree.

You see, they always had one up and one down. Why? Why not? I suppose Mrs. Truhart, with such a large family, thought it would make for less confusion.

One year, at Christmas, there had been sickness in the family, and that was when it started. Little Lily had pneumonia that winter, and they put a stove up in the front bedroom. She was better at Christmas, but very weak, and not able to come down with the other children, so the upstairs tree was begun.

"Hello girls," she said, cordially. "Alfred, take the cat off the rocker."

"No thanks, Mrs. Truhart," I said, "we just wanted to see your upstairs tree. Everybody said it was so beautiful at Christmas so we came to visit it."

The puzzled look was still on her face.

"Oh, of course, you are welcome to see it."

Just then Mr. Ten came in, and was as surprised as his wife to see us.

"No, don't tell me, let me guess." he said. "This one is Billie Dix's daughter and as sure as the sun is shining, this is Dollie Nelson's little girl."

"You're right, Mr. Ten," I said. "I'm Effie."

He looked at Thelma, and she said, "I'm Thelma."

"Tennyson, the children want to see our upstairs tree. They're visiting Christmas trees today."

Tennyson—the name struck a chord in my memory, every night Aunt Sallie read to me from Tennyson's poems.

I had started up the stairs, stopped and looked back.

"Mr. Truhart, what is your whole name?"

"Alfred Lord Tennyson Truhart."

"Mr. Truhart, do you know whom you were named for?"

He laughed softly. "Yes, for the poet. Alfred Lord Tennyson. Born 1800, died 1892. He lived to be ninety-two years old."

Thelma had come down a few steps, and said, "He probably didn't have a tooth in his head."

Mr. Truhart laughed loudly at this, and then went on. "My father was a preacher. He loved poetry and poets, and I do too."

"Half a league, half a league
Half a leaguer onward
Into the valley of death
Rode the six hundredth."

"I know that," I said, "It's *The Charge of the Light Brigade*."

"Do you know Lady Clare?"

He began softly "It was the time when lilies blow, and clouds are highest up in air."

"Oh," I said, "It's my favorite of Tennyson's. So dramatic, when she flings the diamond necklace … My Aunt Sallie reads it to me." I said, dreamily.

Mrs. Truhart said, "Tennyson, show her your book."

It was lovely, brown leather, with gold decorations. *The Poems of Alfred Lord Tennyson* in gold letters on the back. I opened it, and in the front, I read. "From a proud and happy father to my son Tennyson, on his twelfth birthday."

Thelma said, crossly. "Effie, are you going to visit the Christmas tree, or not?"

"Yes, I am." Thelma was on her way up the steps again.

"Mr. Tennyson," I said, "what is your favorite poem in this book?"

He didn't take a second to think before he said, "Almost the shortest one in it. A little one called Fragment" and he began,

"Flower in a crannied wall
I pluck you, out of the crannies
I hold you here, root, and all in my hand
Little flower- -but if I could understand what you are,
Root and all, and all in all
I should know what God and man is."

Thelma said, sharply now. "Effie!"

The tree stood in a corner, and we looked, while all the family came to look with us; Elizabeth, Mary, Lily, Fanny, John, Charles, Hope, Willie, Earl and Alfred, all ten.

Alfred! A thought came to me. "Is Alfred named Tennyson, too?"

"Yes, indeed," Mrs. Truhart said, proudly. "He is named for his father."

Going along the road, Thelma said. "Why does he be a drunkard? He's got real good sense."

"Yes," I said, thoughtfully. "I wonder why?"

It was not for us to ponder this question. We were only two little girls.

"Effie, do you think we should go to see Miss Agatha's tree or go home?"

"It feels late to me," I said. "Let's go home, Thelma."

"Yes, let's," she said. "We can go another time, and her tree not so pretty anyway."

I stopped suddenly.

"But, Thelma, you always tell her that it's the most beautiful tree of all that we go to visit."

"I know, but it's one of those little white lies, you hear about all the time. Her tree really is skimpy, not tall enough, and the balls and the angel are so old and the tinsel is straggly and …."

"But a lie," I said

"But it makes her so happy."

"Thelma?"

"What?"

"I'm not sure I'm going to visit Christmas trees, next year."

"Why not? It's fun."

"Yes, but it's a little bit sad, too. I think they should be just for Christmas.

Maybe God intended it that way. They're only truly beautiful at Christmas, when they are fresh and green and new."

"New, like the little baby Jesus, on his birthday, when the wise men brought him presents," Thelma said.

I changed the subject. "Imagine, Mr. Ten being named for Alfred Lord Tennyson," I said, thoughtfully.

Thelma said, "Yes, imagine that," and then sensibly, "Well, he had to be named for something. Let's run. I am hungry as a bear. "

THE END

MY FATHER HAD A DREAM

My father had a way of showing his love. It was easy for him to speak of love, not only to our mother, and us three children, but to everyone. He was a completely sincere person. I had gone to school quite a few years before I ever knew people could be insincere in their speech. Such phrases, indicating sarcasm, were not used in my home. Perhaps it was from a teacher that I received this shock. Some of them were masters at this cruel form of speech. Anyone who hopes to know love will not use this. If one has not love, there is nothing. There is only love. It is all. Love and sincerity.

Nor did I know that all children were not as happy as we. It was the day of the telling of my father's dream, and our happy acceptance of it, that I learned this to be so. I had just assumed that all children had a loving father and nice mother and relatives like ours, and a nice town to live in and grow. Of course the truth is, I didn't think at all at this time. I just lived and enjoyed the happiness of the days.

Growing up is such a pleasurable experience. It is the parents love, first. Then, if one is extremely fortunate enough to have grandparents a child is blessed. They enter another dimension. If this isn't realized, and of course it isn't always, it is sad. If it is, it is thoroughly enjoyed, even into those years of life when memories tumble over each other.

Today walking down Main Street we were on our way to see some of these relatives, but we had begged our mother to go straight to the new five and ten cent store first. It was so pleasant on a summer day to walk down the pretty street of our town. All the beautiful homes had trees in their yards and the branches met in the center, making an archway over the street to walk beneath. The birds sang and the maples, elms and oaks gave us lovely shade.

On the side yard could be seen weeping willows, cedars, and flowering small shrubbery. Croquet stakes and swings with striped, gay tops in some places.

In front of us, as we walked along, a tiny bird took backward steps, reminding me of the little sandpiper poem in my reader. The one, by Mary Mapes Dodge, where the little birds dart back quickly to escape the incoming waves on the beach. Halfway down Main Street there always seemed to be a woodpecker and we would stop to listen.

"Why does he peck?"

"I know, he saves the chips for his nest."

"Au, Effie."

"It's true. Thelma's grandfather told her and she told me." I used the old argument. "You don't see any chips falling, do you?"

"No…."

"Well then."

"Just because Thelma's your friend, don't say she knows it all," my brother Charles said. "It was her grandfather that knew, not her."

It was so leafy and lovely, as we walked on. All the way to the shopping section, the shade lasted. Here, the very first store was the new five and ten. Wonderful things could be bought here. Alger books for a dime! What if the binding was slight? The story was there. Not all things were five and ten cents. Some were twenty five and fifty cents. The punch bowl and dear cups for a little girl to play tea party with. The set of tiny water glasses (six), the set of sugar bowl with cover, butter dish with cover and cream pitcher were one half dollar. A lot of money!

They were so darling then, and priceless antiques now. Ten cent stores are just that now, but that first one was untrammeled joy. It had candy, many kinds, by the quarter, half and pound. The day of penny candy was waning. Sad, but this was progress.

No! No! We really didn't need the ten cent store yet. Oh years, please wait and let a little girl be little a little longer. She doesn't need a quarter pound all alike. Let her decide. Let her choose: Two of those, three of these in front, one all day sucker, strawberry flavor, some of those in the back of the glass case, two cents worth of cinnamon hearts, one peppermint patty, a penny, but a big circle, mottos, shape of hearts, I Love You, Love Me, Hello, Dear One. There was imagination in penny candy.

A small town is made up of three types of people.

- The ones who are born there and stay there a lifetime.
- The ones who leave after high school for a job or college and never return to live, just on visits, but they leave their hearts.

- Then, there is the third kind. The ones who come. They arrive in unique ways. Some to run the Western Union office, the Adam's Express, etc., etc. Some young men come on coast or navy ships, during a war. Then, later, they return, marry town girls and spend their whole life. One came on a showboat, loved the town, stayed, married, and played the organ at the Methodist Church, also the movies, until he was an old man. Some were from other countries. One young man was from Norway.

The first category sometimes win fame just by staying. They build a better mousetrap. Success is thrust upon them. These have real talent, superb intelligence, and undying love for their hometown. They will not go.

The Lavalette family came before 1900 from France. They built a home on the shore of our Little Annamesic River and had furniture shipped from France. The Lavalettes stayed a lifetime. Their daughter Ruth and son Junior graduated from our high school.

Our town was nice, and people liked us. We took all strangers to our hearts. We found them jobs if they had none waiting. Their children were always in the local plays with good parts and won prizes for tap-dancing. There were boys and girls of school age who came, perhaps to live with an aunt or uncle or a preacher, for some reason.

They were new and different, we liked this. Their names enchanted us; Ethel Glunt, Isabelle Sinn, Caroline Surface and Elizabeth Benson, they all seemed so very different. We had never heard such names. Maybe it was their clothes; their ways, city ways, maybe. One wore all hand-knit sweaters, and one wore white coats, winter and spring, and white shoes. Unheard of, and unusual up to now but beautiful; a welcome change to ways that were not wholly our own.

Surely the next small town of any size, Princess Anne, did not take strangers to their hearts. Oh no, they were nice people but could not be called friendly. Only the ones who had been born there made up the pretty town.

A beautiful town, yes, the homes were far finer than ours. There was a hotel, with columns, like a southern mansion, where George Washington had slept on his way from Virginia to Philadelphia but they were just not like us. We were loving and giving.

We cared and did something to help. A small town is a perfect place to live, but sometimes rough for everyone to make a living. Everyone can't have a drug store or be president of a bank.

Many must leave and stay away though they leave their hearts. There is a nice little story of how Paderewski carried his native Poland with him. Unlike the Polish pianist, they need no little bag of soil in their pockets.

The soil is always crumbling through the fingers of small town wanderers. The Brown-Eyed Susan fields blow in that bright sunshine, under that blue, blue sky. The pine trees give their fragrance and the wild roses bloom in memory. Is there any shade of pink so vivid? It is time for a visit.

A Baptist preacher came and gave the small congregation a challenge: a new Church, the replica of Jefferson's Monticello. He made a list of members, both men and women, to preach each Sunday. He went off on a lecture tour and came back with thousands of dollars, a real modern day Emerson.

The Church stands today, proudly and beautifully, a monument to a man who loved our town, liked us, and stayed. Some Sundays we did a breathless thing when my father said, "Today, we will go for a sailboat ride." We were so happy that we almost stopped breathing.

It wasn't my mother's favorite thing to do, but she always tried hard not to let her terror show, and made chicken sandwiches. She put pieces of molasses cake in a shoe-box, for we always became hungry. It would seem that sail boating on a Sunday was not to be enjoyed, but I never heard anyone say it was not right. It felt right, like taking a walk in the woods or along the bank where the prickly pears bloomed, their tiny roses, holding my father's hand.

My father put up the sail and did the other things necessary to start, and off we sailed, and we knew just where we were going. "I hope Mrs. Lavelette has some of those good cookies." my brother Charles said.

"Charles, we have nice sandwiches and cake with us."

"Yes, but I hope she has some."

"She doesn't make them, Buddie. Her cook does."

"I don't care who makes them, just so she has some."

I was six, one brother eight, one eleven on this happy summer afternoon. The Lavelette home was the showplace of our town. Built on the bank of the river, it could be seen for many miles, both by land and water.

A gabled home, painted a bright red (crimson would be the pretty name for it) trimmed with bright green. It may sound strange, but it was perfect for this particular place and is still the same today. They came in 1897 or 1898, a nice family. Different of course, but we liked this. They and their house were an adornment to our town.

The father was unfortunately handsome, and the mother and children dark and very, perhaps the word is exotic. Everyone commented that the whole family had black hair and blue eyes. Yes, there are such people and they are quite sure to be handsome.

We arrived and Mr. Lavalette came out to meet us. "Mr. Dix, I am so glad to see you. Mrs. Dix, children, go up to the house. I'm sure there's lemonade."

My mother and all three of us walked up the broad boardwalk toward the pavilion. Mrs. Lavalette came out, welcomed us, and told us to go in and tell cook to bring cookies and lemonade.

The pavilion was a screened octagonal shaped summer house, with wicker furniture. It had sliding glass windows for cold weather and when the wind was strong. All around the top were electric lights. It was a sight to be seen for miles by night, beautiful. At this time electric lights were very new.

I seem to remember two pavilions and I think I remember rightly. I asked my brother who is seventy five. He thinks two also. My brother Charles, rests. I am generous in my remembering, but one or two, they were beautiful! Our Sunday visiting was brief. Soon we were sailing along.

My father said, "Yes, the Lavalettes are fine people. The only French citizens I have ever met. That is a beautiful home. A fire place in every room with tile borders, squares with miniature paintings of rosebuds, forget-me-nots, violets, tiny pictures of windmills and landscapes."

"Yes, a lovely place, but our home is nice too, Mr. Dix. Our trees are so big."

After a while my father sailed close to the shore and put down the sail. "Mr. Dix?"

"Don't worry, Annie. Charles, lean out and tell me what you see in the water. Look closely."

"Sand and the water is as clear as glass. I never saw water so clear. Fish are darting about."

"Now, look up, all, at the shore. The Lavalette's have a nice piece of the Annamesic shore, but it isn't the only one."

"Oh," I said. "There are millions of star flowers, millions and how the shore makes two half circles, is so pretty."

"Yes, our house will be set back in the exact center."

"Mr. Dix? Our house, we have a home."

"Yes, Annie, this is my dream for my family."

"Would it be painted red and green?" I asked, never doubting it be there and soon.

"No, Sweet. It would be pure white, sparking in the sun and gleaming in the rain."

"An upstairs porch and a downstairs porch, both front and back. I can see it," I said suddenly.

"Effie!" Imagination and falsehood were very nearly related in the Victorian mother's mind. My father laughed.

"In her imagination, Annie."

"Well, first I have to get the State of Maryland to sell me the land. It has to be filled in with shells, many, many shells. It would take years it would seem but no, I have friends who would help and ample shells would cover the star flowers. There will always be star flowers. The marsh is a vast expanse of their beauty."

"If we had a home like Mr. Lavalette's our front yard would be water."

"Where would we play croquet?"

"Maybe on the backyard," my brother said.

"Willie, did you ever hear of anybody playing croquet in the backyard?"

"No...."

"Well then—."

"We will have a croquet field and in the front yard, I promise. Maybe one of those grand sets, like your grandfather's."

"Papa bought that a long time ago. It is the only one I have ever seen."

"Well, we will buy a new one anyway. Oh, we will have fun. Now we will put up the sail and head home."

We sailed into the sunset with my father's dream.

We had a vision of a sparkling white house and millions of pink star marsh flowers at our back. I wanted all children to be as happy as we. I felt kindred to all the families in the entire world, who loved one another.

It was a happy day, sailing home in the deepening twilight. The name of our boat was on the side in bright blue, *The Banner*, and a bright American flag painted beneath the name.

After we were ready for bed, my brother Charles was still asking questions. "Will we take our things? What about our organ?"

"No, no indeed," my mother said. "Our home here will stay as it is."

"Could we get a talking machine with a horn with pink roses and morning glories on it?"

"Now, that is an idea, perhaps. We will see, Charles. And perhaps I will ask Sister Sallie if my violin is still up in her attic. Our new home will be a fine place to practice."

"I love the violin but always things stood in the way of enough time for concentration. Time for music, there must be time," my mother said.

"Annie, I'm glad you have kept up your music. It is a real pleasure to us all. Charles, would you like to take violin lessons?"

"No Sir?" Charles spoke with decision.

"Willie? Perhaps Willie would like to start the organ first, Mr. Dix."

"Yes, Sir, and take violin lessons later, after I learn the organ."

"That seems a good plan. Of course, Effie will learn organ very soon now. Yes, indeed." My mother was emphatic in her statement.

A year later, my Uncle Sam, my father's brother became very ill. He had to go to a Baltimore hospital for an operation. This put the burden of the seafood packing company on my father.

"Sam will be well soon. I can manage," my father told my mother.

Uncle Sam did return, so thin and pale. It was a long time before he could work again, but eventually he took up his work again but not with the old zeal. This kept my father away from home a lot as Uncle Sam had to get lots of rest. In the fall, a tragic accident occurred taking his life. The life of my Uncle Sam was over.

The Dix, Sterling and Company failed. Our house was sold to pay debts, and we went to live with our Aunt Sallie.

Her husband, the Sterling of the firm, had died three years before and she had remarried. Her property was in her new husband's name as was the law then, and exempt from such debts.

The law is changed now in Maryland. I suppose laws are both good and bad. In this case, it was good, for it would have been very sad to have lost the house in Calvary. Very shortly after we went to Aunt Sallie's her husband, a fine gentleman, died suddenly.

Her two boys were at college, and Priscilla, her daughter, lived at home and taught school.

My Aunt Sallie ran the small farm with the help of a hired man, two horses and one mule. My father went to work for a salary in town.

Sometimes I would say, "Aunt Sallie, why don't you go in and read? It's so hot today."

"In a little while Effie. Your father and I have some debts to pay." She continued. "I want to get these sweet potato plants in. This crop is already sold to George Mason and Jim Brinks." These men were the grocers of Calvary.

My father and Aunt Sallie paid every penny owing against Dix, Sterling and Company, a firm that is long forgotten in our town. The history of our town I would like to read but suppose it will never be printed. There is no one to write of those days.

I used up all the pale blue paper, embossed with a darker shade of blue. There were many, many sheets. My father was generous in many ways. No, I cannot believe generosity is a fault. It was said that my father fed every man who worked on the water from Jenkins Creek's crumbling bridge to the Baltimore harbor.

At their place of business, there was a kitchen on one side, always stocked with groceries, and anyone was welcome to come in and cook and eat.

It seemed to me someone was always there, frying something. My father or Uncle Sam would say, "Put in a couple of crabs for me, I forgot to eat any dinner." They enjoyed being generous. It was a way of life.

It was early Fall, school time again, our lessons done.

We had been in the parlour singing and now we were back in the sitting room, where Aunt Sallie had made a fire in the "Spear" stove. I think "Spear" was a trade name like the Franklin stove that Benjamin Franklin invented to put in a fireplace and is still used. The heat felt cozy. The parlour had been chilly.

My father sat down in a rocker. He seemed very tired. It wasn't easy working for someone else though he had worked long and hard at his own business. There was a difference.

"Effie, look in my inside pocket and give me the letter you'll find there. I was in the post office today and the clerk said there was a letter addressed to the old box number."

I got the letter. A long envelope, and noticed that it had a picture on it, a gold picture, a seal of the State of Maryland. I noticed that hardly being able to imagine it! Father opened the letter.

Mr. William J. Dix, Sr.
Box 96
Crisfield, Maryland

Dear Mr. Dix:

Hoping these lines find you and your family in the best of health. I wish to inform you that the committee formed to make a decision regarding your request for the sale of five acres of marsh land on the Little Annamesic River, had this week decided in your favor.

These five acres are to be deeded to you by the State of Maryland as a gift. A good business man, an upstanding gentlemen and citizen, we salute you.

Until your surveying and land fill are finished there will be no tax due. However, when a structure is erected for dwelling or business, there will be a fee of ten dollars a year, payable on January 1st of each year.

Very best wishes,
Emerson C. Herrington,
Governor for the free and fair
State of Maryland
October 25, 1913.

My father folded the letter and put it back in the envelope and said thoughtfully. "Five years ago this letter would have made me very happy. It is said everything happens for the best and I believe it must be so."

My mother said, with tears in her eyes. "Mr. Dix, I am sorry."

"No, Annie, don't be sorry. Perhaps some dreams are not supposed to come true. They have their place in life, as they generate happiness, increase endeavor, instill pride, and…."

He continued, "Yes, I did try to be a good business man, upstanding, an old fashioned word."

"And you succeeded beautifully, Billie, and upstanding is a good word,"

Aunt Sallie got up as my father made a motion to put the letter in the fire. "Oh, no, no, Billie, that is a rare letter, the State giving you a gift. No, don't destroy it. No."

"No, I want to draw the picture!"

"Here, then, sweet, when you get through with it, give it to mother to put in the Bible."

Priscilla said. "Uncle Bill, it's like a grant from the King to Charles Carroll or Lord Baltimore or.... It is really unbelievable for these days."

"Who were they, Priscilla?"

"Marylanders, you will read all about them in Maryland history in the fifth grade."

"Oh," I said.

My father got up, "I must go up a story higher. I will answer the letter tomorrow evening and explain that my financial climate has changed since the request 1909, I believe it was."

He kissed me and patted my brothers on the shoulder, as he said, "Goodnight, all."

A little later, my brothers and I took our thoughts and our glasses of water and went up to bed. The day was done.

My father's dream had ended.

THE END

THE DAY THEY SOLD THE WOODS

Fifty years ago, the woods stood, tall and beautiful. The pines towered toward the sky. Other trees of lesser stature grew, lush and lovely. Wild huckleberries were here and there, all over the whole expanse, which was perhaps nine or ten acres.

There were blackberry vines, around the edges, huge cattails, and the largest Queen Anne's lace that could be found anywhere. Holly trees, resplendent with glistening leaves and red, red berries grew all over, and mistletoe clung in a waxy loveliness at the top of the highest trees. Honeysuckle ran riot on the summer using the trees for a trellis. Its fragrance mingled with woodsy smell of pine was delightful.

The birds sang all day long, made their intricate nests, and took care of their little ones, until *pushing out* time came.

Here the children of neighborhood played, bounced on saplings, made play houses, raking straw in piles, using it to outline different rooms, parlour, bedroom, kitchen, and porch.

It was cool here, even on the hottest days, and lacily lovely the sun shone through filtered down upon us at our play.

Sometime our mothers would bring a picnic basket out, and lemonade with large chunks of ice, in a big white porcelain pan, the fragrance of the lemon, and the smell of the pines.

But one day the news was circulated around the neighborhood, they were going to sell the woods. Worse than that, they were going to cut it down, scrape the ground clean, measure it off into lots, and sell it for home building sites.

My playmate came over early in the day and said, "They are going to cut our woods down. They are going to sell it." Tears came to her eyes as she went on, "the poor baby birds, the pretty huckleberries that made such good pies. I can't bear it." And she put her head down on her arm and cried.

Suddenly she looked up and said, "Effie, who are THEY? I've heard about them all my life, but who in Heaven's name are THEY?"

From my almost eight years of experience I said, "Thelma, I don't really know, but I think THEY are people, and I am quite sure THEY are rich people, for the woods must be worth a fortune, and they probably will make millions, cutting it up and selling it in little pieces."

"I can't stand it. They'll burn the cattails to cinders, and the blackberry vines won't be there anymore, and the beautiful Queen Anne's lace that I pick for my mother's bouquets, they'll scorch them, and they'll burn them all up. I wish THEY were dead."

"Oh, Thelma, I think that's a sin."

"I don't care, it's the THEY that are sinners to chop up our woods, and burn it up and sell it away," and she sobbed on my shoulder.

In the evening when things were quiet, I asked my father why this had to be, and he said, "Darling, its progress. The old must give way to the new. Families will buy the lots, build homes on them, and you will love playing with the children."

"But there are enough children to play now, Father. Thelma, Edith, Aldine, Nancy, Joe, Royce. Irene, and Ben, and Russell, and…."

"Well, sweet, let's not worry about things we cannot do anything about. This Dixie Realty Company is trying out something new, so just let's go along with them and see what happens.

Maybe it will come out alright. Most things do, you know. Here's a dime to go get yourself something, and here is a kiss to go with it."

Perhaps my father knew, or at least had a feeling of what was to be. Anyway, it made me feel a little happier about all.

I said to Thelma the next day, "Maybe it will be nice, having new houses, and new children, maybe."

"But," she said fiercely, "It won't. I will hate them to my dying day."

"Thelma, I don't think you should hate people. Maybe, it's a sin."

"I don't care. I shall hate all the people who buy lots and build houses. I will hate every nail that they drive into every board."

"I'll...."

"Oh, Thelma, let's have a tea party. Mother made gingerbread."

"Well, Effie, you won't play with those children, will you?"

"Thelma, as if I'd ever play with anybody but you. You're my best friend."

"And you're mine. Let's go get the gingerbread..."

The weeks went by and industry reigned in the woods. They chopped the trees down and hauled them away. They dug up the stumps. They raked the straw. It was bare and ugly. The Dixie Realty company may have seen some promise here, but to me, and the other children, it was desolation.

The men came to survey, to measure the lots, and at last they set a day to auction them off.

They even gave the woods that was no longer there a name; Summer's Rest. Doesn't it look lovely written, and doesn't it sound perfect? The name was the one thing nice about it all.

Some people said it could be a cemetery with that name, but it didn't seem so to me. Anyway no cemetery was needed as quite a few people had them in their yards, and there was a large one at the church.

Somehow, it seemed sad to me that the woods was named Summer's Rest AFTER it was cut down.

At last they set a date for the auction, August twenty third, nineteen hundred and ten. My father came home with the Wayfield Times, and there was a whole page telling about it all. There would be band music, things for sale such as peanuts, popcorn, ice cream, pink lemonade and a new drink in bottles called pop. Sarsaparilla we knew, a brown drink, but this pop was said to be pink, red, orange, purple and green. We could hardly wait. It sounded so entrancing. It also said there would be pony rides for children and of course balloons.

The day dawned, clear and bright, a summery promise of sunshine all day.

There were hundreds of people dressed in their best, everyone excited and gay. The auction began. A platform decorated with bunting and flags flying from all four corners had been built for the auctioneer.

Back of the auctioneer sat a fifty piece band, the town's finest. The Star Spangled Banner started the proceedings with everyone singing loudly.

Then they sold the woods in squares to this one and to that one. To me, all the gaiety could not overcome the fact that the woods was gone, forever....

My mother held my hand, and said, "Well, Effie, we will have some new neighbors sometime not too far into the future. Of course, it will take time."

"But," I said sadly "I just wanted the woods to stay there. Me and Thelma...."

"Well, there's Thelma now," said my mother, "and she doesn't seem to be thinking about the loss of the woods."

It was true. Thelma was laughing and happy, dancing around, with a balloon on a stick and a flag, and eating popcorn with a group of children. Her eyes were sparkling, and when they fell on me she said, "Effie, why are you holding onto your mother's hand for? Come on. Let's have some fun. I'm going to ride a pony. I've got two dollars to spend."

She whirled and twirled her balloon and munched her popcorn.

"They've got strawberry ice cream cones," she said, "and pop."

"Oh, boy is that good. I've had three already, pink, green, and purple. And I saw a whole load of little cantaloupes, and the man will cut them up for you if you buy one. Come on, listen to that band, tum de dum...tum de dee....de."

I took hold of her arm and said, "Thelma, they've sold the woods now."

"Well, what of it. Think of all those houses they're going to build, and all the nice children we will have to play with, and our mothers and fathers will have new friends. I know the children will have pets, dogs and cats and such. I think it's wonderful. I can hardly wait. Listen Effie, they're playing *Over the Waves* now," and she danced through the crowd.

My mother still held my hand. "Never mind," she said, "You will always have the woods. No one can ever take away the memory of our happy times there. Let's get some of that strawberry ice cream."

It was a gay and exciting day in our small town. The memory of it is still clear, as if it happened yesterday. Years have come and gone. I have only memories of my mother and father, and with them in memory I have the woods. Yes, I have it in memory and also anytime that I want to see my woods I can go and see it.

Tall and beautiful, the pines tower to the sky. The trees of lesser growth, lush and lovely, make up the whole. The holly trees in season are full of red, red berries, and the mistletoe grows in the topmost branches of the tallest trees. The Queen Anne's lace grows large and beautiful at the edges, and the cattails are huge and deeply brown. The honeysuckle perfume is so sweet. Isn't it nice that some things never change at all? Like the beauty of things like parents' love and flowers?

No one ever built a house on Summer's Rest. Why? Perhaps God had just planned for a woods to be in that particular place.

The years went by. And softly here and there a little pine tree would lift up its ferny little self. A sweet gum tree would start to grow and flourish. A huckleberry bush would begin its life. More baby pines, baby cedars, a tiny holly tree, would start to live and … grow. The woods began all over again. And today it stands in beauty, wrapped in God's love.

THE END

THE CROQUET SET

(It was wrapped in rainbows.)

When I was a little girl, I spent a lot of time at my grandfather's house. From our house it was quite a walk to school, but my grandparent's home, was just across the street. Instead of carrying my lunch, I lunched every day with them.

They were always very glad see me. Day after day, I was welcome. My soup was in a bowl, and my sweet potato was peeled, and my bread buttered, my glass of milk poured, when they heard the lunch bell ring.

After lunch, I was given a dime to run up to the candy store. One of that, two of those, some of these, two all day suckers, and perhaps a two cent pickle, which Mr. Johnny Riggin speared out in a barrel of vinegar with an ice-pick, good and wonderful.

Back to school, able to meet the challenge of teacher and schoolmates, with my tummy full and knowing that I was dearly loved, loved double, by my father and mother, and my mother's father and mother. My father's parents, I never knew. His father died the year that I was born, and his mother when he was just a boy.

About every two weeks, my mother insisted that I go have lunch with Auntie, whose name was Effie, and the one that I was named after, and my mother's favorite sister.

Auntie lived a short walk from school, in a large square white house. Everything was extremely neat, both inside and out, and Auntie was very neat herself and particular about everything. My hair had to be replaited before I went back to school, my face and hands washed, and stockings pulled up, without a wrinkle.

She always seemed very glad to have me also. After lunch, she always gave me a nickel to spend on the way back, as I passed Mr. Johnny Riggin's store. She apparently felt that a nickel was plenty, as I had eaten a good lunch, complete with pie or cake.

Whenever I went to have lunch with Auntie, I always stopped by my grandfather's and told him that I had to go to Auntie's today." Mother had said so, I explained. "Auntie's so particularity," I sighed.

"I'd rather eat with you."

"Well, honey, you go on today, and tomorrow you come here. Maybe we'll fry up a chicken, and have blackberry pie."

I was a well fed school girl. So thin, I looked like I might break in half.

Auntie's house had a charm for me that I couldn't have explained, and one day I said to my mother, "Auntie's house is different, mother, from any other house."

"Yes," she said, "she certainly keeps everything neat, a place for everything and everything in its place."

I felt puzzled. I knew this was not it. It was something more indefinable, to my way of thinking.

I loved to sit for a few minutes in Auntie's living room, before going back to school. It was so pleasant there. The couch (everyone had a couch then) had a chintz cover. Pink roses on a pale green back ground, and at one end, a heap of velvet pillows, in shades of green and rose velvet, with silk cords around them and tassels at one corner. The carpet on the floor was not flowered, as most people's carpets were, but plain rose color. The curtains at the windows were of rose net, with lace edged ruffles.

Over these there were chintz curtains, also ruffled and edged with ball fringe. A valance went all the way across the top, with the fringe at the edge. The little soft balls fascinated me. These chintz curtains which seems to be of the same material as the couch cover, were tied back with green velvet ribbon, matching the green background, and harmonizing with the roses, shading from palest pink to a lovely clear rose.

Everything in the room that was of glass, sparkled, the window panes, the prism gas fixture, the mirrors, reflecting the beauty of it all.

"Auntie," I said, "I like this room."

"I'm glad you do, Effie. That clock says twenty of one."

I glanced at the clock on the mantle, China, with small flowers and gold decorations. Ormolu, I think they are called.

"Your clock is very pretty, Auntie" I said, moving toward the door. "Goodbye."

"Goodbye, and tell your mother to plait your hair more tightly tomorrow, and tie the ribbon more securely. Come again, soon."

I went, skipping happily back to school, glad that my duty lunch was over, and for two whole weeks, maybe more, I could go to my grandfather's house.

My childhood was the time of croquet. Every family had a set. Everybody played. Mothers, fathers, aunts, uncles, even grandmothers and grandfathers. It was the thing to do, in the summer evening's twilight. Of course, the children played in the sunshine. They didn't mind the heat and it was a nice change from other forms of play.

I loved it. If there was no one to play with me I played alone. Sometimes with imaginary people, using two balls beside my own, and making all the turns. It really took a lot of walking, but I had plenty of time. As this was, I became an expert, in a small way. The adults never minded me, making up their evening crowds, as they knew I could offer competition.

There was one person, who especially liked to play with me, Mr. Livingstone. He was a friend of my mother's childhood, so you can see he was quite old, when I was a little girl. He had come from Missouri, and said that he was a neighbor of Jessie James' people, and they were a fine family when he knew them.

Mr. Livingstone had been a preacher, but now that he was old, he lived with his daughter in town. We lived in the suburbs, though we didn't call it that. Our section was called Calvary and the nicest people in all the world lived here. My mother had lived in town and belonged to the Baptist church from childhood. Mr. Livingstone was also a Baptist.

He was a very interesting man. He used to say that all important things, started with an M ....Missouri, Maryland, Money, Merry Christmas.

Some mornings in the summer, we would be awakened by the sound of the croquet balls being hit together. My mother would say, (my father always left very early for his work), "Come on, children. Let's get up and get Mr. Livingstone some breakfast. If you hurry, Effie, you can play a game with him, while I am getting it ready."

We were always supposed to put the croquet away in its box at night, and then put it under the porch, but we very often forgot. Children are very forgetful people.

I loved to play croquet with Mr. Livingstone. It was so early, the grass was heavy with dew, and I was still sleepy. Soon, my two brothers joined us and we played until our mother called us to breakfast.

Mr. Livingstone had a good appetite, and loved my mother's hot biscuits. She apologized for the jelly, which had not turned out well. It was like soft strawberry taffy. As he wound it around his knife, he would say, "Annie May, the texture unique, but the flavor. Ah, the flavor of sun kissed strawberries. You have captured it. It is superb. Effie, expert croquet player, please pass the biscuits."

Oh happy days, expert croquet player! You can see why liked Mr. Livingstone. He liked me.

Mr. Livingstone's visits were part of the good weather, early spring, summer and the precious fall days. In winter, he only made a few visits. When he did come in the winter, he wore a huge fur coat of raccoon. It was the first fur coat that I had ever seen.

He would lay it across a chair and I would sit in that chair and lay my cheek against the softness, while he talked with my mother.

Something that Mr. Livingstone dearly loved to do was to hold meetings. He still loved to preach and was never happier than when doing so.

In winter, which was so cold and long, on his visits, my mother would invite the neighbors over for the evening, make a fire in the parlour stove. Mr. Livingstone would give a little talk and we would sing hymns.

I loved it when they sang, *No Not One -There's not a friend like the lowly Jesus, No not one., God will take care of you, Onward Christian Soldiers, Work for the night is coming, I think when I read that sweet story of old, When Jesus was here among me, How he called little children, as lambs to his fold.* Lovely, I felt like a chosen child, happy. Happiness was the breath of life to me.

It seems so strange, that everything that happens to a person now, it is blamed on their childhood, troubles they have, I mean. Why? Well, anyway my childhood was sheer delight. I have never found it necessary to blame one thing on it. No disappointment or unfortunate greed that I had is in way connected with my childhood.

On Saturdays, my mother would go into town to shop and visit relatives. When we stopped by my grandfather's house, I would say. "Mother, please, let me stay here until you come back. I want to play with grandfather's croquet set." She would agree.

Grandfather's croquet set was very old. The colors on the balls, mallets, and stakes were getting dim, but it had another charm. It was a giant croquet set.

The balls were much larger than ours, or any other set that I had ever seen. The mallets were so big and the sticks to them so long the tallest person had no real leaning over to do to play.

I said, one day, "Grandfather, this is the nicest croquet set in the world. Where did you get it?"

"Well, Effie, it is very old. The game was new, when I bought this for your mother and aunts. A long time ago." and he sighed.

I looked at it lovingly, with a feeling of sadness, for its shabby colors, though otherwise, it was as good as ever. It must have been so bright and beautiful, long ago.

"Grandfather, does anyone ever repaint a croquet set?"

"Now, honey, I never thought of that, but I could redo it. Probably make it last another lifetime. We'll see."

"Oh, I can hardly wait. Please do it tomorrow."

"Maybe not tomorrow, but before next Saturday, for sure," he said. "Now, here's a dime, go get yourself some sweets."

The week began. I had to go to Auntie's for lunch. It had been three weeks since I had lunched with her. When I got there, she was upstairs in her bedroom, sewing, and she called to me to come up there.

The beauty of her bedroom made me draw in my breath. It was like walking into a garden. The walls were pale blue; with tiny bunches of violets with green leaves here and there all over the entire wall. At the windows pale lavender organdie ruffled curtains, tied back with bunches of purple velvet violets and lavender satin ribbons.

On the floor was a pearl gray carpet, and all the furniture was painted a soft, misty gray, with golden hardware drawer pulls in the shape of eagles.

"Effie," she said gently, "how are you today?"

"Auntie," I said. "I didn't know there was gray furniture. Ours is brown."

"Do you like it?" she smiled. "I made it gray."

"I love it. It's beautiful. It's as beautiful as the sky, just after the rain has stopped."

"All soft shades remind one of the heavens," she said. "Like the rainbow. I choose all my colors that way. Soft shades make me feel contented."

"Do you like red, Auntie?" I asked, suddenly.

"Red, yes, at Christmas," she spoke dreamily. "Red satin ribbon, wide and beautiful, red, red holly berries. Yes, I love red, but only for Christmas. I take it back, there's one exception, strawberries. In strawberry time, I love red. Come on, let's go down and get some lunch. Your hour is going fast."

We went down the stairs, through a jungle of hollyhocks, swaying in the breeze. The hall wall paper was so real. I could almost hear the pictured bees, buzzing.

The kitchen was shining bright, as usual. The walls here were palest yellow. Yellow dotted Swiss curtains blew in the noon time air. The dishes and glassware sparked and sent sunbeams over the tablecloth of snowy white. The flowers in the cloth were there but you had to look for them, large roses, leaves and butterflies. Later I knew this material to be damask. Then I just knew it to be perfect. In the center of the table there was a round mirror, on tiny gold legs, and on this was a glass bowl, with three sunflowers in it, reflecting themselves in the mirror below, enchanting.

On the wall over the sideboard, there were four pictures: Spring, Summer,

Autumn and Winter, Currier and Ives, of course, to me, Auntie's pretty pictures.

"Auntie," I said. "It's sort of funny, having pictures in the kitchen."

"Funny," she said, frowning slightly.

"I don't mean funny, Auntie," I said quickly. "I meant beautiful."

"Oh, Effie, you must endeavor to use the right word, to express exactly what you mean."

"Yes Auntie."

"And Effie...."

"Yes Auntie."

"Tell your mother to put more starch in your dresses next time."

The lunch had been good, but I didn't have time to stop at Mr. Johnny Rigging store. I had used too much time absorbing beauty, my legs had to hurry. The bell rang, when I was almost there, but I made it inside my room, breathless, but not late.

Saturday, a magic day anytime of the year, but especially so during school months.

This one I was so eager for my mother to get ready to go down town, and leave me by my grandfather's. Today the croquet set was going to be ready. Painted new, for my grandfather had promised and he kept promises.

He was not home, but my grandmother said he would soon be there. I sat in the yard swing a while, read a while, and soon up the street came my grandfather.

"Effie," he called. "She's all painted up, and as soon as I put these things away, we'll set her up,"

I didn't have long to wait. He came around to the front yard, bringing the big wooden box, containing the croquet set. He had painted the box gray. It looked very clean and neat, I thought, for the box had been shabby too.

Grandfather was happy and singing, "You're a million miles from nowhere, when you're one little mile from home," one of his favorite songs.

Now, you run tell your grandmother to make some lemonade, and I'll have it set up when you get back.

In minutes, I was back. The stakes, the wickets were in place. The mallets and balls were propped against the stakes, all ready for a game.

I felt a little dazed, as I looked. My grandfather had painted the whole set gray, even the wickets and he was waiting for my approval.

I dropped down on the front steps, and instantly he was at my side.

"Effie, baby, what's wrong with you? Are you sick? Where do you hurt? Don't you feel like playing a game?"

"My head hurts a little grandfather, and my stomach feels a little bit bad, and my knees, they feel a bit weak."

"Maybe you'd better go lie down."

I loved him so. I wouldn't have hurt his feelings for a hundred bright croquet sets.

Just then, Auntie came up the walk, and saw the gray croquet set, and his concern about me, huddled forlornly on the steps.

"Papa," she said, "what on earth have you done to the croquet set? They should be bright and gay, never gray."

Grandfather looked at the set, and then at me.

"I did have a lot of gray paint on hand, very best quality. A nice soft shade, I thought."

"Oh," said Auntie, "Papa, the gray is fine for a background, but you haven't finished it yet."

I brightened up. "Isn't it finished, grandfather? I thought it was finished."

"No, indeed, this set is not finished. If your head has stopped aching, we'll march ourselves up to the paint store, and get ourselves some finishing paint."

Auntie said, "Wait, I'll go make a list of shades, Papa, just tiny cans, but lots of shades of each color. Maybe three shades of each, though four would be better."

With list in hand, we went off, and grandfather said, "Has that weakness gone out of your legs, honey?"

"Yes, Grandfather. It's gone now. I feel fine. Let's hurry."

It was time to go to Auntie's again this week, so here I was, breathless and hungry.

"Auntie, if I eat real fast, can I sit in the parlour a few minutes before I go today?"

"Of course, child, but don't eat fast. It isn't good for you."

After lunch, she said, "Effie, don't break the stereopticon, or smudge the views with your fingers. Maybe you had better wash your hands again."

"But Auntie, I'm not going to look at the, (ten thousand times is a lot of times to look, after all).

I'm just going to sit in the different rocking chair, and look at the room."

"Oh, the platform rocker, alright, but that clock is not standing still. It says twenty to one."

I sighed. Didn't it always?

The parlour or parlor as it would be spelled today, a shrine of yesterday, where all of the beautiful things were put in one room, and the door closed upon them, for safe keeping, from fading sun, and little children's hands.

Auntie's parlour was different. First, the door didn't close the usual way. It was double, and slid open from the middle.

Most of the time, Auntie kept the doors open. A very unusual aunt was Auntie. I think she liked to look upon the beauty, that she had created there.

This day the doors were closed, but they opened easily at my touch, and I took a deep breath, at the thrust of so much beauty upon me.

Gold velvet hung at the windows, edged with gold braid fringe, with cream net close to the glass. On the floor was a thick golden brown carpet. There were a few scatter rugs of a lighter brown, with wreaths and bunches of pastel flowers in the center, shading out to rosebuds and green trailing vines to a border of gold. There were three of these, one quite large beneath the piano stool. Not a bench. The seat was a round piece of monotony, and the legs held clear balls of glass, encased in gold filigree.

This piano stool was the cynosure of the whole room. It shone, like just washed glass. I fell down on my knees, and looked at my reflection in it, before sitting in the chair. If only I had curls, I just had plaits, oh well. It was just a passing ambition.

Over the mantle, there was a mirror, which went all the way to the ceiling, framed in gold and giving back a picture of all the beautiful things in the room. There were candle sticks on the mantle, with many prisms, and each one held twelve candles. I always counted. In the center was a low crystal bowl, with fall asters.

Later there would be just ivy. My Auntie couldn't abide artificial flowers in a bowl that was supposed to contain water. She had told me so. There was nothing else on the mantle. No vases, no family pictures, just order and beauty.

I had to enjoy a little more looking before I had to go, and a little more rocking as gazed.

A few pictures adorned the walls of pale green, with a vine cut out border. All of the pictures were interesting, but over the piano was the loveliest. Pansies, all shades, grouped together in a pleasant color medley, and framed, not in just a gold frame but gold and pale green one.

"Effie, do you know it is ten minutes to one. You'll have to run all the way. You don't have time to stop at Johnny Riggins today."

"That's all right, Auntie, goodbye." I stopped a second, and said, "Auntie, I don't know which of your rooms, I like best. I'll have to think."

"You do that. Always think, and do put your mind on your lessons, so that you will get good marks, to please your mother."

"I didn't mean that kind of thinking, Auntie."

"Hurry child, and don't stay away so many days this time. I am going to make a black walnut cake tomorrow."

The next Saturday was the day. When my mother and I got to my grandfather's house, Auntie was there, though it was quite early, about nine o'clock, and my mother said to her, "Effie, I didn't expect to see you this early on a Saturday. I thought you wouldn't leave your work on Saturday morning."

She smiled and said, "This morning is special. Papa has been working on the croquet set all week, and I want to see Effie's eyes when she sees it for the first time."

Grandfather came in and said to me. "She's all ready. I'll go set her up. When I call, you come out."

At last he called. I ran down the steps and stood, absolutely bewitched at the beauty before me. The croquet set was wrapped in rainbows. The stripes went around the stakes, lovely shades of blue, pink, violet, green, yellow, with variations of every color. The mallets were the same, and the balls were also wrapped in rainbows, two ways, this way and that way. The wickets were each painted a different color.

I gazed and gazed, and suddenly a problem, long puzzling to me, was solved in an instant. Instead of beginning to play, I ran back into the house, calling, "Mother, Mother, Auntie, Auntie!"

"Effie, what is it?"

"Mother, now I know why Auntie's house is different. It isn't because it has a place for everything and everything is in its place. It's because everything that Auntie has is beautiful.

Everything she has is as lovely as grandfather's croquet set," I said happily. "I'm going to beat Grandfather today. I can hardly wait to hit the beautiful balls with those beautiful mallets."

My grandmother, a very thoughtful quiet person, said softly, as she came over and kissed me, "Effie, I hope beauty will be yours, all the days of your life." She gave me a little push and said, "Now, don't let your grandfather win."

"Grandmother, he doesn't stand a chance." And that part was true. Mr. Livingstone had not called me expert for nothing. I knew just how hard to hit that rainbow ball with that rainbow mallet to put it just where I wanted it to go.

THE END

TO MEMORY DEAR

Yet in this hearts most sacred place
Thou shall dwell forever
And stool shall recollection trace
In fancy's mirror, ever near
Each smile, each tear, upon that face
Though lost to sight, to memory dear.
Sir Thomas Moore

It was late spring, the last of May, and though the days were sunshiny and warm, the evenings were chilly. For a treat and surprise, for us, my father had made a fire in the fireplace this evening.

In the early nineteen hundreds, fireplaces were old fashioned. Everyone used stoves and burned coal in them.

The stoves were pretty, made ornamental with iron flower decorations and little doors all around the sides, with glass, through which one could see the blaze, and the door in front with its glass panels was very cheerful. But now, the stoves had been polished and put away in the closets for the summer.

My father pulled a comfortable chair closer to the cozy blaze, and took me on his lap.

"Yes," he said, "Every day that I live, I feel more convinced that heaven is right here on earth. Here, with my little girl, my two boys and my beautiful wife. Our warm fire and our nice house and just across the way my brother and his family in their happy home, and a short walk away my sister Sallie, and..."

"Yes" I interrupted, "Uncle Sam got Aunt Sarah a new carpet, roses and roses and buds and buds—."

"Father?" my brother Charles said.

"Yes, Charles."

"Effie got down and smelled the roses."

"Yes, and they were sweet."

"And I know why," he teased.

"Why? Because they were roses," I said innocently.

"Effie, carpet roses are not roses. I'll tell you why they were sweet. Uncle Sam just put some of Josie's perfume on the ones you smelled for a joke."

"Well, it was a rosy smell. I liked it. Next time I go over, I am going to smell them again, so there."

"Children, children."

There was a path between our houses, just a daisy field between. "Straight ran the pathway. Never grew the grass upon it." From the time I was three I was allowed to go across the field to Uncle Sam's, whenever I wanted to go.

How does one explain how families are different? There are no two families alike.

My mother's family was so nice, and certainly there was love there, complete accord with one another, and they knew the art of living each day happily. They lived in a neat white house, with always cut grass, cedar trees on each side of the front brick walk, and hydrangea's on each side of the porch steps. Look, you can see it.

There, was a garden and a glorious wisteria vine of fragrance and beauty. These grandparents I loved devotedly.

The families of all my friends were nice. Thelma's family was most interesting, and others had goodness and earnest endeavor.

But it is of my father and my Uncle Sam that I want to tell you. They were not just ordinary people. They were unique, and perhaps ahead of their time. They were not afraid of the word love. It was easy for them to speak of love. Love and poetry were a part of their life. Love was in their voices when they spoke of one another.

My father would say, my brother Sam, my sister Sallie, with pride and love in his voice, and they speaking to others would say, my brother Billie. To each other, they were Sallie, Billie and Sam. These three children had been raised with great care and understanding.

They had love and respect for humanity. They were kind, tactful, and generous. So generous that some considered it a character fault. I don't agree not true, generosity as they practiced it, with no thought of remuneration in any way for themselves.

Aunt Sallie was the oldest, then my father and then Uncle Sam, the youngest. Uncle Sam was young and gay and handsome, black curly hair, laughing blue eyes and vitality unbounded, a warm hearted person. He looked at the world around him as if he considered himself fortunate to be a part of it.

He would say that the greatest need of each human spirit was to walk with his head high in the dignity of his own self respect. To the children he would say our business on earth was to make ourselves better and others happy that kindness is the central and supreme simplicity of religion as Jesus taught and lived it, that life can be full of meaning and music, if we have faith to love and learn. I think my grandparents found the secret of bringing up children in the very right way.

Human nature is built of truth, knowledge, the power of beauty, and the fitness of things of social life and manners. He gave them righteousness with wisdom the power to grasp comprehensively the whole like of their times. They knew that eternal hope is happiness, that dignity and serenity are necessary for the completeness of one's life. Though my father and Aunt Sallie were admirable and intelligent to a great degree, I would say that if my grandparents could have lived to see all three through middle life they would have considered the fruition or their hopes to be culminated in Uncle Sam's character.

Uncle Sam had an ease and grace exclusively his own. There was a complete sanity about his way of life and his attitude toward books, nature and men.

He really looked at the sky, and was alive to the great sights and sounds of life. He loved the seasons and realized their influence on life and actions. He kept his own individuality in spite of pressure of work and family. There was no sarcasm, no irony in words or manner, just the knowledge that he had a life to live and the resolution to live it well.

The little key that my grandparents found and gave these three people, caused them to have a cultivated mind, tenderness and wisdom, honesty and courage. Their father taught them that love is a flower that grown in any soil works miracles and gives blessings.

They all three had refinement that only a loving home influence could teach, gentle manners, love of children, respect for all. They led by example and encapsulated benevolence and patience into their children. They gave them the art of saying and doing everything in a pleasing manner. They were conscious of a reliance on themselves and God. This in itself makes a happy and useful person.

I think the little key, was love. Then an understanding of the childish mind, early enough to obtain results, early enough to instill principles of right action. The keynote was a profound respect for everyone and everything that manifests; itself as worthy.

It was a busy path through the tangled daisy field. My little feet, eagerly ran to Uncle Sam's house, when I knew he was home from work.

The springtime was fun. I would help Uncle Sam plant flower seeds. He would make a little depression in the fine soil and I would drop a seed in. He told me that in those shriveled brown bits, there were flowers asleep, and we could awake them with warn soil, water and sunshine. Tired and hot we would sit under a tree to rest.

"The maple is so pretty, Effie, look at the fresh green leaves. Look at the shade of green. Only for a short time in the springtime are the leaves this shade of green, a magic green. Beautiful, unforgettable, look closely. It will change soon. Look at the old Willow tree."

He continued softly, "Pale green, lace trims the willow tree." The fronds of the willow moved gently in the warm spring air, and if Uncle Sam said they were green lace, I believed him.

"The bark is pretty, too," I said. "A darker green to match the lace." we laughed merrily.

I knew about matching shades. Aunt Sarah was always doing it with her dresses, hats, gloves and such.

While we were sitting there, my brother Charles ran across the field trying to get his kite up. It was windy, so the kite was soon up in the sky, high up.

"Buddie, can I hold it," I called.

"Effie, you couldn't hold this kite. She is pulling strong," he said proudly. "She might take you up with her. Isn't that so, Uncle Sam?"

"Well Charles, let's be…"

I said, "I would like to hold a kite. Everybody says I am too little."

"Charles, the next time you make a kite, make two, one for me, and gets two balls of string. Put the tail on, ready to fly and I will give you a quarter for making the kite. Here is one now for the string."

"Thanks, Uncle Sam. I will make it tonight. Oh boy, a quarter."

The next day Uncle Sam put the kite up.

"Effie, this kite is yours, your very own. Hold tight now." He transferred the string from his hand to mine. The tug of the wind was terrific, but thrilling, a never to be forgotten gesture of love and understanding.

The summer evenings were long and we played croquet until it became too dark to see the balls.

Our neighbor across the road, Mr. Jim Carman came over and played with us. We loved Mr. Jim. He was Aunt Sarah's brother and very dashing and good looking. His wife, Miss Mary, was quiet and gracious to everyone. They had no children and all the children liked to go there for there was always coke and candy, and homemade ice cream on Sundays. There was also some on Mondays, too, as their ice cream freezer was a large one.

Mr. Jim played the organ so beautifully that no one ever grew tired of listening. From the time I was very young he would take me on his lap as he played. He had a deep love for all children. Even with none of their own they had swings on their trees, a hammock between two trees, and a yard swing in the back yard.

Miss Mary would say, "Effie, how about some fresh bread and butter, or some coconut cake?"

I would say, "No thank you."

She would answer, "Little Effie, you put that no thank you in your pocket and eat this good cake."

I helped Mr. Jim with his grass cutting using the scissors to cut around the trees and flowers. Yes, our recreation was croquet and we loved it. At Uncle Sam's, the recreation was not croquet.

The girls Josie and Monie were always on the front porch with other boys and girls. Joking, singing, or in the parlours playing the organ or games. Sometime, they were even allowed to join in this sport that their father and two brothers loved so well.

Uncle Sam, with Sammy Jr., Leroy and friends were shooting at a target. A red and white target set up beyond the wild blackberry vines and peach tree. This was their sport that they loved so well.

Most of the men of the neighborhood came over and joined in the fun. The pistol shots rang out on the evening air. It never seemed to be too hot for this sport. It was an every evening thing, until twilight deepened into night.

My father was not an advocate of this sort of fun. He did not like any kind of firearms. There was a pistol at our house on the top shelf of the hall closet and a box of ammunition. On the same shelf there was a bottle of unopened whiskey for medicinal purposes. This was never opened or the pistol loaded. Here was also a fruit cake in a tin box. My mother cut slices from this when we had special company.

My father said the pistol was for protection which was very amusing, for he never would have fired it under any provocation, and it made my mother nervous even to know that it was there.

It was almost dark when Uncle Sam finished cutting the grass and trimming around the front walk and trees and flower beds. I helped with the large pair of scissors.

We sat down on the porch steps to rest. The noise inside the parlour was terrific. Josie, Monie and their friends were singing and dancing in high spirits. Aunt Sarah came in and said, "Boys and girls, you make by head ache."

Uncle Sam murmured low "A handful of quietness."

"What did you say, Uncle Sam?"

"Oh, Sweet," I was just thinking out loud. "I said "a handful of quietness." It is a phrase from the Bible, Ecclesiastic, I think, yes I believe that is right."

"But you can't have a handful of quietness. You couldn't hold it."

He answered with a smile. "But you could feel it."

Just then the boys and girls came running out madly, almost running us over.

Monie said, "Dad, are you still cutting grass? Effie, go tell your mother she wants you." Monie was full of fun and jokes. "Come on, I'll take you home."

"That's all right Monie. I'll walk over with her."

Aunt Sarah came out, "Sam, I'm going to walk over to Bessie's for a little while."

"Let's sit in the swing a little while, Effie." so we sat in the yard swing together, close together, and he put his arm around me. The fireflies flitted here and there over the yard. Locusts droned loudly with the promise of a hot day tomorrow. The sound of music came on the evening air. Mr. Jim playing the organ, and from across the road, Miss Bessie's talking machine was playing the Blue Danube Waltz. It all made a kind of summery magic.

"Say a poem Uncle Sam," I said, caught in the summer enchantment of quiet, contentment and love.

"And the night shall be filled with music
And the cares that infest the day
Shall fold their tents, like the Arabs
And as silently steal away"

"I like that, but I think it has a sleepy sound." Perhaps, Monie was right. Mother may want me. For me the day was just about over.

"Come, child, I'll walk you over. You were a big help with the scissors."

My Uncle San had married early in life and my father late, so his children were older than my brothers and me. They were teen age. For instance, Monie was seventeen when I was seven. Josie was nineteen. Sammy Jr. was twenty one and Leroy was twenty three, really grown up, though Uncle Sam was only his late forties.

They were a handsome family, full of life and happiness. Aunt Sarah was just as nice as she was pretty with curly brown hair with golden lights, brown eyes and a glowing complexion, an old fashioned adjective to describe her would be lightsome. She was of average height. Her neck and arms were like a painted picture, and little brown curls were always escaping from the soft hair piled high on her head.

The fashion of the day was that everything fitted in a lovely way. It was the time of ostrich feathers on hats, plumes they were called. Most women had black or white ones, but Aunt Sarah's were pink. They had been ordered from New York.

One Easter, I remember, she wore a pale beige suit with a lighter shade of shoes and a beige hat, with shaded pink plumes, a beige lace blouse over pink satin. She was so lovely, and Uncle Sam was so proud of her. The girls had new outfits too, but Aunt Sarah's out dazzled her daughters.

As summer came on, a dark cloud loomed for a while over our lives; Uncle Sam had to go to a hospital in Baltimore for an operation. But in a few weeks he was home again and back at the business of providing for his family.

Being so young, I didn't realize that he didn't have the same energy as before, or notice the look of worry that he and my father wore these days. Business problems were not for children. We went our happy way. We were told to be good, and I think we all three really tried to be.

The six peach trees at the back of Uncle Sam's yard were his pride and Joy. He thrilled at their blossoming every year and awaited their fruit. Can there be anything more lovely than a peach blossom, that intense pink at the center shading to almost white at the edges and the heavenly perfume? He would say, "Effie, take this little bunch into Aunt Sarah for the table."

Alas, one hard cold winter was the death of all but one. This one tried to be so valiantly beautiful. One time, when I was about five and out in the yard alone, I innocently picked all of the very tiny peaches that I could reach off of the little tree and put them in my apron pockets. They were so cute and green and fuzzy.

When Uncle Sam knew, he looked sad for a second and said, "The baby didn't know. I'll tell her how it is and next year it will be different. So he told me how the tree had to have blossoms, how the little peaches formed from the blossom, and how the sun and rain and even the wind all had a part in making the beautiful fruit. I was enchanted with the story and promised never to pick the little green balls again."

"I know what to do, let's throw them at the target," So merrily, we did. Oh, Uncle Sam was fun.

Uncle Sam built a little fence around the tree and he would take the trowel and lift the soil around the base now and then, to let its roots breathe, he said. I loved to follow him around and help.

"Someday", he said, "soon, I am going to work on these blackberry vines, take out all the weeds and make a trellis for them to lean against so that we can pick them easily. Yes and very soon too."

"I'll help, Uncle Sam."

"Yes," patting my lightly on the head, he said, "you can help and we'll get done in a jiffy, you and I. I will paint the trellis white."

Uncle Sam didn't get the weeds out, or the trellis made.

It was so much fun to shoot at the target and he only had so much time for fun. There was work all day, and lots of nights to keep a family happy and contented. To keep Aunt Sarah and the girls in pretty clothes, to keep rose strewn carpet on the parlour floor, and satin damask upholstered furniture new and beautiful.

To his family these things meant happiness and he worked for them to have them, long hours, getting large shipments of seafood off to the big city hotels in Chicago, New York and Philadelphia. This meant working sometimes all night so that it could be on the refrigerated cars early in the morning.

"Dad," said Monie one day, "Anybody would think that Effie was your little girl. You are always talking to her, and...."

"Monie, I love Effie and I love you. I love Josephine and the boys and your mother. I have lots of love. The love I have for Effie is Effie's love, and the love I have for you is your love. Oh, I have plenty of love.

The sea hath its pearls,
The heaven hath its stars
But, my heart, my heart
My heart, hath, its love.

I have enough love to divide and give forever and ever," he said gaily. "Let's go make some lemonade."

It was a nice day, and a tramp was cutting wood for my mother. We burned wood in the kitchen stove in summer for cooking, and it took a lot.

He'd enjoyed a good meal, and my mother would also pay him for the work. Some people just gave them something to eat, but my mother also paid, so we had quite a few tramps stop by. I was tired of playing so I was watching him work.

He stopped working and looked around at the flat fields and woods of our southern country, and he said, "The State of Maryland is a puzzle. Western Maryland is so beautiful, mountains, valleys, scenery, but here," he waved his hand at the daisy field.

Then he explained to me, that at the summit of the Blue Ridge Mountains there was a lovely blue haze that floated between heaven and earth, and edged the clouds with blue.

"Oh, Oh," I said, entranced. I had that breathless feeling.

"Why" he said "it's like living in a ditch, after seeing the Blue Ridge."

"A ditch," I said, "Oh, no. We do have very nice ditches, but they are made to let the tide go away, so that the gardens will grow and they're fun to jump across too. Thelma and I, we—."

He didn't say anything.

"But the people," I said, "in the western part, are they as nice as us?"

"Well now."

"Are they, Mr....?"

"Brown. To that I would say no, if I am to judge the other people here by your family."

"I would really like to see the Blue Ridge" I said dreamily, I've never seen a mountain."

"You probably will if you live long enough."

"It must be a little like heaven."

"I'll be going now."

"I thought to myself, where does a tramp go?" and as if answering my thought.

"I'm leaving town"

"Thank you for telling me about the other part of Maryland. I am going to tell my father tonight."

"Obliged, I'm sure, kid."

Every few weeks I would go with Uncle Sam to cut the grass in the graveyard at the very end of the Jenkins Creek Road. It was a sweet place, honeysuckle, pink and white, delicate wild roses, and tall brown lilies grew around the edges. Here my grandparents were at rest. It didn't seem sad to me. It seemed right for them to be there and Uncle Sam seemed happy to cut the grass and trim the weeds away from the stones. I helped with the scissors. I picked a few quick flowers and put them on a grave. Uncle Sam smiled.

"On the graces, yet unforgotten," he said. "These graves will never be forgotten. It will be beautiful here forever," I said looking around at the elm trees at one side and breathing deeply of the honeysuckle fragrance.

"I'm afraid someday they may, child. That line from Mr. Longfellow is full of thought. Let's sit down under the oak a little while."

"Say a poem, Uncle Sam."

"How about *The Schooner Hesperus?*"

"No, the little girl got too cold, and her father, he—, say, *Under the Spreading Chestnut Tree.*"

I loved the sound of his voice, and the story the poem told.

"He goes on Sunday to his church.
He sits among his boys.
Each morning see's some task begun.
Each evening sees it close."

To me poetry seemed a part of life, of everything. It was intermingled with the summer, the smell of cut grass, of walking on dandelions and oak tree shade, Uncle Sam's voice and manner and love.

While he was working I would look around for small flowers, interesting bugs and worms. In the clustered ivy on the largest elm tree, I saw a birds nest.

"Oh, Uncle Sam, there's a bird's nest here, but no little birds," I said sadly.

He came over to look.

"Yes, that is last year's nest, see how dry it is, and the soft lining has blown away."

Softly, he continued, "All things are new, the buds, the leaves, that gild the elm trees budding crest and even the nest beneath the eaves. There are no birds in last year's nest."

"That is pretty poetry Uncle Sam but is it true? Do birds just use their nest one time?"

"That is true, just once, but other birds will use the materials if we scatter it widely around, see the bits of wool. They are woven in with the twigs and sticks. It is some bright red knitting wool."

Uncle Sam lifted the nest, and gently took it apart and scattered it around the base of the tree. Little bits of milkwood feather and dandelion down fluttered for a second in the breeze.

"Now we are helping to make some mother bird happy. A bird's nest is a beautiful intricate weaving of sticks, twigs, and soft cozy lining for the baby birds comfort, made of the fluff of dandelions and milkweed pods and mother's love."

He picked up his rake and I began to pull weeds from around a stone. Roses were all over, moss roses, with many close petals, thorny, but so beautiful; cabbage roses, like a tiny pink cabbage, on a stem, with a different rose perfume, calico roses, speckled ones, pink and white. These roses had been planted by another generation. They were old fashioned now. Over one large stone there was a bush of tiny white roses, the ones Uncle Sam called Baby sweetheart.

"Uncle Sam, this graveyard is alive with roses."

He laughed. "Yes, Effie."

"Time brings the roses. Pick all you want, there will be plenty left."

I made two bouquets, one for my mother, and one for Aunt Sarah, and put them under the oak tree until we were ready to go.

In one corner of the graveyard, there were five little graves in a row, and on each stone a small curly stone lamb, asleep. These always fascinated me, and I would pat the little lambs, and think about the babies buried there. Once when Uncle Sam saw me do this, he said, "They were Mrs. Nelson's babies. Only one of her children grew up, and he had the misfortune to be drowned."

"But where is his grave," I said looking around.

"It isn't here, Effie. He has, what is called a watery grave."

Very sad for his parents, it was very hard for them to be reconciled.

They had the sympathy of everyone. "No Mound, No Stone, No Violets."

"Uncle Sam, why is everything sad?"

"Everything isn't sad. I am not, you are not, nor the roses. The sun is shining. Come little one, we are all through here for another few weeks. We must hurry home now. Aunt Sarah wants me to make a flower bed for her annuals."

"Are they flowers?"

"Yes, they are ones that must be planted every year, nasturtium: petunia and others. I should have done it a month ago, but the time slipped away. When they all bloom you can pick all that you want. They have a short life, but a merry one. The other kind of flowers that reseed themselves are called perennials."

"Like the violet and snowdrops in the graveyard?"

"Yes, that's right."

He began to sing "After the Ball Is Over", above the noise of the grass cutter on the hard shell road. Uncle Sam did everything with such verve and gaiety, even rolling a grass cutter.

I skipped along happily beside him. When we were almost home, Monie came up the road to meet us.

"Dad, it's too hot to cut grass. Why didn't you get Mr. Dave Bailey to do it for you?"

"I will, when I get old." He put his arm around her. She took the grass cutter and rolled it the rest of the way.

Monie looked at me and said, "Effie, go tell your mother she wants you."

"Now, Monie, that old joke, don't you ever get tired of teasing Effie?"

"Goodbye, Uncle Sam."

"Come over tomorrow, Effie, we might make some taffy."

On Saturday, I always had a tantrum, crying, acting up. The reason, I wanted a piece of cake. Not because I was hungry, but the cake looked so pretty and good, four layers, a different icing every week, and it was for Sunday's evening supper, a long time away from Saturday morning. It happened every week, as soon as my mother had the cake finished, I would start. I want a piece of cake.

Every family did it this way. In fact, they did most of the Sunday cooking on Saturday, as Sunday was a day of rest. Going to church three times a day left very little time, only to dress and get to church on time.

One Saturday, I was acting this way when Uncle Sam came over to bring some fresh vegetables from his garden, and was really alarmed.

"Annie May, what is the matter with Effie? She will make herself sick."

"She wants a piece of cake," my mother said wearily. My tantrums made her very nervous. He knew the custom. It was all over.

"Annie, did you ever think of making her a Saturday cake?"

"A Saturday cake?"

"Yes, a little layer cake all her own. You can bake the layers in coffee tin lids, and she can put it together as you do yours, and eat it right away. She might even want to keep it a while."

"A Saturday cake!" I got up right away, I was interested and so was my mother anything to stop my weekly tantrums.

"Yes, we will do that. We will start next Saturday, but right now we will all sit down and have some of this cake, and some lemonade to go with it."

"Here comes father. I'll go wash my face."

A summer day, not deep summer, as the middle of August, but still fairly new, the lilacs, violets, daffodils and hyacinths were a memory now, but the fragrance of the roses came to me, as I was swinging in the rope swing on the maple.

Suddenly, I decided to swing as high as I could and try to touch the drooping branches high above me. I gained momentum to fulfill my desire, but as all times before I couldn't quite make it. It was fun trying. Well, I could try again.

The green leafiness of the big maple was so beautiful. I gazed at the beauty as the swing began to go slower. I thought, how nice, we have three rope swings. The two in the front yard belonged to my brothers, and the one in the side yard mine. Somehow my brothers seemed to go the highest.

I jumped out of the swing to go get a jelly and bread sandwich. Swinging made me hungry and thirsty too. I would get some lemonade.

Just then my mother came out to cut some flowers. We heard at that moment hard running footsteps out on the road, and saw it was Sammy Jr.

My mother hurried to the edge of the yard and called, "Sammy, what is the matter?"

He slowed down for a second, "Dad, shot, accident."

"Come, Effie, put your bonnet on. We must go and see if we can help."

We went in the side door. Monie said, "Oh, Aunt Annie, please help me with mother, I don't know what to do." She took my mother's arm and they went upstairs to Aunt Sarah.

I was alone. I was forgotten in the excitement. There was no one else downstairs.

The backyard was full of people. I couldn't go out the back door but I could see Josie sitting on the low porch that would be called a patio today. She was holding Uncle Sam close to her. Tears were falling on his face.

I went through the parlour and out the front door, through the crowd and sat down by Josie, who was saying, Daddy, Daddy, in a broken despairing way.

She turned around and saw me, "Oh, no, Effie. You shouldn't be here! Go find your mother." I have never seen such pain in anyone's face.

"They won't let me come upstairs."

"Effie," she said in desperation, "Go dust the parlour," this time she didn't say, "and don't break the Shepardess," or anything. She just kept saying, "Daddy, Oh my daddy."

Uncle Sam, Sammy, Leroy and the neighbors had been shooting at the target, all having fun enough.

The boys went in to dress for the evening and Uncle Sam said, "Tell Sarah, I'll be there in a minute."

Seconds later, a single shot rang out, and Uncle Sam lay in the tangled blackberry vines, that he had never found time to weed, or make a trellis for.

There was no time for hope. Uncle Sam died in Josie's arms.

There was no one in the parlour. I went to the closet and got a folded dust cloth and then looked around the room. I rubbed my fingers on the center table, and on the mahogany arm of a chair, and on the mantle. The glass dome under which the shepherdess stood her pink sprigged flowered dress with faniers and crook in her hand and little curly white china lambs on the green simulated grass and the tiny flowers sparkled with cleanliness.

I couldn't dust. There just wasn't any. Josie had probably dusted the room and forgotten, I thought to myself. I put the dishcloth back and stood undecided. A murmur of voices came from the open door of the stairway, and a louder sound of voices from the yard.

I felt that Josie didn't want me with her, so I sat down in the platform rocker.

The next thing I knew my father was lifting me up in his arms and saying, "This is going to break her heart."

So, when I was seven years and eight months, my heart was broken.

Afterward, when I had that terrible feeling, that wouldn't go away, I knew it was because my heart was broken. I had heard my father say so.

A feeling of loss, it stays and stays. Time, everyone says, that is the only thing that will help. People keep repeating the saying, "This too shall pass away."

Yes, but it takes some sorrow as long as life itself, as long as forever.

It was being decided what I should wear to the funeral. I had a black and white checked dress, piped with red around the collar and at the edge of the long sleeves. Small black and white checks were very fashionable for little girls then. Over it, I wore a white organdie pinafore with fine Valenciennes lace. It had a white organdy sash that tied in the back.

"The red" my mother said, "it will never do!"

Auntie, my mother's sister said, "Annie May, just turn the collar in, and turn the edge of the sleeves under, that will take care of the red. Here, give me a needle, I will fix it."

"And now, about the hat," She held my best in her hand. White straw with black velvet band and streamers at the back, looped up with bunches of forget-me-nots. Around the hat was a circle of the forget-me-nots in pale shades of blue and pale pink and green leaves.

"Shall we take the flowers off?" asked my mother uncertainly.

"Well," Auntie began.

My father came in just then and my mother turned to him, "Mr. Dix, what do you think? Shall we remove the flowers from Effie's hat for the funeral, or do you think…?"

My father looked at the flowers and at me.

Forget-me-nots, aren't they as he turned away, he said, "Leave them on Annie. They are very appropriate, and after all, she is only a child."

The church was as full of people as it was on Children's Day, for Uncle Sam was loved. The funeral was on Sunday at one o'clock.

"Still, still with thee, when purple morning breaketh
When the birds' waketh, and the shadows flee
Fairer than morning, lovelier than the daylight
Dawns the sweet consciousness, I am with thee."

The last hymn was over, and the preacher stood by Uncle Sam and recited, Tennyson's *Crossing the Bar.* Sunset and evening star, twilight and evening bell.

The crowded church, the profusion of flowers, and Aunt Sarah sobbing and her voice as she looked at Uncle Sam for the last time, and said, "Sam, Sam."

This is as sad in memory, as on that Sunday afternoon. In the cemetery, at Aunt Sallie's request these two verses were read.

In the valley, shadows rise
The lark sings on
The sun, closing his benediction, sinks,
And the darkening air
Thrills with a sense triumphing night
Night with her train of stars,
And her great gift of sleep.
So be my passing,
My task accomplished and the long day done.

Some late lark singing
Let me be gathered to the quiet West
The sundown splendid and serene,
Rest.

So Uncle Sam was at rest. No more would he desire a quiet time, no more happily cut the grass, say poetry to me, or make things right with a quick idea, or endeavor to keep his family happy, by his industry and love.

Coming back from the church, I gazed through a mist at the rippling, dancing fringe at the top of the surrey. My father sat up front with the driver, and my brother Charles and my brother Willie, and my mother and me on the back seat.

My father helped us out of the carriage, and said to my mother, "Annie, change Effie's dress, the sleeves are quite wet."

The long sleeves were sticking to my arms, wet with tears.

I heard my mother ask my father later, "How could a little child cry so much, so silently."

"Heartbreak", he said, turning away.

In the evening, I said, "Father, did Uncle Sam think heaven was here on earth, or…?"

"Uncle Sam had a very happy life, dear."

"But, was it heaven," I remembered something, "or did it have mist over it, or maybe gray all the time or…"

"What do you mean, child?"

"A tramp told me that up in the Blue Ridge Mountains, there was a blue mist between Heaven and Earth. It even edged the clouds with blue, he said."

"Yes, I have seen it. It is very beautiful. I will take you to see it someday. There is a mist over Heaven just now, for all of us. It is more gray than blue, and is called sorrow, loss of a loved one. We will try to forget the sorrow and remember only the good and happy days of his time with us. On Sundays, when the flowers are blooming, we will always take a bouquet for him, as we go to church. In winter, we will take ivy, and evergreens, in his memory.

Yes, we will keep the memory, dear, but let the sorrow be forgotten."

"I will always pick the flowers very early in the morning," I said, "and some weeks maybe there will be rain, and the flowers will live until the next Sunday."

"Yes, they may. Uncle Sam left fond memories and they are the treasures that will give us peace of mind."

I'm sure if my father had known these lines, he would have thought them very beautiful for he kept saying we will forget the sorrow and remember the love.

Let the sorrow be forgotten as a flower is forgotten
Forgotten as fire that once was singing gold,
Let it be forgotten forever and ever,
Time is a kind friend
He will make us old.
If anyone asks, say it was forgotten,
Long, and long ago,
As a flower, as a fire as a hushed footfall
In a long forgotten snow.

How missed my Uncle Sam! I still walked the path through the daisy field, but when I got there, stayed only a little while.

I spend some time, helping Mr. Jim Carman and he was very nice and Miss Mary couldn't have been more kind.

One day, I was sitting in their porch swing, when I heard Mr. Jim and some friends talking, as they were leaving.

"Yes, that's the way it must have been," one gentleman said, and Mr. Jim agreed.

"Yes, Sam must have been despondent about his health and the way the business was going, and he took his own life." They said a few more words, and then Mr. Jim saw me.

I ran home and threw myself on a chair, sobbing.

"Effie, what is it?" my mother asked in alarm.

"I don't like Mr. Jim anymore. He said," I sobbed louder, "I'm never going there again. I told him I would never darken his door again. He said my Uncle Sam..."

My father came in and put his arm around me.

"Now, now, everything's all right, don't cry."

"He called me a quiet little spitfire."

"It's all right. Don't cry, child."

"Effie," my mother asked, "Why did he call you that?"

"Because I was mad and screamed and stomped my foot, like a cake tantrum used to be."

"Effie," she said sadly, "Oh, Effie."

"Now, now it's...."

I wouldn't stop until my father said quietly, "We won't be neighbors to Mr. Jim anymore. A fine man, we will miss him and Miss Mary. We are going to live at Aunt Sallie's."

"Live at Aunt Sallie's?"

"Yes she wants us so much."

"But who will live in our house?"

"Oh, someone," said my mother, tears her eyes. "I hope, they will."

"Now, Annie honey, let's take things easy. Here come the boys."

It is said that everything happens for the best but I can't imagine who said it, the Bible? Not Benjamin Franklin, I wonder who? But it seems to be true, and at times the thought has given me comfort, and also has caused deep thought about some things in life.

Leaving our home to live at Aunt Sallie's made my life different certainly I was closer to Thelma. We were now on the same side of the woods, closer to church and closer to school.

I adored Aunt Sallie. As a poet said of his great Aunt Augusta,

"There is a warmth about my heart for her,
and a sadness that never more I will see her,
for she died and left all her memories
of happenings and interesting people,
and her love for one small child,
who afterwards remembered her with joy."

In the evenings, my father read me stories and comforting poetry, and explained that what is once loved is always yours in your mind and nothing can ever take it away.

My memories of Uncle Sam, I can compare to putting my hands deep down in a fairytale chest of jewels, amethysts, emeralds and pearls, and bringing up double handfuls to admire their scintillating rays in the light of memory.

The Bible says, "The kingdom of God is within you," and a psalm says, "In quietness and confidence shall be your strength." It was that way with Uncle Sam's life.

And forever afterward, when those who had loved him spoke of him, it was with love in their voices, and when they thought of him, it was with love in their thoughts.

Stronger than steel is the sword of the spirit
Swifter than arrows,
the light of the truth Greater than all,
is love.

Little Key:
Though lost to sight, To Memory Dear. Sir Thomas Moore.
The Sea hath its Pearls. Heinrick Heinie, translated from the German by H.W. Longfellow
Time brings the roses. Thomas Carlyle.
It is not always May. H.W. Longfellow.
A handful of quietness. Bible.
Aunt Augusta. Rostrevor Hamilton. English.

Stil, Still with Thee. Harriet Beecher Stowe.
Crossing the Bar. Alfred Lord Tennyson.
Some Late Lark Singing. William Earnest Henley.
Flame and Shadow. Sarah Teasdale.
What is Once Loved. Elizabeth Catesworth.
No Mound, No Stone, No Violets. Mrs. L.C. Quinn.
Straight Between Them Ran the Pathway.
Never Grew the Grass Upon It. H.W. L. Hiawatha.
On the Graves, Yet Unforgotten. H.W. L. - Hiawatha.
Greater than All is Love. The Nun of Nodoras. H.W. Longfellow.

THE END

WE WILL REMEMBER HIM

The springtime was coming, slowly. This year it seemed reluctant to separate from the winter and begin a cycle of its own.

It was the eleventh of March, but one had to look very closely to see that the trees were showing any signs of rebirth. Yesterday, in a secluded place under a large lilac bush, had seen the green points of the lilies peeping up, and had run in breathlessly tell my mother.

This evening, as we all gathered in the sitting room after supper, my father said, "I think we are going to have a spring snow," and as he said it, I looked out and the snow began to fall. Thickly white, the big flakes fluttered down, and I thought of the lily points and wondered what it would do to them.

As I gazed out of the window I saw someone coming up the lane to our house. The snow made the person just a soft blur through the haze, as it was almost night now.

"Someone is coming," I said. Then a thought came to me. "Maybe it's a tramp."

"Effie, no, it's too early for tramps. What ideas you do have, honey," said my mother fondly. "Do your lessons now and perhaps we'll pop corn later?"

There was a knock at the side door and my Aunt Sallie said, "I'll go."

Our family was so happy together, my mother, my father, my two brothers and my Aunt Sallie and her daughter, Priscilla, who was a schoolteacher. It could have been said we were seven.

At the time of this story we were spending a year with my Aunt Sallie, for in her loneliness at the loss of her husband she had asked my father to bring his family and live with her. The house was large and she and Priscilla really wanted and needed us. The arrangement was such a happy one that it lasted a long time.

Aunt Sallie really ran the little jewel of a farm, for my father went to his business in town. She had, as I heard one of the neighbors say one day, the constitution with the resolution. She loved the earth and the things it gave back for her labor.

The strawberries were so big, the pears so yellow and the crabapples so deeply purple and velvety, the vegetables so good and plentiful.

There was a hired man, Bill Bibbins. Bill had a room in the barn, very cozy. It even had a rocking chair and curtains. It was really a room made inside the big barn and all his own.

In the hot summertime, he stayed at the Old Place across the road, because it was cooler to sleep there. The Old Place belonged to Aunt Sallie's first husband.

Bill was a big help with the work, but he was not the energetic type. He had to be kept working and never liked to work alone. As long as Aunt Sallie was in the field with him, he worked, but when she went into the house he stopped and rested under a shady tree, until she came out again. Bill was honest and could be trusted.

The years from nineteen hundred until the First World War could be called, *the day of the tramp*. The words hobo or bum, I never heard. They tramped from place to place so in my days, they were called tramps. I suppose the economic situation of the country was partly the cause.

They came, all through my childhood. We would see one coming and my brothers and I would run in and say, "Mama, a tramp is coming," and she would say, "Now Children, sit quietly until he knocks."

The knock came and my mother went to the door and timidly, but kindly, said, "Good morning."

Battered hat in hand, he would say, "Morning Maam, do you have any chores that need doing? If so I'd be pleased to help you out."

There was always wood to be cut, weeds to cut down and the grass was always getting too high.

Always, before my mother let any tramp do anything, she would say, "Wouldn't you like cup of coffee before you start work?" and they always did.

While the man was working, my mother would cook him a meal, fried potatoes, dried beef and gravy, hot biscuits with preserves.

We three children would be very interested but shy to converse with him. Anyway it was a time of children being seen and not heard, and we were quite good children. It was love that made us so, I'm sure, for we were given it in good measure.

It worried my father that my mother was not afraid of tramps, for some of them were disreputable looking characters. I think my mother was very frightened at times but the kindness in her nature overcame the fear.

She would say, "They are just unlucky men, who may have lost something or someone dear to them. A good meal and some kind words may put them back on the right path."

Who knows? Perhaps, it helped. Anyway, they all really liked my mother's fried potatoes. I remember one time a tramp who had been by the year before said, as mother turned away to get a meal ready, "Maam, your fried potatoes are the world's best."

Why is a tramp a tramp? Who knows? The tramp perhaps. Well, all the ones that I saw through my childhood certainly were not talkative people, they were extremely reserved. They worked in quietness for a good dinner and sometimes a small amount of money.

Some seemed happy and would leave whistling. Others worked and left with only a nod toward my mother and a so long to me and my brothers. Charles would say, "He has no manners. Do you think they didn't have an etiquette book at his house?"

"Well, they do cost three fifty Buddie," said my brother Willie, who was very thoughtful and earnest.

We had one. Every family did. It was as important as the Bible or the dictionary.

The knock came again, and Aunt Sallie opened the door and said, "Good evening."

She knew the etiquette book. She could have written one herself. It was a tramp. And that very first evening that he came, he read *Snowbound* to me.

We could see Aunt Sallie through the glass door talking earnestly with the man, and a few minutes later they came in together.

She said quietly, "This is Mr. Walter Jordan. Mr. Jordan, this is my brother Billie, his wife, Annie May and their children, Effie. Willie, and Charles, and this is my daughter, Priscilla."

My father looked at my Aunt Sallie, and then reached out his hand to Mr. Jordan.

My Aunt Sallie had unerring judgment.

"Mr. Jordan is going to help us out for a while with the plowing and planting. There is lots to be done."

Mr. Jordan started to speak, and Aunt Sallie said, "There is only one way to do it, and it is not complicated. Sit down, Mr. Jordan, and have some hot coffee and some food. I know you are chilled coming through the snowstorm."

He said, "Thank you."

I jumped up and said, "Take my chair, Sir, I'm going to pop corn."

Walter Jordan's brown eyes smiled into mine and I was won, forever.

After I got the corn popped, we all sat around eating it, and after a while

I tired of listening to older people talk and said, "What can I do now Mother? I've got my lessons done."

"The evenings are too long. You could go to bed early." answered my mother sensibly.

Mr. Jordan was sitting by the stove, where Aunt Sallie had insisted, to warm himself. In the corner was a table, within his reach, with a few books on it. He reached out and picked one up that I knew was a book of poetry.

"Would you like for me to read to you?" He asked me. The he opened the book of Whittier's poems and said, "How about *Snowbound* ?" And he read the whole poem, and we were all entranced with the beauty of the story and the unique way he read.

The people in the poem lived for all of us in that cozy room. They lived forever in our memory. Walter Jordan put them there.

Aunt Sallie said softly. "Splendid, Whittier's best. Mr. Jordan, I'm sure you are ready to get some rest."

He said goodnight with an almost imperceptible bow.

Aunt Sallie had fixed a place for him to sleep in the summer kitchen, where there was a couch. I had noticed earlier that she had carried in lots of blankets and things.

My father said, after Mr. Jordan had said goodnight, "Sallie, do you think...." and she said, "Yes, everything will be all right."

So we all went to bed, with a strange man sleeping in our summer kitchen.

The snow didn't stay long. The next day the sun shone brightly and by evening there was not a trace of it left.

A week went by, and each day the lily points came up a little higher. The lilac bush was looking alive, and the tips of the tree branches were showing that they had only been resting and waiting for the warmth of sun. Aunt Sallie, Bill Bibbins and Walter Jordan were making, as Bill said, "hay while the sun shines."

I'm sure Walter Jordan had never been behind plow before, but he was eager, and so willing to work.

Once I said to Aunt Sallie, "Mr. Jordan looks so sad, but he seems happy."

Every evening now he read. It was so wonderful. Priscilla said he was an elocutionist, and explained that meant to read properly with expression and the right timing for periods, commas, exclamation marks and such: *The Wreck of the Hesperus, Hiawatha and Lady Clare.*

Hiawatha took three evenings for the work that Walter Jordan was doing made him tired by nine. He enjoyed reading, as much as we enjoyed being read to. We could hardly wait for evening to come.

When he had been with us about a month, and the spring planting was well started, we began a flower garden. While we were working diligently one day, the Methodist preacher came up the lane and asked for Priscilla.

She came out on the porch and walked over to us and he said, "They are burying old Mr. Sears today, and there is no one to play the organ. Our Church organist is away and the family wants some hymns sung. There is a good organ in the home, but …."

"No I'm sorry, Mr. O'Brien, but I can't think of anyone."

We were all listening to the preacher, and Mr. Jordan stopped digging, and said, with that small bow that could hardly be called one,

"I play the organ. Could I offer my services?"

Personality was a word not used much in those days. I'm sure I had never heard it, but I knew it when I saw it. His browns wavy hair and brown eyes, his warmth and good manners all mingled together in such a pleasant way to look upon.

Now in the evenings, we sang. You can believe it or not, when Mr. Jordan played the organ, the organ not only played, it sang right along with us. It was magic! I mentioned to Priscilla and my brothers, and they said they could hear the organ singing too.

It was so wonderful to sing. We sang the hymn books right through. The Stephen Foster book, and Heart Songs, a collection of many beautiful songs, Toyland, Do They Think of Me At Home, Juanita, In the Gloaming…

Mr. Jordan's voice was so nice, tenor, I think my father said. The beauty of it blended with the old songs and became a never dimmed memory.

The spring came slowly and beautifully and fragrantly on. The lily points were six inches high now and there were curled up little bunches on the lilac bush. Soon they would uncurl into leaves, very soon, maybe tomorrow; I could hardly wait. The peach, cherry and apple trees were a mist of pink and white, and the perfume forgotten from last year? No, they were just a memory that had been asleep.

After Walter Jordan had been with us for some weeks, and he was getting to know some of the people of our community, he said one day, "Effie, I believe all of the nicest people have been gathered together here."

"Yes." I said "Calvary."

"Calvary", he said softly, "The place of prayer." He spoke as if he were talking to himself.

"And," I went on, "everybody is good here. They all go to Church three times every Sunday."

"Three times," he said, "Everybody?"

"Well, most everybody, unless they are too old or too sick and then the preacher goes to see them."

Someone was running up the lane. It was Thelma, come to play.

Mr. Jordan said, "Hello, Miss Thelma. Would you like to help us with the flower garden?"

"Don't mind if I do," said Thelma.

We worked a while, making the soil into fine powder, so that the seed could push through easily, then Thelma, getting tired, said, "Effie, let's go over to Aunt Jane's and ask her for some apple blossoms. My mother would be so happy to have some."

Mr. Jordan said, "Effie, will you bring my jacket before you go? It's on the porch."

I picked up the jacket and as I did something fell out of a pocket.

"It's a gold piece," said Thelma picking it up. But it wasn't. It was a locket.

"Effie, it's beautiful and it's got an *E* on it, your initial. Why don't you ask Mr. Jordan to give it to you?"

I looked at the deeply and beautifully engraved *E* and then turned it over. On the back was "To Earnestine, with love."

"Ask him," said Thelma, nudging me in my side.

"I can't."

"Oh, well, the catch is broken anyway, but it sure is pretty, how there is a pearl here and there in the chain and the clasp has tiny diamonds and baby pink pearls too."

It was lovely. I slipped it back into a pocket and said to Thelma, "I'll hurry, and take Walter Jordan his jacket."

Summer was with us. The lilacs had been fluffy bunches of lavender beauty. The lilies, yellow ones and the white ones called narcissus had bloomed, and I had almost crushed them lying in the grass and smelling their fragrance so deeply.

Here Mr. Jordan found me one day when only a few were in bloom, and said softly,

"Lo, the winter is part
The rain is over and gone
The flowers appear on the earth
The time of singing has come"

"I know that," I said. "It's from the *Song of Solomon* in the Bible."

"Right," he said, "2:11:12."

"Mr. Jordan, why does it say the rain is over and gone? I like rain."

He laughed and said, "Effie, you are almost too discerning. I think it means the really bad weather, not the summer rains."

"Mr. Jordan, I'm glad. Just smell this one."

Our flower garden was so beautiful that everyone came to see it. Even

Hattie Sluting who was the best flower gardener and who made her garden in shapes of stars, half moons, hearts and circles said ours was perfect.

Walter Jordan had put a formal personality into the garden. It had a brick walk through it made to wander to observe everything, and you could pick flowers and not walk on any of them. There were shells and stones placed here and there, adding charm and a difference from other gardens that we knew.

Together we had transplanted young hedge for a border and now it had grown to about ten inches high and six inches thick, and this was trimmed neatly, enclosing our garden.

It was a hot afternoon and we were sitting under the big maple. Bill Bibbins, Walter Jordan, me and Thelma. My brothers were always off on jaunts of their own fishing, playing ball, boy's affairs.

Aunt Sallie came out with a pitcher of lemonade and four glasses and put it down on the edge of the porch.

"Effie, you and Thelma can get the cupcakes. They are on the kitchen table."

"I'll go." said Bill Bobbins.

After a few minutes Thelma said, "Effie, your Aunt Sallie does make the best lemonade and cupcakes. Give me another chocolate one, Bill."

"Yes she does."

"Well," Thelma said, "everybody says she is as smart as a steel trap anyway."

Mr. Jordan laughed. "Your Aunt Sallie is better than smart. She is intelligent."

"You mean she likes everybody," said Thelma.

Mr. Jordan seemed to be far away as he said, "She loves humanity and she has compassion, the best trait of all to have, and she gives courage to others by her way of living."

"And she makes good cupcakes too" said Thelma. "Give me one more, Bill."

The happy summer days were coming to an end. The grocery store now had new composition books, tablets, pencils and companions, now called pencil boxes, new pens, and bottles of ink. He even had a sign saying, "School supplies for the year starting September 5, 1911." My mother was having new school dresses made. It was inevitable.

As I came into the house, returning from having these dresses fitted at Miss Jennie Moores', who made everyone's dresses in Calvary, Aunt Sallie called me in.

"Effie, there's a package for you on the dining room table."

"A package for me?"

"Yes, you will know from whom, when you open it."

The package was small, wrapped in white paper and had the name the town jeweler printed on it. I took off the paper and opened the box of white velvet. Inside to my surprise was the locket that had fallen out of Jordan's jacket that day. The clasp had been repaired and the tiny diamonds shone, and pale pink pearls gleamed as a stray sunbeam fell upon it.

"Aunt Sallie, it's Mr. Jordan's locket. Why?"

"Let's go out in the yard swing." She took my hand and we got into the swing.

"Effie, Mr. Jordan has gone away. He had some obligations that he remembered had to be taken care of at once. He left early this morning. Bill took him to the train."

"Gone away," I said. "Forever? He didn't say goodbye."

"No, he said he couldn't. The locket is his goodbye to you."

It is so bad to miss someone. The sun shines less brightly, the flowers look pale and you ache and it doesn't go away. It's with you all the time, wherever you go and whatever you do the ache is there.

School took lots of my time now, but in the evenings every one of us missed Walter Jordan's presence.

My mother played the organ and we sang of course and we went to church socials, bazaars and life went on and the fall changed into winter time.

My father read the paper in the evenings, some items aloud, his custom, as my mother sewed and my brothers and did our lessons on the dining room table.

One evening, as he opened the paper, he said some excitement his manner, "Sallie, will you come here a moment? There's something I want you see in the paper."

He spread the paper out on the table and on the front page was a picture of Walter Jordan. We could hardly believe our eyes. It said that Dr. Walter Earnest Jordan had returned to his work at the university, which he had left when tragedy overtook him some months before.

He had returned from a lecture tour, when he was met at the train with the news that his wife and three daughters, Elizabeth, Elsie Lee, and Earnestine had lost their lives when his home had burned the night before.

The article said he seemed dazed by the news but he said he would go the hotel for the night. The university town was stunned at the calamity for everyone in the town knew and loved the family. Next morning, Dr. Jordan was missing. The hotel bed had not been slept in, though Dr. Jordan's suitcase was the room.

Suddenly, in the fall, after months of absence, Dr. Jordan had returned and resumed his work. When asked where he had been, he told reporters, "I feel that I have been to a faraway place, where everyone was kind to one another, and that he hoped someday to find it again, and prove that it was not just a dream."

Dr. Jordan, the doctors agreed had been suffering from amnesia, rare, but not infrequent when too great a shock occurs to alter one's way of life.

"A-m-n-e-s-i-a," spelled my father slowly. "Sallie, are you acquainted with that word?"

Aunt Sallie picked up the dictionary from the pile of books on the table so suddenly that Whittier's poems fell to the floor. I picked it up and put back, remembering.

"Amnesia - forgetfulness, loss of memory due to injury, shock, fever, repression, also - a gap in one's memory," Aunt Sallie read.

I said, "Aunt Sallie, do you mean Mr. Jordan won't remember us?"

I burst out crying, and threw myself in my mother's lap.

Aunt Sallie said, "Effie, you remember the beautiful hymn that Mr. Jordan used to sing, *God's way is the best way, God's way is the right way*?"

I wiped my eyes with my hands and said, "Yes, I remember."

"Well, if God wants Walter Jordan to remember us, he will, and if he doesn't…."

"Oh, you do think he will, don't you? You do think God will let him?"

Another thought came to me and I said sadly, "The organ will never sing again. It will only play.

I want to hear the organ sing again," and I cried and no one could comfort me.

Aunt Sallie put her arms around me and held me close, and as my sobbing grew less she said,

"We can hope that someday Walter Jordan will remember us, but this we know, we will always remember him.

THE END

LOVE IS FOREVER

My father loved me, enchanting phrase.
Four words, so heavenly sweet.
He kissed me when he went away,
And when he returned at close of day.
- My eyes were very blue.

He walked proudly, because of me.
Plain plaits, bows of blue, not a curl
You see, I was his dearest treasure
And I was given devotion in full measure.
- I would put my hand in his.

The curls were not missed by him
My plaits were perfect to his eyes.
A little girl, full of earnest endeavor.
Promising, to be good forever.
- He said my smile was sunshine.

He called me names, not my own
That made me feel cherished, loved.
Baby, sugar. honey, sweet, pet.
I can hear the love in his voice, yet.
- He gave me a locket on a golden chain.

His stories had a quality, originality
That has never been surpassed.
And when all goodnights had been said
He spoke softly, "I love you," before he want to bed.
- I said it softly too.

Once, I said that I hated a little girl
I was very mad with her, and he quoted.
"Love is Sunshine, hate is a shadow, love.
You and I know God is watching from above."
- He loved the freckles across my nose.

Shower of nickels and dimes fell on me.
The general store was quite close by.
They had ice cream cones for a penny.
Half the time, I didn't care for any.
- Sometimes, I put money In a little bank.

Some children would take the babies back
If there was no penny inside, after the pin test.
But, not me, they were so very, very good.
I had to eat them right away, delicious food.
- Sometimes, there was worry about my appetite.

The glass bowl on the dining room table
Was always piled high with fruit. A picture,
Drew it once; watercolored, in my childish way.
But my Father was sure I would be an artist some day.
- Everything I end was perfect.

He brought me candy in a green striped bag,
A new kind with little motto on them -
"Do you love me? I love you."
Pink hearts and white - Be kind, be true
- They had a strawberry flavor.

Whenever I wear the color, blue
I feel my father's love all around me.
He said, "Blue is true." and he loved the color so.
Blue was part of my childhood, long ago.
- I forgot to say his eyes were like mine.

My hair ribbons were always blue.
Once I had a polka dot dress with blue dots.
If had a checked dress, it was blue.
And of course, my satin sashes were sky-color too.
- All little girls wore sashes on best dresses then.

We had a bed of forget-me-nots, blue, tiny.
They were his favorite flower.
Their beauty reminds me of my little girl
The nicest in the whole, wide world.
- They grew beneath the white lilac bush.

He would bend down low for his comin-home kiss.
His overcoat collar was of velvet, brown.
Cozy soft as kitten fur, as milkweed feather.
Oh, it was nice to be together.
- Dinner was ready, when he came.

The years have come and gone, so many.
But, I can feel his love, wrapped around me still.
It encircles me, as in that so long ago.
I am happy now, because my father loved me so.
- I smile, remembering.

Time cannot break the golden chain of love.
Its links are strong.
They hold secure.
They last forever.

THE END

I LOVE HER VERY MUCH

Two summers before and after I had been to school one year; my brothers Charles, Buddie Widdie and I were sitting on the grass under the big maple, talking.

Charles, age 12, said, "Ef, I got to give it up to you this summer. I want to keep on, but I just can't. My stomach caves into my backbone and it leaves a terrible sick feeling. I get it when the first vinegar doesn't work. I turn into a coward with every thunderstorm."

"Oh, Buddie," I protested.

"It's the honest truth," my brother insisted. "Now you're a girl and I know, and not caring what boys say, girls are braver than boys. They grow up to be nurses and—," my brother rambled on.

"I'm not!" I argued back at him.

"No, what are you going to be, then?"

"I don't know." I thought a second, "Maybe a missionary."

"Oh, Ef, you can't! They go to Africa. You wouldn't be here for thunderstorms."

"Well, I don't have to decide now." I replied.

"But will you do it, the water and the vinegar? I'll make the tea and Willie will spread up the couch. Please, Ef, please!"

I felt brave. "I'll do it, but let's not tell our father about the change, until we know I'm brave enough."

"Oh, Ef, I'll help!" Buddie Widdle spoke up. "If I was ever here alone with Mother, I would get the water and vinegar and not be afraid a bit, but I think, like Buddie, that you are a girl and braver and would do it better."

Charles spoke up, "Yes, I'll have the tea ready, and Willie will spread up the couch and let's not tell our father until summer is over because he has worries. I heard him tell our mother."

I somehow doubt if any three children had our unique problem. It was very real and took the bravery of all. There was always that fear. I suppose that water and vinegar treatment; then the tea and a short rest were all the doctor ever prescribed. He didn't know any more than we why our mother left things.

Strange, when our father was at home, it was a rare thing for her to faint. After we went to live at Aunt Sallie's, we believed that it was over. It almost was, but I think some imbalance in her must have caused my mother's problem. Her love for us made it impossible for her to cope with being alone with three children. There were woods on one side and two fields between Uncle Sam's house and ours. I wasn't taking any chances with my cut leg that looked so much like a faint thing. I found out then that I could keep a secret.

If there was the least chance of my mother having to cope with a bad situation, I kept it from her. My Aunt Sallie was brave and my father being home every evening helped a lot.

All of our summers were happy, but this one was different. Our mother fainted only twice; one time during a terrific thunderstorm and the other because of one of Bud Charles' friends. My mother and I were sitting at the kitchen table eating rice pudding happily. The pan of pudding was in front of us when a boy rushed into the kitchen and said,

"Miss Annie, Charles fell out of the barn window and we think he's killed!"

My mother put down her spoon, got up and turned toward the door. She took one step and crumpled on the kitchen floor.

Quickly I pulled the cushion from the kitchen chair and put it under her head. I got a glass of water and half of a large glass of vinegar. I was alone. Oh, where was Buddie Widdie? I had no way of knowing if Bud Charles was hurt or worse. The water I put on my mother's wrists and temples did no good. I quickly tried the vinegar, and then held the rest of for her to breathe in.

Just then, Bud Charles came walking in the back door. He explained that he had fallen on a bale of hay.

He glanced at Mom and ran out to hit Freddie, the cause of it all. By the time Bud Charles returned, Mom came back to us and seemed her usual self.

In the third grade, we had Miss Nellie. A nicer person, a lovelier woman or a more perfect schoolteacher never walked upon the earth. She was so nice that we all, thirty little girls, longed to be as nice as she was, and we tried. She was so beautiful that every day we had a real desire to be pretty as a reflection of her. We wore our starched cotton dresses, with hair ribbons to match and really cared about shades that were in harmony. If a plait became undone during the day, we asked someone to redo it and tie the ribbon back on.

Miss Nellie wore her brown curly hair in a sort of Gibson girl fashion. She piled all her long curls on the top of her head and the ones in front that slipped out, she made little circles of them and fastened into the curly pile with invisible hairpins. These were very tiny and lived up to their name. She did the same from the back and it was a delightful hairstyle. When it was warm in the room sometimes, little curls would fall on her forehead and make her even prettier.

She had some shirt waists (blouses) that had painted buttons of white china, with forget-me-nots hand painted on them, matching her eyes. The double halo of her brown curls will linger in memory as long as my forever. Her way of asking us to help her, made our endearment complete.

One day she said, "Girls, when the day is done, please see that I leave the stove door open. Yesterday I left with it closed and the janitor met me on the steps this morning and told me by doing that I was burning up the tax payer's money and could have burned down our school; so please, everyone, just glance over at the stove." We all promised.

Miss Nellie taught her third grade with the wisdom of Solomon. If a child started the third grade missing twelve words out of fifteen in their spelling, at the end of the year they would only be missing seven or eight out of fifteen, a big improvement.

She would change a poor speller's seatmate and have them sit with a good speller. Privately, Miss Nellie would ask the better student if she would please help Ada to do better, and of course she would agree to help. She asked me to sit with Ada at times. It was hard to be as nice as Miss Nellie, but we were learning patience and kindness for one another.

The year was coming to a close. Miss Nellie's desk was full of violets, lilacs, and perfect shades of tulips. Everyone would pass of course; no one failed the third grade. It was the last week of May. As Eve talked, sitting on the grass at recess and lunchtime, the conversation was of next year. The news was that the fourth grade teacher was Miss Nellie's sister. We would have another happy year with Miss Nellie's sister, but we were not really sure that this was true. Sarah Ward said, "As soon as we get in, I'm going to ask Miss Nellie."

As soon as we were all back in our room and quiet, Sarah raised her hand.

"Miss Nellie?"

"Yes Sarah?"

"Will you answer a question for me?"

"Yes, I certainly will, if I know the answer."

"Is the fourth grade teacher we are going to, if we pass, really your sister?"

"Yes, Sarah. She is really my sister. I love her very much."

I just wonder if I wondered then why Miss Nellie told us that. I suppose not. After all, I was only nine and not even nine and a half until June 20th. So it was true. She was, now we knew, a happy year again. This year we had lived with beauty, learned about patience, kindness and understanding.

The last day came with the reports. Then Miss Nellie said goodbye to us all and wished for us a happy summer.

Summer was coming to a close. The happy days, the woods picnics, croquet was ending. My thoughts were on my new fourth grade teacher. Imagine she was Miss Nellie's sister! Was it possible for anyone to be nicer than Miss Nellie? Soon I would know. Every day brought me closer and I could hardly wait to know.

I had two new composition books and a new pencil box. I needed no lunch box since my grandfather would be eagerly waiting for my coming to lunch. My sweet potato would be peeled, my soup in the bowl and my cake or pie already sliced. Of course, once every three weeks I would go to Auntie's. There was no fourth-grader happier than I as I skipped along with my composition book and my two sharpened pencils.

Miss Lena was really Miss Nellie's sister. Oh, how lucky could we all be? I could hardly wait for the loud beautiful bell to ring.

We had all chosen our seats. The last sound of the bell was stilled and Miss Lena had closed the door and stood on the platform before us. She had on a blue summer dress and white slippers. Her brown hair was piled on top of her head but it missed the loveliness of Miss Nellie's. The shade was all right, but it was straight. She looked very neat and very strong, but beauty was absent although she had pink cheeks and was smiling. Alas, there were freckles on her nose and the low neck she wore showed more. Her short sleeves revealed more on her arms and on the back of her hands.

My mother would have been outraged at this show of a lady who had exposed herself to the sun's rays, wearing no sunbonnet or sun gloves. Girls never looked like this. I wore my bonnet and gloves all summer through. I never wanted to be freckled as badly as she was.

Miss Lena began to speak, and school was beginning for the year. She stood up and smiled in a friendly way.

"Now, I want to learn your names. Start with the first aisle and stand one at a time and I want your first and last names. If you have a first name like "Mary Ann" or "Nancy Sue", just say both names." This we all did.

"We will do this again tomorrow after opening exercises and I think I will know everyone."

"Today will be only a half day, tomorrow a full one. As time is going fast, I will tell you at once how I conduct my class. I wish some things to be understood from the beginning. I do not allow the use of chewing gum. The first time, I will ask very nicely for the person to put the chewing gum in a piece of paper and bring it up to the wallpaper basket. When a student is chewing gum, it makes me very nerv—."

She had started to say "nervous," but changed it quickly to "Unhappy."

"The next time the same person is asked to put it in a piece of paper and bring it up to the waste basket. I will ask kindly again. This will be the last time!"

I thought, now how does she know that? It had a strange sound, and another thing most teachers said just plain "gum", not "chewing gum."

She kept talking and we were all attention.

"I do not like flowers. Please do not bring any to school. I will bring some ivy for the window sills. I have a great dislike of apples. Please do not bring any, only as part of your lunch."

Oh, all those big ones I had ripening on the window ledge at home. Miss Nellie had brought a pretty basket to put her apple gifts in and every once in a while, a paper bag to carry them home. One time a pupil had been sick for a long time and Miss Nellie had brought a glass of pink apple jelly made from gift apples from some child to take to the sick student. It had green crepe paper frilled around the top and a ribbon tied in a bow.

Miss Lena was still talking.

"At Christmas, I accept no presents. Do not bring any, only for one another. We will have a small tree at Christmas. That is all unless I remember something of importance. We have one half hour left. I see you all have your paper and pencils. I will give ten spelling words and then I will write them on the board. Tomorrow you can check with me so that I will know your spelling ability."

My seat mate whispered, darkly, "It's not going to be a good year!"

"Quiet, Adelaide Long," commanded Miss Lena.

In the first six grades of public school, the children are from every kind of family. There are the ones whose father knows how to make money in some mysterious way, the doctor's children, the dentist's children and the ones that there are the most of in every class, the children who are said to be "from the wrong side of the tracks" a phrase that puzzled me.

These children came to school in unstarched dresses. Their hair looked like it had been given a lick and a promise. They were, as the others, some smart, some not so smart, but nice. They were all nice. I liked them.

I can remember there were five and Miss Lena was even more severe with them than with the rest of us. They could hardly speak that she didn't find some reason to be displeased and she would rush down the aisle with her steel ruler to hit one or to slap one, to shake one or whatever violence she wanted to enjoy. I won't say "employ" for these children had nothing in the first place.

Lois Smith was the one who got the most brunt of her displeasure. Just moving Lois to another seat or moving Nancy Lee would have made this turbulence in the classroom unnecessary, but Miss Lena loved that kind of thing. This was her way of teaching. Miss Lena said to us that she had to keep order or it was impossible to teach us.

She just couldn't take thirty-two children. She did not have what that demanded. There were so few jobs for women before World War I that no wonder so many were hired to be teachers who should not have been. Miss Lena was certainly one of them.

The second week of school was beginning. The last sound of the pretty old bell was leaving. I just wonder what happened to that old school bell. I hope some church bought it. I remember the September of the year after I graduated when I heard it. I wrote a poem and felt very sad, "The school bell rang this morning, and all went but us." That's all I remember. Before another September, the beautiful old wooden school was torn down, the bell silenced.

Miss Lena closed the door and as soon as she did, it was opened again. Hilda came in, with the ever-present note in her hand. I knew there had been something missing, but I had been so scared of Miss Lena, I hadn't been able to think.

Hilda was beautiful. The Bible speaks of "burnished gold", referring to utensils, vases, musical instruments and such things. That was the color of Hilda's hair, burnished gold, not yellow, not blonde. It was the golden color of a wedding ring that has been worn many decades. It was combed straight back with a narrow ribbon, but little curls were escaping all around her face and ears and the back part rippled down her back and ended in these similar curls. Imagine the palest pink rose leaf and that was her complexion. Her brown eyes matched the glinting light shades of this same brown color when she walked and the waves of her hair moved.

Miss Lena said, "I see you are Hilda Sterling."

"I am Miss Lena," said Hilda.

"You cannot miss a whole week and keep up with the class. Don't let it happen again this year," said Miss Lena.

"If my grandmother can stay well; if she is sick I have to stay home," said Hilda.

"Get a neighbor and you come to school," said Miss Lena.

"I will try to come every day I can," said Hilda.

"See that you do! Take the sixth seat down the third aisle with Lois Smith," commanded our teacher.

I would talk with Hilda at recess.

Later we had morning recess and Hilda, Lois Smith and I were sitting on the grass talking.

"Hilda that is the prettiest dress I have ever seen. I love pink," I said.

"Granny made it. I drew a picture for her and she made it just like the picture."

"Your Granny made that dress?" Lois was amazed

"Yes, Granny can do anything when she feels good but most on the time she is sick." Hilda replied.

"What is the matter, Hilda?" I asked.

"I don't know, Effie, and the doctor doesn't know and we have the best one, Dr. Hall."

"Maybe she could have an operation." said Lois "but she…."

"Yes, I know. She might die," Hilda answered

Lois looked sad, "Yes, maybe she had better just rest a lot."

The bell rang.

How badly I would have felt if I had known that this was the last time I would sit on the grass with Hilda. It was a bad afternoon for the fourth grade. I should not have mentioned Hilda's pretty dress, for it was a sad fact that Lois had only two dresses.

They were cotton gingham made with short sleeves; one was a pink and green plaid and the other a blue. Actually, it had been blue, but was now almost white from many washings. Lois wore one on Monday, the other on Tuesday, then the Monday one on Wednesday and the other one Thursday. She had no sweater and before the room got warm, she kept her coat on. Now this coat was a nice one, a pretty shade of blue| with a squirrel collar and cuffs and carved buttons, also her two dresses had been very nice, the style pretty and the material of good quality.

Lois' mother had been dead for about a year. It had happened when we were in Miss Nellie's room; very probably from an operation, since she had looked so sad when we were talking at recess. While we had been talking, Hilda had been curling Lois' yellow curls and she pulled the ribbon off her own hair and tied to Lois' curls.

"There" Hilda said, "It is a present. You look beautiful!"

"Oh, Hilda! How will you keep your hair up?"

"Oh, I have some invisibles in my pocket. I carry them. See, Granny made pockets in each side of this dress. They are very handy."

"Thanks, for the ribbon, Hilda," Lois said.

I wondered about Miss Lena's ruler. Did she buy it at a hardware store or was it in the room when she took over?

I had seen such a ruler before one time when a carpenter was doing some repairs to the top of the well in Calvary. He had used one just like it. I asked,

"Mr. Riggin if I go and get some paper and a pencil, can I sit here on the steps and use your ruler? I won't take it way."

He replied, "Sure you can. They are a dandy tool. Help yourself."

It was sixteen inches long and wider than the usual twelve inch ones. At the top was an extremely thin piece of copper to be sure your line was straight. The inches had many graduations.

This was the kind that Miss Lena had and it was hardly ever out of her hand. She used it for many things; to rap for attention, to point out things on the board and for her kind of violence, more toward Lois and the others as poorly dressed, but I don't believe there was a child in that room who during that year didn't feel the force of that piece of wood and metal.

Even Adelaide, who was a model pupil in all ways, was hit on the back by Miss Lena and told to sit up straighter. Adelaide wrote on a piece paper for me to see, not daring to whisper, "I've a great mind to tell Mama."

"You know what she said about tattlers," I wrote back.

Then she tore the paper into little pieces and put them in her pocket. You didn't take any chances around Miss Lena.

Lois sat with Hilda and back of them was Nancy Lee, sitting by herself. We all wondered about Nancy Lee. There was no Lee family in town. It was whispered that she was a gypsy and lived in a caravan in the woods outside of town. She was old for the fourth grade, as Hilda was. Probably the gypsies didn't stay in one place long. She was pretty with black hair and blue eyes. She was full of mischief, to the sorrow of poor Lois.

When it was what we called *the most quiet* time, like before reading or during copy-book time, then Nancy Lee would poke Lois in the back with a pencil. Lois would scream, "Nancy that hurt!"

Then down the aisle, Miss Lena would go with her ruler to hit Lois.

It was impossible for Miss Lena to hit Nancy Lee. She would tear off a piece of paper and go up to the wastebasket with it. Miss Lena would not give up her dignity and chase Nancy, so she could make her do nothing.

Today, as Lois screamed, Miss Lena got up from her desk and as she did, her eyes met mine, not hiding the contempt I felt for her ways. As she went by, she hit me on the top of my head, and said, "Shut up!"

It didn't hurt as I had a large bow made of ribbon flat on the top of my head. My back hair was divided into two parts and plaited, then pinned in a half circle. It was neat and stayed fixed all day and I couldn't have cared less how my mother did it.

"Now, why did she hit you?" Adelaide whispered.

"I know. I'll tell you later," I whispered back.

Miss Lena was mad as she could be because Nancy Lee got away from her again. She hit Lois over and over again.

Hilda, sitting by Lois, got out of her seat and pulled Lois into the aisle.

Then, Miss Lena tried to hit Hilda, but Hilda took the ruler away and started for the door. As she put her hand on the knob, she paused, as if knowing she should not take the ruler with her.

It had been hot in the room earlier and Miss Lena had asked someone to put a back window up. These windows were of immense size. Hilda stepped back in line with the window and threw the ruler with all her might. It flew over the heads of everyone and went out the window.

She turned around to leave, and as she started to open the door, I Jumped to my feet and said, "Hilda!"

I knew something was ending that should not be happening. Hilda went out and closed the door. Her school days were over.

Miss Lena came back and pushed me into my seat and said, "Effie Dix, sit down and shut up!"

Later, Adelaide was saying as we sat on the ground.

"I would like to talk it over with Papa, but then he would tell Mama, since they are so close, and he would feel that he had to tell her. Then Mama would go straight to Miss Lena and she would be very angry."

"I have never been hit in my life before. It makes me feel degraded"

"Effie, we have no rights at all."

"Did it hurt when she hit you?" I asked.

"No, but through no action of mine, I was struck. I was sitting up straight. I always do. I never slump for my health's sake."

"Adelaide, if my father knew how Miss Lena is, he wouldn't even let me come to school. He would get a permit of something and teach me himself."

Adelaide said thoughtfully, "Effie, I wonder how it is that we all never speak of her ways?"

"I hate to say this and to use a word I don't like, but we are ashamed of our teacher."

"Yes, we are, but what can we do? You know that Miss Lena said that tattle-tale tellers would be in the same class as second offense chewing gum people."

"Yes and poor Ada still says her neck hurts from being slapped on both sides of her face."

The bell rang. Recess was over, a short fifteen minutes.

Why anyone would risk Miss Lena's violence was a mystery to me.

I gave up chewing gum for the year, even if "O.K." was such a bargain, a five inch stick for one penny.

Most of us did and I'm sure Mr. Johnny Riggin's sales on O.K. dropped, but it continued. Some thought that they could get away with not being seen chewing gum and some may have been absent on the day that a second offender was seen. No more O.K. for me, after all, it wasn't candy. It couldn't be eaten.

Miss Lena did meet with a strong personality in Dorothy Legere's father which offered us some diversion.

Miss Lena stood up and said nicely, "Dorothy, bring your chewing gum up in a piece of paper and dispose of it at once."

Dorothy replied, "I'm not chewing any, Miss Lena."

"Don't tell me that! Bring it up at once." commanded Miss Lena.

"I don't have any. It's the truth. Yesterday I had a tooth taken out and it left such a big hole that I can't keep my tongue out of it."

Miss Lena said "You bring me a note from your mother and have it on my desk by nine tomorrow."

"I can't," replied poor Dorothy.

"Don't tell me you can't," shouted Miss Lena.

"My mother is dead," Dorothy replied quietly.

"Is your father dead, also?"

"No, he went to the dentist with me."

"Then, have him write the note."

The next morning, just as we were all seated and the bell had ceased, there was a knock. Miss Lena opened the door and a handsome man stepped in.

"Good morning. I am Pierre Legere, and you are Miss Lena? Let me assist you to your chair." He escorted her up the one step and pulled her chair out for her.

She asked him to accept the visitor's chair, but he declined, saying, "Thank you, Miss Lena. I prefer to stand. Now you relax completely, and I will briefly explain. It has been brought to my attention by my daughter that her truthfulness has been doubted in a truthful child. I let no one cast aspersions on my daughter's word. There must be three words said to her. I am a busy man and would refer the swift way, right here and now or I can go bring the principal down here or we can go up to his office. Now, which shall it be?"

"Here," we could barely hear Miss Lena.

Dorothy's father said, "Dorothy?"

Dorothy came up the aisle and stood by him as he put his hand on her dark curls. "Now, Miss Lena."

"Dorothy, I am sorrow," said her reluctant teacher.

"Thank you, Miss Lena," replied a subdued Dorothy.

Dorothy's father bowed to Miss Lena. Dorothy returned to her seat. At the door, with his hand on the knob, he turned and said, "A good day to you all," and with another slight bow, he left.

Some of us who were friends of Dorothy sat on the grass at recess, telling her how good looking her father was and how we all liked his manners.

"Oh, my father's wonderful, so good to me. We have been in many countries. He builds unusual things. Here, he is doing a terrapin maze for Mr. Lavalette. It keeps them happy and healthy until they are shipped to big city hotels and to ocean liners. Once, on a ship, the menu read about some terrapin dish that had the sketch of a miniature terrapin beside it called Crisfield the "Seafood Capital of the World". My father says that of all the places we have been, he likes this little town best. The people are so nice. We live at the Hotel Crisfield and they knew that I like my eggs only scrambled and they always are."

The bell rang and we had to go, but Pierre stayed in our memories. We wondered if all Frenchmen were so charming.

Easter was a whole year away. I had happily worn my new hat with my good last year's coat which still was nice. Spring coats don't seem to get to be worn much. The rule of no flowers still held in Miss Lena's room although it was May and violets were all around in bloom.

Today, Daisey Lee broke the rule. Every desk had a built-in ink well of metal and a sort of glass cup that fitted in the metal so that could be filled with ink. Today, Daisey had thrown her ink away, washed the glass and had put in a bunch of purple and white violets with some green leaves - a breath of spring.

We waited, but it wasn't long until Miss Lena saw them.

"Daisey, take the flowers and put them with the trash."

Daisey tore a sheet of paper and carefully put the violets in it. As she got close to the waste basket, she put the violets on the floor and deliberately put her feet on them. Then she picked the paper up and folded it over and said, "There, sweet little violets, you're murdered. You didn't want to live in this room anyway!"

Miss Lena met her half way up the aisle and slapped her on both sides of her face and said, "Daisey Lee, you're expelled! Don't come to this class again!"

"How about my report?" Daisey asked.

"Your mother can come and get it," replied Miss Lena.

"I have no mother."

"Then your father," retorted Miss Lena.

"I have no father," Daisey replied. "The reports will be given out on the 29th of May. I will be here myself to get it, for I will need it for my next school." Daisey informed Miss Lena.

It was springy but that gladsome time was not celebrated in Grade 4, girls only. The fragrance of spring was all around. In the halls, on the stairs, passing children carried bouquets of flowers for their teachers. We had almost survived a school year with Miss Lena, but not Daisey.

She gathered up her pencil box and collapsible drinking cup and left.

"Bye all. See you on the 29th."

We all said, "Goodbye Daisey," and Miss Lena said, "Quiet! That's good riddance of bad rubbish!"

One morning in April, Lois Smith came to school in a light blue dress with a blue ribbon tying her hair on top. She had not tried to put her yellow hair in curls, but had brushed it and combed it until it went into ripples, as Hilda's did. She looked lovely. She had stopped by my desk before the bell rang and said,

"I have something to show you at recess."

"Lois, move to the back seat in the same aisle as you are in."

Lois had been begging for this all year, but was there hope for Miss Lena? Could she change?

At recess, Lois and I sat on the grass and she took a letter from her pocket. "This letter came from Hilda," and then she gave it to me to read,

"Dear Lois, when I came home the day I threw the ruler away, I said to Granny—," "Granny, Lois Smith liked my pink dress so well!" she replied, "I wish I could make her one just like it." Hilda, I should have taught you to sew. Though you can't, I still can. Get me the blue material and I will cut it out now."

"Granny, this drawer is full of material."

"Yes, I can cut out a couple more - maybe the yellow gingham and the green linen. I am never as happy as when I am turning straight material into a pretty dress. Get a catalog and show me her size."

So I did, and Granny felt good so she made them in no time at all. She loved doing it and they are a present, with ribbons to match. "When they wear out, tell your father to get you some. I don't know much about fathers since mine died when my little brother was three. I am sending the package in care of the barber shop, as I don't know your house number."

"Lois, that is wonderful, how sweet of her Granny." I sincerely replied. I wrote both Hilda and Granny a letter.

Hilda had put a P.S. at the bottom, "I may get a job soon if I get picked. I hope I do."

It is the last of April now, no hyacinths, lilies or violets to make the room pretty. We had respected Miss Lena's bad wish and brought her no apples, no flowers in the fall or in the springtime, Christmas present, nothing at all. Well, she didn't deserve anything. The room was desolate, not even a pretty homemade map of the USA. Some of the teachers could and did make beautiful ones.

I love how some old movies fade back and show another dimension of a person's life - seems to be always a good story when they do this.

Well, this little story is going forward a year.

I am walking down Main Street with my mother and it is one week from Easter. We are going to get my Easter hat from the millinery store. I am excited, thinking of how beautiful it will be, with rosebuds and velvet ribbons, pale green, soft pink, maybe with leaves too. We picked out the hat quickly, for I always knew the one I wanted as soon as I saw it. It was put in a pretty round box, with a silk cord and, as the milliner gave it to my mother, she said, "Don't you want to choose one for yourself while you are here?"

Mom said, "Not today. I like to take my time choosing a hat and it is late. Send the bill to Mr. Dix at the first of the month."

"Of course, Annie May, goodbye."

"Goodbye." we replied.

We passed the Lyric movies, swinging my hat box. Just beyond was the new Rexall Drug store, just opened and giving a balloon away with each orange julep sold at the fountain. I quickly gave the hat box to my mother. She gave me a nickel and said, "Don't be too long. I'll walk slowly and look in the window."

I entered the drug store and was fascinated by all the light and beauty. All the electric lights were on around the large mirror back of the soda fountain with a marble top. The mirror went to the ceiling and I had never seen anything like the frame that was around it. It was partly an ice cream parlour and partly a drugstore. There were four little tables with their pretty chairs around them scattered around the room. I sat down at the fountain and looked up into Hilda's brown eyes, and she laughed, "I thought you would never see me."

"Oh, Hilda, I am so glad to see you again!"

"What would you like?" she asked.

"Oh, one of those orange juleps."

She put the small glass down and put a straw in it.

"How's school this year, Effie? I hope, better."

"We have Miss Scott this year," I replied.

"Is she nice?" asked Hilda.

"Well, she is nicer than Miss Lena."

"Oh, not nice."

"Well, not as nice as Miss Nellie."

"Effie, I am starting school again, tonight."

"You are Hilda?"

"Yes, I am going to Melvin Horsey's business school in the Ward Building. I am going to be a typewriter."

"A typewriter? Type-print?" I asked.

"Yes, you do it on a machine, and you study spelling, and grammar and I can learn to be a secretary. I can learn all those things like periods, commas, all of those things and where to put them. The whole course lasts two winters and I'm going to learn it all. Then I'm going to get a government job in Washington, and you know that pays a fortune."

"But, Hilda, will your Granny be able to go?"

"Effie, Granny died."

"Oh, Hilda I am so sorry."

"Yes, I miss her. She was glad that I had a job. Here, try your drink."

I took deep draw and strangled. I felt terrible and couldn't get my breath. Hilda came around and beat me on the back and a man who had been sitting at one of the little tables shook me and got me to take a drink of water. Finally, I got over it.

"Effie, this is Mr. Claire."

"Mr. Claire, Effie is a friend of mine."

He bowed slightly as a flower bends in almost no breeze. The slight bow brought back memories of Mr. Legere. It is a gentlemanly gesture that they hardly know they make. It is a part of their upbringing and it was charming.

"Mr. Claire, I'm going to give Effie two balloons." Hilda said.

"Make it three, Hilda," he replied.

"Mr. Claire is going to help me with my lessons, Effie," Hilda said.

He bowed slightly, "Of course I will, Hilda," he replied.

I wanted a world of loveliness for Hilda, so good, so beautiful. When I was eight my father explained beauty to me like the *Filigree Button*. Since then, I had been a beauty-seeker, people, things, nature and how great a pleasure my search has been. With Hilda, to look at her beauty was joy, and when I found that she was kind to everyone and helpful, I adored her. Yes, truly, I wanted God to weave a web of loveliness for her, but such was not to be.

When Hilda was seventeen and a half, a tragedy came over her that was as intricate as a circle of Queen Annie's lace. Why? I was only 4 ½ years younger than Hilda. I didn't understand then nor do I now, six decades later.

How is it possible to choose the right person to have charge of thirty or more good children, for that we all were. When that schoolroom doorknob was turned at nine o'clock, those children were at her mercy. Of the seven teachers I had in elementary school, four did not have the needed patience. Children made them very nervous and brought out real violence. Choosing elementary school teachers should be taken very seriously. In High School years, this violence was not present. The teachers could take that age. I liked all of my High School teachers and two older ones I adored. I liked them and the knowledge they tried to impart to us.

I wonder what those four teachers did to us, psychologically, I mean, anything or nothing? Did the chewing gum incident with Edna harm me or help to make me stronger. I survived.

Although Miss Lena never acquired a new ruler, her strong body and hands only made our school life miserable. The chewing gum second offense ran all year and came very close to disaster. I wonder how much different Miss Lena acted the year after the one I spent with her. I sincerely hope, better.

It was time to go to Auntie's again for lunch, but today it was raining very hard and I decided to go to my grandfather's today. It was only one house up from the school. The undertaker, Mr. Lawson lived on the corner then the next house was for me. I could put my coat over my head and run over there and not get wet.

As usual, they were glad I came. I explained that it was the weather since it was really Auntie's turn. My grandfather said,

"Rain, rain, pour and pour—the blackberry pie is ready to take out of the oven door."

I was wishing a futile wish, like Miss Nellie's sentence which didn't sound just right to me when we asked if Miss Lena was really her sister. I closed my eyes and thought quickly, I wish every little girl and boy in the world had a grandfather like mine.

"You haven't got the toothache or something, have you child?" he asked.

"Oh no, I was just thinking of the pie," I replied.

Happy days, if I write "Grandfather" with a capital "G" and it isn't proper, it is how I feel. There should be a grandfather like him for every child. After lunch he gave me a dime to run up to Mr. Johnny Riggin's store. It had stopped raining and the sun was shining brightly.

I walked slowly up the street on the pavement for I was not really in the candy buying mood.

"What will you have? One filled with nuts, one of the new ones," Mr. Riggin stated.

"I believe I'll have a two-cent pickle and three cents worth of mottoes, seems like I never get tired of reading their little messages."

He speared a pickle out of the big barrel which was half way down now. It was the last of May and he had been selling pickles all year.

"I'll be!" he said. "A giant if ever saw one, but you've been a good customer all year, so for you - just two cents!"

"I'm not sure I can eat this big one."

"Share it with a friend." He put it in a small paper bag measured out the candy and gave me my nickel change.

"Goodbye!" I said, as usual, and he again shook his head.

I pulled my pickle a little way out of the bag and took one bite.

No, two slices of hot blackberry pie had been too much and I could eat no more. I crossed the street and hurried back to school.

It seemed strange that I should get two bargain pickles in one year, but it turned out to be a blessing. Or did it? Should Miss Lena have received her just deserts then and there? Maybe what happened reformed her a little. I rather think so. Then there was Miss Nellie. Who would ever want to hurt her? Miss Lena was really her sister.

Adelaide complained again this afternoon about the pickle juice running down on her side of the desk and gave me some of her drawing paper to wrap the pickle in.

"Why do you get such huge ones?" she asked.

"I don't. They just come to me somehow," I replied.

"A two cent one is big enough," she said.

"I know," I replied. "I wonder why it happens to me."

Dear Summertime, I shall enfold your loveliness this year, hurry. Why didn't I write a school story? See, there was so little to say. To the end, in Miss Lena's rooms we kept quiet.

As Adelaide said that day that Miss Lena hit her on the back, "I feel degraded!"

"What?" I queried.

"Like a slave must have felt."

"But it didn't hurt."

"No, my white wool sweater was thick," answered Adelaide. "But that was not it. It was the indignity!"

I still felt later that I should have told Papa about Adelaide. Helen Brian told me that her father was organizing meetings for next year to find out some things. He had been having too many children for patients. One girl had such a neck pain that he thought she should be taken to Baltimore to Johns Hopkins Hospital.

"Adelaide, do you think it was?"

"Quiet. Get to work," replied Adelaide

We talked more about it later. We had heard that the society will be called the Students, Parents and Teachers Group. It will meet once a month in the evening at someone's home. The first meeting will be at the Brian home in

September with ten fathers and mothers, ten children and will include two teachers from two different grades.

Adelaide said softly, "School could be a happy place."

"Yes, if all the teachers could be as nice as Miss Nellie," I sighed.

Suddenly, Miss Lena commanded, "Edna, put that gum you're chewing in a piece of paper and bring it up to the paper basket!" Her voice was sweet and low, but her expression was not pretty.

As Edna turned to put her gum in the basket, Miss Lena slapped her with all her strength! Edna was a small girl and she stumbled backward down from the platform, fell and slid along the floor until her head hit the bottom part of Adelaide's and my desk. It was the nearest to Miss Lena's desk which stood on a raised square.

As I looked down at Edna's closed eyes and still white face, I sprang into action.

"Adelaide, fill your cup with water, quick!"

I got up out of my seat and had to move Edna slightly to do so. Adelaide gave me the water and I put the cup on the floor beside Edna. A glance showed me that Miss Lena stood about three feet in back of us. There was a terrible expression on her face and her arms hung stiff and inert by her sides. I knew that for a while, Miss Lena would be no threat to anyone. The room was as quiet as a church before the prayer.

I turned Edna toward the empty front bench of the next row and tried to raise her up so that she could sit down but did not succeed. Precious time wasted here, but somehow I knew what to do for although I had never heard of shock, fainting was something that knew about and time, that precious things was going.

I knelt by Edna and turned her wrists over. Then I applied the water lavishly to her pulse, then to her temples with a soothing motion and then across her forehead. I checked her breathing, and then reached for my big history book so that could put it the long way under her head so that it would support her neck as well. Then I applied the water again for the third time. There was no change in Edna. The room was very still.

Oh, for some vinegar. If only I had some vinegar! Pickles, I thought. They're full of vinegar. I pulled the brown paper bag off, threw what was left of the water on the floor and tried to break the pickle in half my fingernails. No, my teeth would do better. I bit into the pickle, half way down and squeezed one half will all my might into the cup and then squeezed the other half. Would you believe it? I had almost a cup full of vinegar. I applied the vinegar to her pulse, her temples and across her forehead. There was still no change.

Then I got what Buddy Charles had mentioned. My stomach caved in to my back bone and I almost fell down on top of Edna. I swallowed hard, took a deep breath and made myself use the vinegar, but there was still no stirring from Edna.

I held the rest of the vinegar for her to breath in the fumes. Edna opened her eyes and changed her position.

"Effie, did I slip?"

"Yes, you did, Edna. How do you feel?"

"Oh, all right, I think."

She started to get up but couldn't quite make it. Adelaide got up to help me and we got her standing.

"Can you walk to your seat, Edna?" I inquired.

"I think so," twice without success and the third time, she made it to her feet and started for the platform.

I walked back of her but didn't touch her. As she raised one foot, she had to put it down again and then rested her hand on the visitor's sturdy captain's chair in order to walk. The next time, she made it to her desk. At that second, the bell rang and everyone left quickly, except Edna, Miss Lena and me. She was quietly sitting at her desk.

I picked up all the brown scraps of the pickle paper bag and the squeezed out halves and put them into the waste paper basket. Then I picked up my history book and put it with my other books which Adelaide had stacked neatly for me with my pencil box on top. I tucked the heavy history book under the pencil box and I was ready to go. Edna had just gone out the door.

Before this, of course, I had never been called upon to help anyone, but I just can't help wondering if Miss Lena had fainted because of something one day, would I or wouldn't I have helped her? We just don't know ourselves that well, do we?

When Miss Lena saw Edna on her feet, her expression changed and she made a small try to get up but couldn't. We all waited. In a few seconds, she tried again.

My medical knowledge was truly limited in the fourth grade, but I knew at once that Miss Lena had thought that she had killed Edna.

All I knew was about fainting and doing the right thing. This was told to my father by the best doctor in town; also, I knew when sent to get calamine lotion for poison oak to get it with phenol or it would do no good at all. We all had a lot of poison oak.

I picked up my books and as I got in front of Miss Lena, she said, "Effie, will you….?" she paused and I was getting impatient. "Stop by and tell my sister to come here at once? I need her."

"Yes, I will tell her," I replied.

As the many years have passed, I have wondered why I didn't fill my cup or hers with water and put it on her desk. She needed it. The pure truth of it was that I didn't think of it. As went down the long flight of stairs, I felt very tired. I moved my history book over to my other hand, but it didn't help, so I put it back.

I had no compassion for Miss Lena. I was not an angel. I was just a weary ten and a half year old. I wanted suddenly to be home.

Yes, I would take the short cut today, in spite of Mary Elzie's bull-dog. Miss Nellie's door was open and I gave the message.

She said, "Thank You, Effie," and then went up the stairs in a flash.

Helen Brian, the doctor's little girl, was sitting on the top step.

"Effie, I waited to ask you if you had told Edna to tell her mother about getting hurt. She could have a concussion."

"Concuss?" I said. "What is that?"

"It's something very bad that people get after they get hit on the head."

"But she only fainted, Helen."

"I'm not so sure. It took so long to revive her." Helen replied.

"I know, it's never taken that long for my mother and I've been doing that ever since I was 7 1/2 when my brother gave the job to me because - well, I must catch up with Edna and tell her."

"Edna, wait. I'm going to take the short cut today in spite of Mary Elzey's bull-dog. You must feel brave."

"No, I don't feel brave at all today, but I want to get home."

"I've heard that if you don't run, he won't chase you, but will just go back to the steps and sleep."

"Well, today I'm going to try it out, and I hope it's true."

"Edna, how do you feel? That was an awful hurt." I inquired.

"Well my head feels a little sore and aches."

"Edna, I think you should tell your mother and go to see the doctor. Helen says they either put you to sleep or keep you awake so many hours after you get your head hurt. She didn't know which."

"I'll tell her," Edna said as we parted.

"And Edna, tell your mother to make you some hot tea. That's what we do for my mother when she faints."

"Faint? Effie, did I faint?"

"Yes, you did. Bye."

As I left the pavement and turned down the narrow road where five houses were on one side of the road, I saw the big dog fast asleep on the third front step. I hoped as usual that he wouldn't see me, but no, here he came, barking and doing his awful growling and looking so mean. I walked my usual way, not fast, certainly not slow and could feel his hot breath on the back of my legs, expecting him to bite me at any second.

But no, although scared, I kept walking until I got to the end of the short road, where I turned to go across the field to the path that would take me home.

I had hardly pulled the bright cover over me before I was lost to everything.

The next day was the 28th of May. On the 29th, we would get our reports. We were all seated as the sound of the bell died away on, the 28th, but no Miss Lena. Instead the principal came in and sat in her chair, and said, "Miss Lena will not be in school today. Dr. Hall has ordered a few weeks rest for her. Today you may all have a holiday. Tomorrow, Miss Nellie will be here to give out your reports which Miss Lena has ready for you. Have a nice holiday."

The next day Miss Nellie called us one by one and as each child received his report, he left. I was last.

"Effie, I want to thank you for the help you were to my sister. I appreciate it more than words can say."

I looked her straight in the face and said, "Miss Nellie, I didn't do anything for Miss Lena."

She looked sad, and replied, "I consider that you did, and I want to thank you sincerely,

Goodbye."

I knew then why Miss Nellie's voice was so strange when in the third grade she had said, "Yes, she is really my sister. I love her very much."

It was not a statement. It was a plea, carrying no weight.

As Miss Lena was, when that door was closed, no one could love her.

I hope the little seed that Dr. Brian was seeking to plant with his Student, Parents and Teachers evenings made a very great difference.

Someone, I believe it was Hilda who had said, "Wouldn't it be nice if school could always be like Miss Nellie's room? Everyday happy, sweet with flowers and the lovely smell of apples the air?"

I hope that little seed that Dr. Brian was seeking to plant became very fruitful.

All this seems long ago and far away, sixty-six years to be exact, the fourth grade of 1912-1913.

May everyone's elementary school days be happy with flowers on all the window ledges and all of us liking our teachers very much.

School days—a pretty phrase. Happy school days can be a reality, but only if all three groups help. Dr. Brian had it right, First the students, then the parents and then the teachers who are happy in their work and then the phrase can come true: *Happy School Days.*

THE END

THE CHRISTMAS TREE QUILT

A Story of Your Mother's Childhood

This summer, my little girl, you are away
No plaits to fix, no bows to tie
So, here is a little poem for you
It tells a story, truly true.

The summer days were happy and long
And chock full of things to do
For an eager little girl of nine
When all my time was mine.

When looking back upon this time
It seems to be always summer
The smell of strawberries cooking and flowers;
Rain came, of course, but I only remember showers.

Our house was like a picture, set into its leafy frame
Big, with shutters green, quiet rooms, porches
A friendly welcome was as clear
As if it had been lettered on the door here.

Oh, our house was very nice
Trees, vines, flowers, weeping willows, too
Tall oaks, pecan trees, elms, maples, honey pod trees
Our yard was full of these.

Did you ever see a honey pod tree?
Family of locusts, tall with lacy leaves, lots of shade
It is a tree of pure delight
The pods are a sort of fruit, sweet to a childish appetite.

Everyone loved our lovely white house
Friends, peddlers, tramps, children and all
They found friendliness, understanding here in good measure
And good food too. Our Sue was a treasure.

Butterflies and honeysuckle and humming birds galore
Zigzagging their way to the hearts of the flowers
Hollyhocks, larkspur and lilies the yard did adorn
So many flowers, they even grew among the corn!

From early morn, until twilight came to claim the day
I played, read books, had fun
The grownups at our house were the kind
That any child was happy to mind.

On one side of the yard, there was a well
And fig trees spread their big leaved branches here
Under these our mother cats loved to sleep,
Current kittens in a furry heap.

How very fast the days went by. It seemed
One moment the sun would be shining
And the next one, Mother would say, "Come in, the day is done,
Come get a good night's sleep, rest and be ready for tomorrow's fun."

At our house on one side, the other from the well one
There led a path, thru the sweet potato field, past a place I loved,
Past Aunt Jane's little house, through small woods, lovely and cool
I always went this way. It was a short cut to school.

Of course, it was summer time vacation now
And school was far in the distant future.
Today was mine, and across the sweet potato field I went
Happy to take some fresh cake to Aunt Jane, mother had sent.

We "took care of" Aunt Jane, Our family
She was very old and brown and wrinkled, so nice though
Her eyes were getting dim. This was so terribly bad
For making quilts was the greatest pleasure that she had.

Aunt Jane had lived in her little house a long time
Some people said lived on borrowed time, she was maybe a hundred.
How could she be that old? I thought with a frown
She was so straight, so tall she stood, so proudly brown.

She was always very glad to see me. Her welcome was sincere,
For we both dearly loved to sit in the honey pod shade and talk.
We would sit on her front door steps half the day
Talking, sewing, resting the summer hours away.

"Look, honey, at the morning glories, so heavenly blue."
And I would look and notice, in wonder
As she showed me that each leaf was a perfect heart
And say "Yes, honey, the good Lord has an art."

"The morning glories. They are my favorite flower.
Yes, and honey, they keep a secret within their hearts
After their blooming is over, they bloom some more
That is why I always plant them to grow around the door."

"The most beautiful thing about them,
Is what happens after we think their flowering is done?
Tiny late flowers and leaves come. The aftermath it's called
So very tiny you can hardly believe it, in the fall."

"Honey, while we're resting, and a sitting here,
How about threading Aunt Jane a few needles?"
This was nothing new to me. I did it all the time
Most every day and all spare minutes that I could find.

Taking the spool of cotton and package of needles, I would begin
And not stop until every single needle was threaded.
Sometime I would tire, if the day was hot
For a whole package of needles for small fingers can be a lot.

Guess where Aunt Jane always kept her threaded needles?
Stuck in the calendar that hung on the kitchen wall!
This day I filled up every day in June
Then hurried home as the mantle clock struck, twelve, noon.

"Honey," Aunt Jane said, "This quilt has to be done sometime soon,
I've got to put in a little more time, hurry it a little
The church fair time will get here mighty soon, you know.
I'll just have to sit myself down and sew and sew."

"Aunt Jane," I said watching her industrious fingers working.
"It takes a long time to make a Christmas tree quilt?"
"Yes, it does, honey, more than a whole year, night and day
Spare minutes added, but I'm so happy working, it seems like play."

So I filled up every blessed day in the month again
And some days in the next one too, sticking them in well.
I worked quite a while and was all the way to 24
When suddenly I had finished. There wasn't any more.

"Aunt Jane," I said one day, "Why don't you get some specs?
Lots of people do you know." And she would say
"Honey, I got to get me around to that, your advice is sound
Someday, yes, someday, I'll get myself to town."

Dear patient old Aunt Jane. She couldn't read or write.
I didn't know till later there was no need for specs
It was only for needle threading and for that she had me
Too many years may have passed away, you see.

Sometime after the needles were threaded, I would say
"Aunt Jane, you certainty need a pin-cushion to put them in."
"Just you put them in the calendar there, dear
So that their tails will hang down clear."

Every time I threaded them, I would stick them in securely
June 1, 2, 3, 4, 5, 6, 7, 8, 9, 10
And in a few minutes I would finish out June
Then I would go, after promising to come over soon again.

I ran. I was in a great big hurry now
For I had something very important on my mind.
I must get to work and make Aunt Jane a present quick
Hurrying so fast, I fell. The sweet potato vines were thick.

I knew how to sew, so I cut two small squares.
And sewed the material together and turned it over
Stuffed the little square, but it looks so plain
I wanted it to be beautiful, for Aunt Jane.

"What are you doing, dear?" my mother said to me.
"Just making a little present for Aunt Jane.
She needs a pin cushion to put her needles in."
"That's nice," said mother laughing. "She might even put in a pin."

"Here," said mother, "Take these small pink flowers
They came off of your pretty last year's hat
And sew one on this way and that way, dear
And she will love and adore it, never fear."

It was so lovely. I sharply drew in my breath
When my mother was done.
A violet here, a bow there. A little frill of lace
I could hardly wait, to see Aunt Jane's happy face.

"I'm going to carry it over to her, this minute
I do hope that she will like it, Mother."
She did like it. Oh, she liked it too much
She couldn't bear to use it, for needles and such.

So she wrapped it up, slowly and carefully
And put it in the second bureau drawer with her best things
"Honey, do you have time to thread the needles over now?
I quilted late last night. Worked a little late, I allow."

"Look honey, here comes your little playmate.
She will want you to go and frolic.
Have a real good time, but don't get hurt, honey child
This day is one of God's gifts, sunny and mild."

"What have you been doing?" my playmate asked
Rushing breathlessly up to me.
"Threading needles. You should see the quilt Aunt Jane's making."
"Oh fiddle de dee. Come on to my house, mother's baking!"

"Don't you ever do anything else? Come on and play
You're always and forever over here.
I'll never darken your door again and that's a fact
If you don't play with me today, I'll never come back."

Oh, no pleased don't say that. I want to make a pin cushion first."
"A pin cushion? You made her one last week, I vow!"
"I know I did." Happy inspiration. "You can make one for your mother."
"Oh, alright, but I think it's too much bother."

So we sewed out on the porch, in the shady corner
While the summer day waned, we were as busy as the bees
Cutting, sewing, twisting, fixing, to her sorrow
I had to promise, I would play all day tomorrow.

This one was really lovely. Palest blue satin
With ribbon bows, and forget-me-nots sewn on
"It is beautiful," my playmate said to me.
"She will put it away, you will see."

"Oh, no. I wanted this one to be a plain one
That Aunt Jane will be sure to use for her needles."
"You can't." she said shaking her head, "no matter how hard you try
It's just the way you are." She breathed a resigned sigh.

"You just have to make them beautiful
To please your own self, you know.
Why not? Just forget it, and let's go and play
She will always put her needles in the calendar anyway."

The heavenly rose color in the sunset once I made
The green of the trees for another.
Pink of the dawn, polka dots, plaids, red, blue
I made them of every color, one of every hue.

Some of delicate lace, with velvet beneath
Once I made one in a wreath of fluffy white feathers
Oh, imagination really had its sway
When I created styles in pin cushions, my way.

Every time, I would carry one over to her
Aunt Jane would say, "Thank ye kindly, honey
Do you have time to do any threading today?"
Of course I did. I'd rather do it for her than play.

And for every holiday that came and Aunt Jane's birthday
I made a pin cushion to put her needles in
But, "No, honey, they're just too much beauty," and so
Into the drawer with her *keeping things* they'd go.

It takes a very great number of threaded needles
To make a Christmas tree quilt
Into each square, there was a fully trimmed Christmas tree
With little circles of material, making the balls, you see.

The circles were lovely pastels, and a clear red
Not one, but many lovely shades of each
And festooned in yellow scallops was the tinsel, make believe
How anyone could create such beauty, was hard to conceive.

Around the tree, there was a white picket fence.
With a gate, and sitting on the gatepost, a fluffy cat.
It was a perfect pattern, that one does not see any more
A rare lovely pattern, that anyone would adore.

The squares were very many. Palest green for background
Darker green for the branches of the trees
The gay circles, the angel at the top, white and gold
The cat was very real. A white one. It would be quickly sold.

"Aunt Jane," I said thoughtfully one day. "The cat,
We surely don't have any like him around here."
"I know, he is an angora, from a higher branch of cat family
His like around here, we will probably never see.

Perhaps no one would do all of the work of Aunt Jane's quilt today
The cutting out, the turning under, the whipping
The quilting, the searching for the shades. Though someone may
Someone who loves beauty. It is beautiful. The art of appliqué.

For every shade in the quilt had to be the one
That Aunt Jane wanted, right there
"No, honey, that's a mite too blue, let's have the sky blue.
There, that gold yellow. Alice blue now, yes, that'll do."

So through the pleasant summer, and through the fall
I faithfully threaded the needles
And stuck then in from the first of the month to the last
July, August, September, October, the year was going fast.

And now on my way home from school
I would stop and thread the needles, so happily
November: one, two, three, four, five, six, seven, eight
Mornings, too, if I wasn't afraid of being late.

"Aunt Jane," I said one day. "It takes lot of squares.
You have worked so very long."
"Yes, honey," she smiled, "It's been a long time *a borning*
But ready for somebody's bed on Christmas mornings."

She stopped working and looked at me closely, and said
"I couldn't have done it without you, honey
Thank ye, for your willing help," and with a smile from eyes of brown,
"You have surely earned a star for your crown."

"And while we are speaking of heaven, honey child
I must tell you. Aunt Jane will pretty soon have to go
I've been on the old earth a long time
and when I'm called to go, I won't mind."

"I'm getting old and tired, child, my work is nearly done."
"I love you, old. I love you just as you are. I really do."
I read a lot. A phrase came to me that pleased me well.
"I love you Aunt Jane—I love you better than tongues can tell."

"I know, child. I was a little baby slave."
"A baby slave. Aunt Jane! I can't bear to hear that!"
"Yes, honey, don't you fret yourself. It was a long time ago."
"No more slaves now. Abraham Lincoln made it so."

I wish you could have seen the quilt
When it was spread out, all finished up
So perfect. A Christmas tree each square adorning.
Just like the first glimpse of yours, on Christmas morning.

After Christmas came and was gone that year
There were no more needles to thread. Aunt Jane gave up sewing
And only the needle pricks in the calendar on the wall
Spoke of her industry that had been and was now beyond recall.

The New Year had begun. Aunt Jane was very thin and gray.
She rested half the day. I thought how kind she was to everyone.
The calendar was new now, upon the wall
It looked so strange. No needle pricks at all.

I heard my mother say one day, to my father
"I'm afraid Aunt Jane is fast leaving us
Her sight is getting more dim. Her steps are very slow
It's going hard with someone, when she has to go."

I ran. Through the sweet potato field
Aunt Jane was resting an her step, her head bowed low
"Please, get yourself some specs, Aunt Jane, they'd help, I know
Please, please, please, I love you so!"

"I know, honey. Aunt Jane knows your love
And I know the good Lord in Heaven above
Is putting down white marks in his book for you
I'll think on the specs. I will. That's true."

One morning, after breakfast, my mother said
Coming softly into the room
"Sweetheart, Aunt Jane left us a little after eleven
Her work is over now. She has gone to heaven."

So Aunt Jane was laid to rest. I missed her very much.
The days were long without my visits to her.
But in childhood grief cries itself away
It is well, it cannot stay.

And my mother was very wise and said to me
"Be a real good girl darling, Aunt Jane will know
And be happy in her home up In Heaven above
God is taking care of her. She is sheltered with His love."

Aunt Jane believed in a golden Heaven
Streets paved with gold, a golden crown, golden slippers, too
She used to sing a lovely hymn about it. Above the bright blue
Heaven is waiting for me and for you.

I would look up at the lovely blue
And feel that she knew that I loved her still
I tried to envision just how it was in Heaven
But young as I was, I realized that power God has not given.

A week went by, as weeks will go
And one day Mother came in with a package
When she said it was for me, I looked up in wonder
"Well, sweet," she said, "you don't have to sit and ponder."

"This, my darling," she said, "is from Aunt Jane.
She left it wrapped up for you.
See your name is on it, and a note, yes, I know
She had Daddy write it for her, weeks ago."

This is the note I read, "Dear Child,
The Christmas tree quilt is now all your own.
And here are my beautiful treasures too
Give one to each of our neighbors, from me and you."

"Mother! The beautiful Christmas tree quilt
Aunt Jane gave it to me, for my very own."
"Yes, it will be yours forever, dear.
She wanted it so, because of your kindness to her, here."

"Oh," said my mother . "It is a thing of beauty."
"Yes," my father mused. "A thing of beauty is a joy forever
It's loveliness increases." "A great poet said that and it is true
Of Aunt Jane's quilt. Age will increase its beauty for you."

"Her church, though, Mother?" "She left some money for her church.
Your father will take care of that.
Come, let's see about the pincushions for our neighbors.
1, 2, 3, 4, 5, 6," She stopped at 37, and said, "the fruits of all your labors."

We wrapped each one, and tied them with ribbons
Put on a flower and "Love from Aunt Jane and me."
My mother was very, very good at such
And the neighbors loved the one I choose for each, very much.

The years went on, and in my heart
My love forever grew for, people - good, old, bad
My children, other people's children, for God above
It seemed Aunt Jane had left me, a legacy of love.

She thought she was only leaving me the quilt
But she left love enough for me to share all my days.
Loving her made me love everyone
Made me want to be kind to everything, under the sun.

Illustration Created by Jennifer Ann Jones and Stephen Dakota Jones
03/2010

So, when you go to sleep tonight, my own
Beneath the pale and lovely quilt. Tuck it close
Around you dear. There's love sewn into each square.
I know. Aunt Jane sewed it there.

THE END

THE FILIGREE BUTTON

A Childhood Memory

Beauty -n- That quality or aggregate of qualities in something that gives pleasure to the senses or pleasurably exalts the mind or spirit, a particular grace, ornament or excellence.

The winter that I was nine years old, a lovely thing happened to be. I became aware of beauty, and for me life began that day. It took on meaning and purpose and love. Love of beauty in all things, tangible and intangible.

The object of this life of beauty was a button, or rather quite a few buttons. To be exact, there were eleven at the beginning, later reduced to one, and again much later there were four, but that is part of my story.

The summer was past and the autumn came on. There was talk of an early winter, and one of the family problems was a new winter coat for me.

My mother said to my father, "Perhaps, Aunt Priscilla at Christmas," but be said, "No, you couldn't depend on that. Her mind might run more to a white fur muff or hat, or to a locket and chain, something expensive, but thoroughly impractical, certainly not a warm winter coat."

It was imperative that one was forthcoming, for my sleeves were away up my arms, and the pockets of my best winter coat were not in the right place any more. "Effie is going to be tall," said my mother, and my father said, "I'm glad."

"Of course," mother said vaguely "but …."

My father kissed my mother gently, and said, "The Lord will provide." It was a saying of his.

And the next day, I got a winter coat. It didn't have to be bought. It was given to me. My cousin Ruth gave it to me; or rather her mother gave it to my mother, for me.

Ruth was almost two years older than I was, and getting tall too, so after only one winter, the coat was outgrown.

My Aunt Annie was really my great aunt, and Ruth was my second cousin. Aunt Annie bought things to fit, not to grow into, so the coat came to me.

I tried it on, and my father said. "There's nothing that gives a child such a loved look, as a warm winter coat." And that was the way I felt, loved, warm and happy.

The coat was gray and soft. The color soft, the texture too, and my father, making a little rhyme said, "Just the right sort of color too, for a little girl, with eyes of blue."

How wonderful the feeling of having something really beautiful. How I loved the pearly gray color of a summer's twilight.

The buttons were of silver filigree with one small flower in the very middle. Smaller flowers clustered close around the circle, the open work bringing out the effect of vines and leaves adding to the beauty. Around the edge there were other small flowers, and for a finish a beaded edge of silver. I am not an artist, but I think I can draw one.

A new winter coat a promise of warmth and coziness against the wintery wind and snowy times. And this one had something else. I tried to tell it to my father.

"You really like it, sweet?"

"Oh, yes, the buttons; they are so different, Father."

"Different," he said, looking intently at them. "Yes, darling, they are, and do you know why. They have a rare element called beauty."

"It is not only that the buttons, themselves, are beautiful. You see, it is like this. Into each beautiful thing, are all the beautiful things that you have ever seen? In that beauty that you see there is the beauty of a rainbow, your mother's smile, and stars on a summer evening, an autumn sunset, our wisteria vine in full bloom. I could go on and on. All the beauty that has been, is, and will be, is in each thing that you think beautiful."

"Tell me, sweet, what is one of the most beautiful things you have ever seen?"

I thought for a second. "The ceiling of our Church."

"Yes," said my father, "That is unusually so. An artist from New York designed it."

I could close my eyes, and see it clearly; pale blue expanse of simulated sky, with drifting white clouds, and a star tucked in here and there, a suggestion of a star studded Milky Way.

It gave me an effect of motion, and over all there seemed to be a lovely sapphire haze.

I remembered that when the sermon was long I would put my head in my mother's lap and look up and imagine the stars were twinkling.

Later that day, I said to my mother, "Mother, what do you think are the most beautiful things in the world?"

"Oh, a Christmas tree on Christmas morning, a lilac bush in spring, your father's smile, pink satin under black lace, lighted candles, pale blue organdie, our front yard after a summer shower," she stopped breathless, "Oh, I could go on forever."

The coat was kept for very best. I had the almost outgrown dark blue, alright for play and a second best, little brown checks, with a brown velvet collar.

I was always eager for Sundays to come.

"Oh," said my playmate Thelma. You got a new coat—gray. Why didn't your mother get you a red one? Gray and what kind of buttons are they?"

"Silver," I said. "Filigree."

"Fil-a-who?" she said.

"It means beautiful," I said intelligently. "Like a snowflake, a picture on one, I mean. You know, Thelma, like Queen Anne's lace."

She knew what that was. Our mothers used it in bouquets.

"Well, they are different, and that's, a fact, and there's even one right there on the back."

"Oh," I said, "you made a rhyme. You're a poet and don't know it."

It was true. The coat had a yoke, cut to a fine point in the back, and nestled close to the soft gray wool one large button, for decoration only, was sewn.

Thelma chattered on. "I like red and green coats the best and red buttons or maybe gold ones."

"Where did you buy it?" she said suddenly.

"We didn't. It was gave. It was my cousin Ruth's. She grew too fast last year. It cost a lot of money, and it came from Philadelphia."

"Why didn't her mother give it to the rummage sale?"

I felt myself growing pale. "Oh, no, she couldn't. It was too new. It had cost too much."

"Oh, well," my playmate said. "It's a second hand coat now, mine's new."

I said nothing, but thought happily. Yours is new, but mine is beautiful.

The day, went by, the weeks, the months, the seasons changed and made the years.

For two years, the gray coat was best. For one year, it was second best. Not a button had been lost, for my mother kept them sewed on securely, but alas, my arms, and my legs lengthened with the time, and one day my mother said.

"Effie, though the pretty gray coat still looks nice, it is much too small for you to wear. I am going to give it to Mrs. Barnes, for her little girl Gertrude. They have so little, that I'm sure she will appreciate it."

So, the next day when Mrs. Barnes stopped by with her children, Mother said, bringing out the gray coat. "Mrs. Barnes, would you like this for Gertrude? Effie can't use it anymore."

"Yes, indeed, I'd be glad to have it and thank you kindly."

Suddenly I couldn't bear to lose the beauty I had loved so long.

"Mother, can I speak to you alone? It's very important."

"What is it, dear?" coming into the dining room and closing the door.

"Mother, can I have the buttons? Will you take them off before you give the coat away?"

"I don't think that would be the right thing to do, dear. No, I wouldn't want to do..."

"Mother could I have just the one in the back, the big one? I'll find another in the button jar to put in its place."

"Very well, if you want it so badly, find me a large gray pearl button."

"And Mother, will you sew all of them on again? It will break Gertrude's heart if she would lose one."

Mother gave me a quick look.

"I don't think so, dear, but I'll do it anyway." she said with a smile.

So Mother changed the button in the back for the gray pearl one and sewed all the other ones on whether they needed it or not while Mrs. Barnes and the children waited.

I put the button away, away among my treasures, and went out to play.

* * * * * * * *

One day in the hot summer time a year or so later I had all the children of the neighborhood over in our back yard, having a show.

We were always having shows and charging pins or pennies for admission and serving lemonade for a special inducement to come.

This day there has a shortage of ice at our house, and Bobby Barnes, whose father was the iceman said, "I can get a big piece from Dad" (This was before electric refrigerators).

"Be sure to wrap it up in something for in this sun it will melt before we have the show."

"Ok," said Bobby. "Come on Gertrude."

In a little while they were back with the ice in Bobby's red wagon. I had a pan ready to put it in, and as he was helping me lift it out, I noticed what it was wrapped in, and Gertrude did to.

"Oh, that old thing," said Gertrude, "I wore it to a frazzle. It was pretty when your mother gave it to me.

I saw a glint of silver against the ice, and jerked the coat from under it. There were two tiny filigree buttons on one sleeve, and one on the other.

"Bobby, do you have your penknife?"

"Sure."

"Let me have it. I want to cut these buttons off."

I held them in my hand. They were as lovely as ever.

"Gertrude, did you lose all of the others?"

"No, my aunt cut them off to put on her new spring suit."

So some of the beauty I held in my hand, and some was still giving pleasure to someone.

I went into the house and put them with my treasures. One day, years afterward, quite a good many years, my own little girl said, as she was stringing buttons, a favorite pastime of hers at five.

"Mother, here is one big button and three tiny ones, just alike. Were they on something pretty one time?"

"Yes, darling, they were on a gray coat, when I was a little girl."

"It must have been a pretty coat to have such pretty buttons."

"Yes, darling, it was," I said. "It was the loveliest coat in the world."

THE END

I DO NOT HAVE A HORSE

Some little girls live in mansions
High on a wooded hill.
Some have horses. I do not.
But one thing I have and I always will.

All little girls do not have this thing
I've researched among all and I know
And only now and then do I find one
And they, like me, are glad that it is so.

I have a reading mother, something very nice
She read to me before I could talk you see.
Not a hurried up story at bedtime, oh no.
Because the baby book said read from three.

She read beyond me, my age, you know.
Not for the story then, but for our pure delight.
The snow had begun in the glooming and busily all the night
Had been heaping field and highway with a silence, deep and white.

Oh, how the lively words came and went.
The rhythm was the key that opened the door
And how I would draw closer and closer
And listen, and listen and listen some more.

Long ago, there was The Night Before Christmas.
I know it's every pleasant line
How the stockings were hung by the chimney with care
Later, came the ones that began, Once upon a time.

Mother Goose, I know them all, love everyone
If you like, I can say them for you right now
Little Betsy Baker, take her up and shake her.
Bow- wow- wow, whose dog art thou?

Those magic words, promising so much
I would get cozy and lean against my mother
And when one was all finished
I would say breathlessly. Please read another.

Cinderella, her unbelievable slipper of glass
Mother put touches in, Cinderella's eyes were blue
(But first, how could a slipper be made of such?)
Oh yes, blue as dark blue ink, and nice as you.

Little Boy Blue, a favorite. The little toy dog is covered with dust
So sad, and the Little Match Girl, my tears fell.
The little match would burn, give brief warmth, flicker, and go out.
I know the heart-breaking little story well.

There came a day, fairy stories were stored in memory
I loved them, the red, the rose, the blue, the green.
Why are fairy books named in this way?
Why are the covers the loveliest of any book ever seen?

But poetry, those lovely, lovely lilting words
Enthralled me then, as they charm me now.
The Day is Done, Paul Revere's Ride, I love Longfellow
One made me feel important, The Children's Hour.

The Arab Steed, I still badly want a horse
He couldn't part with his at the last
(I would have done the same) He flung the gold pieces on the ground
And rode away, fast, fast, fast.

The Village Blacksmith, the Barefoot Boy, great the men who wrote
Woodman Spare That Tree, they mean so much to me.
Because of this poem, I really look at trees
And look and look and their beauty, really see.

The Schooner Hesperus, the final verse so sad.
The Last Voyage, in the midnight and the snow
Poe's poems, The Raven, Annabel Lee,
The Bells, how the music of it swells, now loud, now low.

The Curfew tolls the knell of parting day,
This made me love the twilight hour.
The promise of rest at the end of the day.
Evening shadows on trees, and brook, and flower.

Lady Clare, for truths sweet sake,
She cast the diamond necklace aside
And found her love to be faithful and true
And proud of her courage, her loveliness and pride

There were the stories, like Philip Nolan
Unforgiven by his country, who sailed and sailed, until—
Nathan Hale, I only regret that I have but one life to give
Unusual, Great men, did their destiny fulfill.

Of Columbus' first voyage across the vast blue,
The question, what shall we do when hope is gone?
And his swift reply, this answer to his crew,
"Why, sail on and on and on."

We read the speeches of the great,
Patrick Henry: Give me liberty or… his words were strong.
Lincoln: All men are created free and equal.
Francis Scott Key: and his immortal song.

We read Shakespeare, I love the poetry best.
One called perfection, it's pure sacrilege to endeavor
To throw perfume on a violet, to and another color to the rainbow,
To gild gold or to paint the lily. Shakespeare was so extremely clever

All this was something to contemplate and I do love to think.
Lovely phrases, like this one, "Full many a flower
Is born to blush unseen, and waste its sweetness
On the desert air." I could ponder for an hour.

Memories, I have so beautiful many.
And that is good, for I have been told
That only our memories are all that is truly our very own.
Precious jewels, they are ours to treasure and to hold.

Of course, along the path of the reading way
I discovered books for myself
For who hath a book, has friends at hand
My room, embraces them shelf upon shelf.

Of all the poems, of all the everything,
The treasures that are found in poetry and in prose,
I love Hiawatha. I was read to sleep with this,
And still the beautiful cadence will cause my eyes to close.

Then the wrinkled old Nokomis nursed the little Hiawatha,
Rocked him in his linden cradle, bedded soft in moss and rushes,
My eyes were growing heavy, already I was getting sleepy
Then she put the cradle among the tall flowering bushes

He saw the rainbow, bowed across the heavens,
"What is that, Nakomis?" he softly said "Tell me true."
"Tis the heaven of flowers we see here. All the wildflowers of the forest.
All the lilies of the prairie. Make this beauty for you."

And she looked prideful at little Hiawatha, as she said,
"When on earth the flowers fade and perish,
They blossom in the heavens above us"
It is a beautiful thought to cherish.

"Mother, is that true?" I asked in wonder.
Blue eyes looked straight into eyes of blue.
"That, my darling, is as true as beauty,
As true as my love for you."

Before the end of a verse, slumber would come to claim me,
But one last thought before I slept, yes, lest I forget,
"Mother, I'm sure, I'm very sure of this.
I do like Longfellow, the very best."

I am not a baby any longer, or a very little girl.
I'm 1, 2, 3, 4, 5, 6, 7, 8, 9, 10, then you can add three,
And, oh how glad I am, the hours are mine
That my mother read, and still reads to me.

THE END

NICE PEOPLE I HAVE KNOWN

These people had the kindness of true sympathy, of thoughtful help. As Emerson has said

"Kindness is a great power in the world. Power has not one half the might of kindness."

Kind hearts are more than coronets. –Tennyson.

Basy and Lola

All around us was that quietness that comes before a storm, the thunder almost too low to be heard yet. The trees were bending and turning and twisting, sending showers of dry leaves to the grass. The wind to me was glorious, but to my mother, with panic in her dark eyes, it was something else. She was afraid of storms, for the distant thunder would soon change to reverberating peals of sound and fury, and the lightning, awesome and terrible to her, would light up our world. "Our world of two little boys and one little girl."—me.

Now the branches would go straight up toward the dark sky, then they would swing down, sometime touching the ground, then swirl around this way, that way. The poplar and aspen trees looked all silver, as their green leaves blew upward, showing their white lining.

"Oh, if only Daisy and Lola would come," said my mother.

My father was often away at his work, but he had asked Daisy and Lola to promise that when they saw a storm coming they would come as quickly as possible to be with us. A few drops of rain fell, the wind grew even stronger, and my mother's eyes darkened with dread as she drew us all three even closer to her and started into the house.

Just then, Lola gave her "La-Low" call, and we saw Daisy and Lola running up the path in the back of the barn. Daisy was out of breath, but for Lola it was a lark. We all went in and closed the door on the storm.

Daisy had stayed with us off and on for a long time. She came before Bud Charles was born, and when he was learning to talk he called her Basy, and we all did forever after.

My mother didn't need her to stay to work as much as for company, for I'm sure it was very lonely for her, when my father had to be away at his business at night. The packing and shipping of seafood was done mostly at night, for it went to the cities by train and very early.

On one side of our house, there were woods, and there was a large field between our house and our Uncle Sam's. Daisy was a real treasure and so nice and so pretty. She had the curliest black hair and a lovely smooth complexion.

She would read to us, and she especially liked to read bible stories. Once when she saw me draw away from a picture of bad people being burned in the bad place, she was very concerned. The picture was in black and white, for there was very little color in books that long ago, but in this particular picture, the fire was a bright red - leaping red fire.

"What is the matter, honey? Are you cold?"

"No Basy I'm afraid. Let's put the book away and you sing to me."

Basy said to my mother later, "Miss Annie, why don't you tear this page out of this book. There is no reading on the back. It frightens Effie, and I don't think it is good for her to see it."

"Perhaps we had better ask Mr. Dix first, Basy. It's an expensive book."

My mother called my father Mr. Dix in the Victorian way. There was twenty-two years difference in their ages

The next time I looked through the book the picture was gone - but never forgotten.

Maybe that's - why - I don't - like red!

How we all loved Basy. She was the very first nicest person I remember. We loved the molasses cake and white taffy she made for us. When we felt bad, she sat and rocked us and sang. She gave us true love and devotion.

Lola was an adopted child, but Basy loved her as a real sister. They were both a happy part of my childhood.

One nice thing! Both Basy and Lola were brave. If a snake came up in the yard, they would run it away. No matter what happened, they could take care of us, storms, tides, anything. They were a comfort and joy to my mother. Even after we grew up, we called Daisy, Basy and had deep affection for them both.

Summer evening: Listen and you can hear it tuning up for another day, the fireflies flickering, the locusts droning their promise of a warm day tomorrow.

The fragrance of the roses all around and the frogs with their summer croak of, "Rain, more rain, we want rain." It really sounded like that.

Summer afternoon, a great writer has said, is the loveliest phrase in the English language. To me the in between time was best of all, Summer twilight.

Lola is taking care of us. She tells us a story every twilight. My mother is sure she is telling Cinderella, Red Riding Hood, or the Three Bears. I am little. She is not telling these stories tonight. She is telling ghost stories, and Bud Charles says to Buddie Widdie (William) (Willie), "Widdie, don't listen too hard. You'll be afraid to go to bed tonight."

"How about Effie?" asks Buddie Widdie?

"Oh, she's too little to listen. She don't know from nothing."

"Now, Charles you know your mother wouldn't like for you to use slang."

Four other children came up the path. "Are you telling ghost stories? We want to listen too."

"Well," Lola began. "This man was coming home from work. It was midnight, and he was going by Asbury Church. He looked up, and the choir loft lit up, and the choir stood up and sang, "Nearer My God to Thee". Three days later his mother died, and they sang that same piece at the funeral."

"And one time a lady heard the piano playing in the parlour. She opened the door, and there were three keys going down, and in three days she was dead!"

A cool breeze made the leaves rustle, and I shivered. Lola held me close to her.

"Maybe we'll play La-Low now," said Lola. "Effie, you can hide with me."

How we adored Lola. She was always ready to play, to picnic, to go swimming, and our mother always knew we were safe with her. She was young enough to be fun and old enough for responsibility.

Always we took Lola with us, the 4th of July that we spent on the water sailing, picnicking on Old Island, and staying overnight at my father's and Uncle Sam's place of business. We always had more fun because Lola was there.

Mr. and Mrs. Dave Bailey

"Yes, you could set your clock Sunday mornings by Mr. Dave and Miss Millie. They go by at exactly ten o'clock."

"They never do miss church, do they?"

"Almost never, they are good members of Shiloh. After their little girl died, they didn't have the heart to go. It's hard to understand the why of things. She was only eight and their only child."

I drew my chair closer to my father.

"I'm your only little girl."

"Yes, you are my precious little girl."

"And Thelma is her father's only little girl. Of course, they have that baby now-Thomas. Thelma said she didn't know why they wanted him, when they already had her."

"Well, everyone also wants a son. I see he is named for his father. Fathers want sons as well as beautiful daughters."

Mr. Dave and Miss Millie came by driving toward home again going very fast. This was most unusual.

"That horse can really go, and he is so beautiful."

"Yes, Mr. Dave likes a fast horse. This one is really a high stepper. I've heard this last one was a race horse."

In a few minutes they came back slowed down, and called out.

"We forgot our collection envelopes."

"Fine people," said my father.

On Mondays, Mr. Dave went into town on business, and Miss Millie went with him to shop. Their small open buggy with red wheels was good looking and at the back, there was room to put their light shopping. Their horse had one fault. He was afraid of trains and loud noises. Because of this, Miss Millie could have lost her life, though luckily it was only a broken arm, and, as people would say today, shock.

She was setting in the buggy, her shopping all completed. Mr. Dave remembered another errand he had to do, not remembering that it was just about time for the three o'clock train. The buggy was lightly hitched, not ten feet from the railroad track. The train came thundering in. The horse reared and pulled the reins loose and was off at breakneck speed toward home and safety, and Miss Millie was really in danger. All she could do was to get as low down in the seat as possible and brace herself to keep inside the buggy. We heard them coming, for we were in the yard. Just as they neared our house, Dr. Hall's automobile came toward them with its loud chug-chug of the motor.

This was too much for the horse after the train. He reared backward, and the horse and buggy jackknifed, as they say, and the force threw Miss Millie into our yard then he raced toward home.

Dr. Hall stopped his car and come over. He leaned over Miss Millie and gently turned her on her back. The breath had been knocked out of her, but now she was stirring and moaning softly.

"She has a broken arm. Let's hope that is the extent of her injury. We will get her into the house and get it set and put her to sleep for a while."

Later he said, "Perhaps she should stay here tonight. This couch looks comfortable."

"Yes, yes, indeed," said my mother.

Just then Mr. Dave rushed in. Someone had brought him from town as soon as he had realized what had happened. Miss Millie recognized him and smiled faintly but was too sleepy to talk.

"She will be fine now. Just let her rest here until morning, Dave. That horse of yours is too high-spirited. He will cause trouble yet. A race horse is a race horse forever." He just wanted an excuse to run and took the advantage.

Next morning, Miss Millie went home. For a long time my mother and I went down to her house; did her ironing and brushed the floors until her arm was taken out of the cast. Mr. Dave did the cooking, as he worked in a restaurant at one time.

One day Miss Millie came, her arm well now, and said firmly, "Miss Annie May, every Saturday during the summer I am going to do your Sunday cooking, and you can take the children and go visiting."

Though my mother protested, it was to no avail. She came early on Saturday. We went to see our grandmother. The next, we went again, the next again. We went to visit friends, aunts, here and there until we were very tired of Saturday visiting and wanting our mother's Sunday cooking again. We didn't want the house so sparkling clean.

Miss Millie had scrubbed the woodwork weekly, and now it had to be repainted. My father laughed, "Next year would have been time enough to paint but for Miss Millie's zeal, we are very grateful for all work."

My brother, Charles said, "I hope Miss Millie never breaks her arm again in our front yard."

Buddie Widdle said, "She makes good cakes, but the lemonade was not sweet enough. The fried chicken was too salty, a little."

"I thought everything was perfect," sighed my mother dreamily "And all that work I didn't have to do. I don't think we will do any visiting for a while though."

Dr. Barkley

"I wish we could know now just what will happen when we get big. Anyway, I want a lot of little girls and maybe one boy."

"Thelma, I think I only want one little girl with curly hair."

"What difference would that make?"

I thought briefly. "Well, she wouldn't have to pray for it."

"Are you still doing that silly thing? You know, I wish we had another little girl to play with, one we would really like, not Edith or Nancy somebody different."

"I don't think we need another one. We have fun."

"Yes, but don't you get tired of just me?"

"No, do you get tired of me?"

"No."

"Well then. Let's go see Leila Ward's baby."

"But it's got whooping cough."

"We've had it so we can get it. Anyway, it might not be whooping cough. The other kids go to school, and they'd have to stay home to keep the germs at home."

We knocked on the kitchen screen door and Leila said "Come in, it's unhooked." Leila stood at the stove, stirring something that was cooking.

"Effie and Thelma, listen, kids. Have you had the whooping cough? The baby may have it."

"Yes we've had it."

"Let us help you, Leila. I'll wash the dishes and Effie, you can get the broom. Then we'll fix up the pantry, wash the shelves, and put on new paper."

Thelma looked at Leila. "Leila Ward, have you been crying?" Her eyes were red and hair awry as she turned from the stove.

"Yes, I have. I just came back from downtown. I went to get some of that new baby food. The doctor said it would make the baby gain weight. It was a dollar and a half a jar. I was running to get home, and I fell and broke it." She cried and sobbed, and we couldn't comfort her. The children come rushing in, five of them.

"Leila, what is the name of that baby food? Write it down and I'll go tell Aunt Sallie to let Bill go to town and get it for you."

She drooped wearily. "No, I'll have to give him condensed milk. I haven of any more money until Billy gets paid Saturday."

I looked at Thelma, and she looked at me. We were both thinking of our banks.

"Write it down anyway, Leila."

She took a piece of paper out of her pocketbook. "Mellins Food. Oh, why does it have to cost so much?"

"Thelma, I don't have much in my bank, do you?"

"Maybe fifty cents."

A car honked at us, and Dr, Barkley leaned out, "Hi, there, what's the rush, girls?"

We knew him well. "Maybe we can ride into town with him, Effie."

"But the money?"

"I'll get it from Aunt Sallie. She'll lend. I know."

"We've got to get to town to buy some Mellins Food for Leila Ward's baby. She broke the jar she bought today, and the baby might have whooping cough, and it is so skinny, it's pitiful. Leila was crying, and we thought we would…."

"What kind of baby food was that?"

I looked at the slip of paper to make sure "M-E-L-L-I-N-S."

"Hop in girls, you can ride to my office for we're in luck. I will give you a whole case of Mellins' Food samples. Very glad I have it. You see, most of my mother's nurse their babies, so I have no use for it."

"Samples," Said Thelma, "they're so little." She was thinking of the tiny tubes of toothpaste and cakes of soap we would send for with coupons from magazines.

"No, No, these are generous and plenty of them, and we can get more when they are used."

"Oh, boy. Won't Leila be happy?"

Harriet

Just a short distance away, to the right, we had a very nice neighbor, Mrs. Jennie Sterling. The nicest person worked for her, it is of her that I want to tell you - Miss Harriet. She came early and left late, so it seemed that she was always there. She had a family of her own to care for and went home at night. Her cooking was a dream of good things and when she found that I appreciated it; she began to tell me things. Apple sauce is much better with coconut in it, and when making cinnamon buns, use currants as well as raisins. Anything that has cooked tomato in it needs a little sugar. All green and yellow vegetables need a pinch of sugar. A few grains of salt added to cake batter before putting it in the pans improves the flavor. Never salt roasts or chickens until ten minutes before taking them from the oven. Little gems I could never forget. Baked apples need a teeny bit or red food coloring to make them beautiful. Also with this, one could change cooked pears to pale pink. Harriet really had ideas like this one: When you roll out your biscuit dough, double it and roll very lightly again; then your biscuits will break open very easily for you!

In the summer, Miss Jennie's sisters from Baltimore came to visit. Naomi was a young lady, but Ethel had a little girl, a little younger than me and Thelma.

Nettie had different clothes, not like mine or even Thelma's. She had one dress that I adored. It had a square neck and puffed sleeves, and the skirt had three tiers. How they bounced and spread out when she whirled around.

This dress absolutely enchanted me. The material was white linen with red pin stripes, and it had a red velvet sash. Guess what she wore with it? Red slippers, imagine red! They tied around her ankles with ribbon, like ballet slippers.

I said to my mother, "I think Nettie's red striped dress is the prettiest dress in the world." I told Nettie's mother that Nettie had the prettiest dress. "The red striped one is my favorite. I like the skirt."

Thelma was with me. "You don't just like it. You love it to death. Why don't you ask your mother to make you one like it?"

"Oh no, my mother doesn't make things. She just sews things up that come apart."

"Well, get Miss Jennie Clipper to do it. She's a dressmaker."

Miss Ethel said, "I'll make you one just like it. Come on, let's go over and see if your mother has some material."

My mother did tiny pink flowers on a light blue background. Miss Ethel made me a three tiered dress. It had a blue velvet sash, and on Sunday, I happily flounced my way to Sunday school. As I was taking my white slippers off I thought dreamily, if only I could have some red slippers just like Nettie's to wear with my new dress.

I wouldn't keep still about wanting them. I couldn't think of anything else. I ached for a pair of red slippers. The idea fascinated me. The more I looked at Nettie's, the harder I wanted them. One day Nettle said, "Effie, you can have my red slippers for I'm tired of them."

"You'd give them away?"

"They'd never fit," said Thelma. "Shoes are not like clothes. They can't be fixed. Try them on."

I did, and alas and alack too, they were too small.

The summer was almost over. Naomi and Ethel were going back to Baltimore.

"Ethel," my mother said, "Will you get Effie a pair of red slippers and mail them to us. She can't stop wanting them."

"Of course, I will, but don't give me the money now. I would just spend it, but tell me the size."

I confided to Thelma, "I've wanted them since the first time I saw Nettie's. I just love how the ribbons tie them on. I hope they come soon."

"Effie, why do you want things so badly? I hate clothes and shoes too!"

"Thelma, not your Children's Day dress with the lace and seed pearls!"

"Yeah, I hate that most of all. Why, oh why does my mother buy that fancy stuff? Why? Why?"

"I know," said Harriet, "because she loves you."

A few days later, Thelma and I were sitting at the kitchen table of Miss Jennie's. Harriet was making a cake.

"Harriet, how long do you think it will take my red slippers to get here?"

She knew of my longing for them. She looked at me with love.

"Miss Effie if I were you, I wouldn't set my heart on those red slippers."

"Why, Miss Harriet?"

"Well, there's a reason . . ."

"Harriet," said Thelma suddenly, "Why do you call us Miss? We're just children."

"Well, Miss Thelma, it's a mark of respect for your parents. They are good and kind, and I respect them, and you and Effie are good children, and I hope you always will be, so I give you respect."

"Oh, I just wondered."

"When do you think they will come, Harriet?"

"Miss Effie, Nettie's mother is a busy woman. She has to work, and she gets mighty tired. Just, please for my sake, don't keep your heart set on red slippers. Then you can't be disappointed."

I waited and waited but the red slippers never came.

At Christmas, a card came for my mother from Miss Ethel with a few lines on the back but she forgot to mention the red slippers.

Harriet knew Miss Ethel and her ways and didn't want my heart to ache. She knew that Miss Ethel didn't know that promises are to be kept.

Maybe that's why I don't like red.

Aunt Susie and Mr. Sam

We rested on Thelma's front porch and looked across the road at the wheat field, with its undulating pattern of gold and green, with a flash of lavender and blue and pink which were the wildflowers that grew all through the wheat. It looked like flower sunshine, the tassels tossing, and the wind making waves, which reminded us of the ocean.

"Ocean City, now there's a place to have fun! I hope we can go on the excursion next week."

We are going, and it's a moonlight one, not an all day. The train doesn't leave Ocean City until nine o'clock at night.

"Imagine, riding on the train in the night time and all the way from Ocean City!"

"Oh boy but that's not until next week. What are we going to do today, Effie?"

"We could go see Mae Cook."

"Ye —ah, but we were there two days ago. We could, though, for I just love that player piano. That is the best thing they've invented yet. All you do is sit there and pump, and it plays. No "C" scale or "G" or any of them. I wish we had one, but we never will, and my mother sure has her heart set on me learning to play that Stieff piano. Six hundred dollars, but I'll never learn. My fingers were just not meant to do that."

"Maybe if you practice they will, Thelma—someday."

"Ne—ver! That day will never dawn. Ne—ver!"

Mae's father had struck it rich, as people said. He had a grocery, but that was not how he made the money to build a big, new house, with new furniture and soft carpets all over, swings on all porches and in the front yard, and the backyard. And a - player piano! He had struck it rich in some place called Wall Street in New York. No one understood how, but it was a fact. He, who had been almost poor, was now very rich. He was also a very nice man with a big family of likeable boys and girls, and a nice kind wife. Mae was the one nearest to our age.

We heard the player-piano before we got to the house.

"Now, that is pretty music," Thelma sighed. "Not a single mistake. Perfect!"

To us the house was so beautiful, the furniture, to use a word of the day, elegant. We were too young to know about good taste and thought the bright red velvet sofa and easy chairs and the flowered carpet was the last word. Everything was so brightly new. The kitchen gleamed, and Aunt Susie Selby reigned there in a white apron with a bow in the back. We knew that she was working for Mr. Jock, and as we knew her well, after we had said hello to everybody we went into the kitchen. The player piano was playing so loudly that the throb of it could be felt even here.

Aunt Susie was stirring something in a big blue bowl. "I'll bet you're making a pound cake," said Thelma.

"Indeed I am. Mr. Jack's favorite! As good as he is to everybody, I'm going to see that he gets just what he wants."

Mae came in and heard Aunt Susie. "That's my papa, Santa Claus!" and she laughed gaily as she went through the swinging door into the dining room.

"Imagine no knobs on the door. What will they think of next?"

"It's called a swinging door, Thelma. All the inside doors are like that. Mr. Jack has a fine house."

"How is Miss Leila's baby, girls. I heard it was very sick with the whooping cough," Aunt Susie paused in her stirring for a second.

"I think it's better now, but poor Leila's worn out. The baby coughs all night, and she doesn't get any sleep."

"Too bad," said Aunt Susie "Poor little Miss Leila. Tomorrow is my day off, and do you know what I'm going to do? I am going to get a chicken ready and go cook Miss Leila a chicken dinner, and what's more, I'm going to make her take a nap while I do it. You two can come over if you want and rock the baby, and I'll stir up a cake too."

"We'll be there," Thelma declared. "Will you put chocolate fudge icing on the cake?"

"That I will do!"

"Her baby's getting a bit of fat now. Dr. Barkley gave us some baby food for him, samples, but big and lots of them."

"That good man, he will have plenty of stars in his crown, and he will walk the streets of gold someday!"

"Did you know him when he was a little boy?"

"Indeed I did, always studying the dictionary, not the regular one, but a medical dictionary. His mother and father died when he was only six, and his Uncle Henry Jewett brought him up, a fine man, Henry Jewett."

"I know Mr. Jewett. He has strawberries!"

"And they are good."

We were walking home when we saw Mr. Sam Ward on his bicycle coming towards us, his big basket with a white cloth over it on the handlebars.

"Hello girls. Tell your mothers I will be by tomorrow with fresh gingerbread. I sold out early today."

As we walked on, Thelma said, "Why do our mothers buy gingerbread and things from Mr. Sam when they make them so much better?"

"Well, it's to help him out and I've heard my mother say it tastes different. Everybody likes some other people's cooking for a change. His wife cooks the things. One day she made gingersnaps and vanilla wafers, and they were as good as the store ones."

"Imagine that, making gingersnaps and vanilla wafers."

I was out in the yard with my mother when Mr. Sam came the next day. It was Friday. We were looking at my father's bicycle that had a badly bent front wheel. He had lent it to someone, they had an accident, and now it had to be fixed.

Mr. Sam got off his bike and came over, and we told him the story.

Mr. Charlie Spires is coming to get it to fix it, but he won't get it back until Monday.

I said suddenly, "He will need it Sunday morning to take the flowers." Very early every Sunday morning my father was up and out cutting flowers to put on Uncle Sam's grave. He put them together and tied the stems with string making a bouquet. Then he got on his bicycle and rode to the cemetery by the church for he wanted them to be fresh when we all walked through on our way to morning church. Mr. Sam knew of this, as everyone around did.

"Miss Annie May, this is my last delivery today. I'm going to leave my bicycle for Mr. Dix to use this weekend. I'll pick it up on Monday."

"Mr. Sam, how very kind you are."

"Mr. Dix would do the same for me." He went and put the gingerbread and cupcakes on the table. Halfway across the field to Aunt Jane's he turned and waved, and I waved back. He was taking the short cut home.

Miss Lillie

Miss Lillie Ward lived next door to Mr. and Mrs. Dave Bailey, with two fields in between. Most of the houses on the right side of the road had fields between one, two, and sometimes three. In these grew brown-eyed Susan, daises among the hedges and weeds. They all had a path through the middle where neighbors cut through to visit each other.

Miss Lillie's little house was brown and small, but neat. Trees gave shade and beauty to the yard. There was a large apple tree, which was a thrill to gaze upon in the springtime.

Then summer came, and Miss Lillie had her troubles. The boys would not leave her apple tree alone for as soon as the apples took shape the boys would pull them off. Of course, they were not good to eat at this stage, but they would take a bite and throw them at each other in fun. When the time finally came for the apples to be ripe enough for apple pies or to make jelly, there were very few left. She was in despair.

One day Miss Lillie knocked on our door.

"Miss Lillie how nice to see you, come in."

"Is Willie and Charles at home?"

"No, they are over to their Aunt Sallie's."

"Well, Miss Annie May, you can tell them that I am telling all the boys this year if they will not bother my apples until they are ripe, I will divide with them in the fall. I've been to all the boys' houses now, and I'm a little tired." She really did look weary.

"Here, Miss Lillie, I've just made some lemonade. Have some of this molasses cake with it. I'm so sorry the boys have caused you trouble. I will have their father speak to them."

"No, no," she said, "just tell them I will divide."

The summer came on. Miss Lillie had a job and worked every day in town, and in the evenings cut her grass and worked in her garden. She was a quiet person. It must have been a great effort for her to make the decision to talk to all of the boys and get their promise. She stayed to herself. Though not unfriendly, she was not friendly, just very quiet.

The 4th of July night that we had all of the ice cream I remember my father had said, "Perhaps Miss Lillie Ward would enjoy some," but Bud Charles had said mysteriously, "Miss Lillie doesn't like people to knock on her door in the nighttime. She is afraid of the Ku Klux Klan. It might be them."

"Char— les!" my mother said.

"There is too much talk before children." My father had been winding the clock, and he put it back on the mantel. "Grownups should be me careful."

"What would they do?" Buddie Widdie asked, "If they did knock on her door?"

"Hush, Willie, you're very tired."

"The 4th was lovely, but so tiring for us all."

"Get ready for bed, boys, while your father and Effie take the ice cream to Miss Millie and Mr. Dave. Then we'll all get some rest. It's been a long day."

The summer was over. The trees were more brown then green now, and the weeds were slowing up in their growing. The grass now needed to be cut less often, and we were a little tired of croquet. We had missed playing on the rainy days.

My mother and I were out in the yard when we saw Miss Lillie coming along the road pulling a cart with two baskets of apples.

She came into the yard and said, "Here is the boys' share for this year."

"Why, Miss Lillie, you didn't have to do that."

"A promise is to be kept. They kept theirs, and I am keeping mine."

"Won't you come in?"

"No, I have to deliver some more before dark."

When Bud Charles and Buddie Widdie came home, my mother said, "Boys, there are your apples from Miss Lillie."

"All those apples? Oh boy!"

Then Charles said, "It would take me forever to eat those apples."

"One basket for you and one for Willie."

"But Willie never did bother her apples. He doesn't deserve any. He never would take them. He said it was a sin to take them, so he didn't."

"Perhaps we had better take Willie's basket back to her. It's not fair to take them," Bud Charles said.

"They would make quite a lot of jelly for Miss Lillie for the winter. She has very little money and has had to support herself since her husband died. She has to pay her taxes, buy her clothes, and food and . . . ."

"I'll take Willie's back to Miss Lillie. Come on, Willie. I'll do the talking."

When my mother told my father the story, he was very proud of his two boys. Later on, Miss Lillie brought us some glasses of jelly, clear and beautiful, deeply pink with rose geranium leaves in it and lemon slices. It smelled like a flower garden and we loved it on our hot biscuits.

I must keep a glass of this to have when Mr. Livingstone comes to call. He does love jelly and Miss Lillie's is perfect!

Aunt Jane

The sun was going down. Another day was almost over. Supper was nearly ready. There would be hot rolls.

"Here, Effie, take these hot rolls over to Aunt Jane. Just stay a little while. Supper soon, for the last pan of bread is in the oven."

When I gave the rolls to Aunt Jane, she said sadly, "Honey, you do so much for me. But I never do anything for you."

"Oh, Aunt Jane, how can you say that? Who ate most of that cherry pie you made? I had three slices of apple. I eat your honey-pods. You let me and Thelma pick the first violets that bloom in the spring. You let me break blossoms for my mother's May basket, and I pick all of your snowdrops and lilies that I want. You let me cut your soap in squares and go to the store for you, and thread your needless I stopped, breathless.

"But Honey, going to the store and threading needles is for me."

"It seems like it is for me. I just love to do it for you."

"Someday," Aunt Jane said, "I'm going to do something big for you, little Effie, for being so kind to old Aunt Jane."

I put my hand over her mouth.

"No, don't say that, please don't. I love to do things. Bye, Aunt Jane, I have to go now." I waved goodbye again as I was half-way across the sweet potato field, as I always did.

Levi

It was late August, and soon school would begin. Already some leaves had brown edges, and many had fallen. Now I had to rake them before I could cut the grass. I was sitting on Aunt Jane's steps resting and she was resting with me.

"You seem tired, honey."

"A little bit, but I've got to go cut the grass soon. Its sky high with dandelion ghosts all over, and the graveyard needs cutting too."

Aunt Jane said, "Seems to me, honey, you do a lot of the grass cutting. How about Charles or Willie, can't they help?"

"Well Bud Charles has to go places and Buddie Widdie back hurts so…"

"There's Bill."

"But Bill is always busy hoeing or delivering groceries or …."

"Well, today you're going to have a vacation from grass cutting. Levi," she called loudly.

"What's up Granny?" A big boy came to the door, still half-asleep.

"I want you to go over to Effie's and cut the grass. It's her chore, but she's too tired today."

"Is the grass cutter sharp?"

"Yes, Bill sharpened it this morning for me."

"I'll do it in a jiffy then. You can stay here with Granny. I'll do it in two shakes of a lamb's tail."

Thelma came running and sat down with us.

"You two sit yourselves down and rest, I've got some work to do." Aunt Jane got slowly up and went in her little house.

Thelma whispered to me, "Some people say Aunt Jane is Levi's grandmother, but how can that be? Aunt Jane didn't have any children."

"Maybe she did a long time ago for she is awful old."

"Maybe, Levi sure is a big boy, and he really can dip that ocean wave. I hope we can go to Nelson's Woods this week. I just love that ocean wave."

The ocean wave was the biggest attraction at the Nelson's Woods Amusement Park.

It was suspended from a post in the middle, and it ran by manpower only. Three big boys started it going with a rope, and then when it was going around fast, they leaped up at its highest and made it dip. It was a real thrill and the main attraction even more popular than the flying horses.

I would like to draw it, but alas, I can only draw filigree buttons and cats, I won't try.

Levi didn't stay with Aunt Jane all the time, just sometime. She seemed to love him. He was a good boy, going to church and never getting into trouble.

"How would you girls like some warm apple pie? " Aunt Jane said. "I made four for Levi has such a good appetite."

We ate it out on the steps. Aunt Jane came out again, and after we finished we were resting some more when Levi came back.

"Don't tell me you did it that quick!"

"Sure did, Granny, and I did the graveyard part too."

"Oh, thanks, Levi, for doing it for me."

"Anytime," he said, "That grass cutter was real sharp. It's a breeze when they're sharp."

"Goodbye, Aunt Jane."

"I guess she is his granny," Thelma said. "Levi Roe. It must be her boy's, boy's, boy!"

"Yes, that's the way it is, I guess."

John Lane

"Hattie's flower garden is prettier than ever this year. I don't see how she does it." Thelma declared. "Stars, half moons and circles and squares all filled with beautiful flowers, and not a weed in sight. And those petunia, how sweet they smell!"

"Let's go see her. Maybe she will give us some for our mothers." As we neared the house, we saw John Lane cutting weeds in the back field with a scythe. It looked so easy the way he swung it, singing as he worked.

"Come in, girls. Take a chair. I just finished the washing, and have to sit down for a few minutes."

"I see you're getting your weeds cut," Thelma said for conversation.

"Yes. I hired John Lane last week for today, as our check should have come yesterday. He didn't come up to the house, just started working. I haven't the money to pay him. It will be at least two dollars, for with all the rain we've had, they are real high. Even my garden has them."

"Let us do the garden for you. Hattie, for if there's anything we do know, it's a weed from a flower, and I'm not sure John Lane does."

Thelma looked out the window. "Now that's a beautiful sight, how he swings that scythe," it was the large one that was held with both hands. I had heard Aunt Sallie say that there was both grace and beauty in a well handled scythe.

"But I don't have…" Hattie looked ready to cry. "How I'll pay him, I don't know."

"Hattie, why don't you pay him in something else besides money? He has ten children, all ages. Maybe…."

"But, Thelma. I don't have any children's things. Not even anything that would fit his wife. She weighs two hundred, I know, and Mother's and my clothes are so small."

"I know! Mine and Thelma's! I'll go get some. My mother puts the outgrown ones in a box. You go talk to Mr. John Lane. Thelma and tell him how clothes for his children is better than money."

"You come with me, and then I'll go."

"Mr. John, how are you?"

"Fine, fine. You girls going to the circus?"

"Circus? When is it?"

"Get's here tomorrow early. I'm going to meet the train and help unload."

"Will they pay you?"

"Maybe, maybe not, might get free tickets, not reserved seats though, that's extra cash."

"Always money, always and forever, Mr. John, do your children go to Sunday school?"

"Well, off and on, Miss Thelma. Right now, no! Girls need dresses, and…."

"How lucky can you get?" said Thelma. "You see, Hattie's going to pay you in children's clothes instead of money. Then they can go to Sunday school."

"Do tell! children's clothes, well, that will be fine. I wasn't going to charge Miss Hattie much, with her sick mother and living on a Civil War pension, which I hear is next to nothing. There's talk of making them bigger. That would be a blessing to folks."

We solved Hattie's problem, and finally went home with a big beautiful bouquet for our mothers, that we didn't even have to ask for.

Bill Bobbins

It was going to be a beautiful day. Thelma came over early.

"What are we going to do today?"

"We could go look at the fairy ring."

"Let's."

The fairy ring was so beautiful, and the magic it held for us drew us back again and again.

"Why did they grow in such a perfect circle and in only one place in all of Calvary?"

The whiteness of the wild mushrooms gleamed in the sun dappled grass, and we gazed in wonder, after we had wiggled our way through the high hedge that grew all around the old house. Tall trees and dense shrubbery grew all around, and there right in front of us was the fairy ring. The circle was about eight feet in circumference. So unusual that it fascinated us. And there's a story! It was said if one came to this place on three succeeding days and jumped into the circle and made a wish, it would come true.

"Do you want to make a wish, Effie?"

I thought deeply. Was there anything I really wanted? I seemed to have everything.

"Do you?"

"Oh, I guess not."

"We never think to come the other two days anyway. I can't think of anything I want. Maybe ..."

"We could wish for somebody else, like...."

"No, that won't work. It has to be the one wishing."

"Who would you wish for," Thelma asked with curiosity.

"Aunt Jane. I wish she could see well. Her eyes are getting dim."

"Yeah. It's too bad it won't work."

I was lying flat on the grass gazing intently at the fairy ring, thinking how perfect and beautiful it was.

"Come on, Effie, you look too long at the old fairy ring. Probably it doesn't work anyway."

"Thelma, we've never really tested it."

"No we always forget. That's the way we are, so busy."

Suddenly Thelma had one of her rare inspirations.

"Effie, do you think that if Mildred Curtis jumped in three days and wished, she would be like us?"

"Like us?"

"Yes - smart, you know."

"I don't know. Maybe she doesn't know she isn't."

"Oh, well. Maybe. Let's go out in the woods and play now."

On our way we met Bill Bibbins, our hired man, with a wagon load of groceries to deliver,

"Want to go, girls? I'm going to the Fluharts. They still have their upstairs tree up."

"Still up?" Thelma asked, "Its July!"

"Well, it was up last week when I took a case of condensed milk upstairs for Mrs. Fluharts to put under the bed. The kids eat it up too fast if it's in the pantry."

"Yes, it's pretty good," said Thelma, "Can't blame them."

"You want to go, Thelma?"

"N-o, we've been visiting Christmas trees enough for this year. Let's play in the woods."

"What are you going to do when you set back, Bill?" Thelma had something in mind and Bill knew what it was.

"Well, first I'll unhitch, put the wagon behind the barn, and . . ."

"Bill, could we ride Stell around the yard a little while, when you get back?"

"I'll take time to let you both ride a few times, but I've got lots of chores to do before sundown."

"Oh boy, we're going to ride Stell!"

We were only allowed to ride if Bill walked along with us. It was a great treat, and one we loved.

"We'll be waiting for you on the porch. How long will you be gone?"

"Bout an hour. Maybe not that long."

Bill stayed at the Old Place in the summertime. It was a piece of property that Aunt Sallie owned, a very old house with two large porches. Over the downstairs front porch was on upstairs one. Enormous oaks grew in the yard end shaded the porches. Bill just lived in the back part. Once in a long while we would beg to do a forbidden thing - go upstairs and out on the shaky old second story porch. It was so beautiful out there. Aunt Sallie was afraid we would get hurt as the house was too old to be safe. Only once in a long time would Bill let us do this. It was one of the most thrilling of all the things we did. He always said when we were safely in the yard, "My heart was in my mouth, for if either of you fell through that porch . . ."

The summer day was almost over. We had played all afternoon. Now Thelma had gone home to get dressed. I had washed up and happily put on my flouncy dress for we were being taken to the movies in town. As I came out on the porch, Thelma was running up the path.

"I'm out of breath, for I ran every step. I thought you might leave me."

"Thelma, you knew I wouldn't. It's early anyway yet for movies."

Bill was sitting under the maple tree.

"Guess you're pretty tired, Bill."

"Yes, I am, Thelma. I wonder if you girls would run up to George Mason's and get me a plug of tobacco. Here's a dime."

"Course we will."

As we walked along, I would twist and swirl around so that my skirt would stand out.

"Effie, stop swishing. You're always doing it. I liked you better before Nettie's mother made you that dress. You're forever swishing around, and you're going to wear that dress out!"

"No, I mustn't."

"Well stop wearing it so much."

On the way back Thelma said, "Why don't we take a little taste of Bill's tobacco. It must be good. Granpop chews it. Bill likes it, and . . ."

"Well, I guess we could. You first!"

She took a nibble. I took one, and we looked at one another in dismay.

"We're poisoned. How do they do it? Never again!"

"As she gave it to Bill," she said, "We took a little taste, Bill. Hope you don't mind."

He looked surprised. "How did you like it?"

"Pure poison!"

He laughed, as he took a large bite.

These people, Daisy, lovingly called Basy; Lola; Miss Lillie Ward, Dr. Barkley, Mr. Sam Ward, Aunt Susie, Aunt Jane, Mr. and Mrs. David Bailey, Levi, Mr. John Lane, and Mr. Bill Bobbins were all colored people, good and kind.

It was a great privilege and a joy, to have known them.

THE END

THE VIOLETS GREW BY THE PINE TREE

The woods was cool
That summer day
A wondrous place
To play

Through the trees
The sun came through
And by a pine
Violets grew

One little girl knelt
In the summer air
And softly kissed
The petals fair

The other little girl
Laughed in glee
Kissing a flower
How silly can you be?

The violets grew
And grew and grew
And made a carpet
Green and purple blue.

Let's never pick them
Just let them grow
And we will always
Love them so.

Here beauty reigns beside the pine
And the little girls play in summertime
When they grow up and are far away
They will remember –That day.

When to the sessions of sweet thought,
I summon remembrance of things past.
Marcel Proust (French)
Softly close the door, but leave a little crack,
That when you meet a little child, you can look back.
Books of Knowledge

ONLY THE VIOLETS REDEEM THE SIGHING

Chapter I

A flash of harmless lightening,
A mist of rainbow dye
The burnished sunbeams brightening
From flower to flower, he flies.
John Bannister,1845-1909
The Humming bird
I was rich in flowers and trees,
Humming birds and honey bees.
John Greenleaf Whittier
Barefoot Boy

Heaven lay all about me, the warmth of the sun, the leafy trees, the flowers and my darlings, the humming birds, so babyish and lovable. They especially liked the tall blue larkspur, and the delphinium, and the hollyhocks, zig zag, zig zag, buzz, buzz.

The bright blue above me, the moving clouds, the beautiful blue that each Sunday in church we were told was waiting - was here.

That heaven could wait. My heaven was here in Calvary, where everyone loved me and I loved everyone. From Bill Bibbins, the hired man to Mr. Wash Tull, who had the most money, and who always said fondly whenever I was near him, "Little Effie, Billie Dix's little girl!"

It was amazing how short the days were, so much play to play, and so much thinking to do. Yesterday, my Aunt Sallie and I had found some clusters of little variegated flowers in a sheltered place. They were nameless, yet as she said, they so beautifully deserved a name. She had asked me to think of names, and she was thinking too.

When we found them, she had said, "Effie, I want to tell you again most earnestly, and I know I am right in this. Look, look closely at everything. You must get into the habit. It is important. Look intently at things, details of all things, flowers, trees, words, and people. When it is words, learn their meanings - the spelling, and look at the beauty of the written word. I believe John Ruskin put this in a paragraph of his; perhaps it was an essay in Sesame and Lilies. You may read this someday."

"Oh, I will," I said. "I want to read everything."

She smiled and continued, "And not only look but listen too. For the sound of a loved voice, clings in the heart always."

She looked up at the blue. "The beauty of the clouds across the sky can look like a piece of fragile valenciennes lace, flowers, vines, scallops are discernible. Yes, remember beauty remember smiles and voices, remember how a rose looks embowered in its own glossy green leaves.

The microscope we have does not create anything new, but it reveals marvels. Just look, and think, and join your thinking with reading. Culture is a great advantage in the daily living of a life."

"How few think justly of the thinking few,
How many never think, who think they do."

"That sounds puzzly, Aunt Sallie."

"Yes, it could be Emerson or Shakespeare, but it doesn't matter. It would be a good idea for you to read both, someday. The acquiring of knowledge is the developing of an avid hunger for books."

"I love books," I said.

Work for the night is coming
Give every flying moment
Something to keep in store.
Lowell Mason

The woods in Calvary were all pine woods, not a wood, as fairy tales say, I like to say woods. Pine trees grow very tall. They tower, they sigh, and they sing.

Sometimes, Thelma, my best playmate, would say, "Listen to the pine trees sigh. Seems sorta sad, like they're sighing for somebody's little dead baby, or somebody. Listen hard, Effie."

"Yes, you can imagine that they sigh, and the pine needles dropping are tears."

"Oh, Effie, I know we're supposed to have imaginations, but that - tears. I know they'll really sigh when you're Aunt Sallie dies, the way she loves their cones."

"Aunt Sallie die!" I said, appalled.

"Well, everybody's going to die - sometime. You, me, you know how many babies die. The food doesn't make them strong enough. Now I ask you, why do babies die?" Tears came to her eyes.

"I don't know, Thelma. I don't feel like playing today. I think I'll go home and start cutting the grass."

"Effie, here's two perfect pine cones. Tell Aunt Sallie they're a present."

We came across a clump of violets on our way out of the woods. We just paused to look, we didn't pick them.

In the woods is perpetual youth.
Emerson

The world is full of beautiful things, and a woods violet is first on the list. Deeply purple at the edges, shading to paler shades of lavender toward the center, then the tiny speck of gold, making the whole flower perfect, the green leaves giving added beauty.

"Now that's a pretty sight," said Thelma.

"Yes, maybe we could play a little bit longer. The grass will still need cutting tomorrow."

The woods were a sort of haven. In summer it was cool. In winter it was warm.

It seemed that Thelma and I owned it all. We owned the sunshine, the tangled daisies in the summer fields; the Queen Anne's lace was ours alone, the wheat fields with their wealth of wild flowers all through them, blue, pink, lavender, yellow. Ours! How beautifully the trembling light of the sunshine played through the pines, or the waving foliage of the low bushes and small hollies and the baby trees.

What tranquility, as the breeze softly moved the long shadows on the ground. If one looked up, and away, there was almost a purple haze and little chirping birds called musically to each other.

Sometimes we noticed the spider webs in the filtered light, and when I mentioned it was pretty, Thelma said, "Ye—s, if you say so, but I am afraid of spiders —a little bit."

She said suddenly, "You know some days the sighing sounds all tangled up, and sometimes it whispers, and I vow, sometimes it sounds peaceful, like sailing in the evening."

"Thelma, did anyone ever read you Hiawatha? It has a lot in it about pine trees. How they smell and the Indians said sometimes the pine trees—sang."

"Is that the one where the little Indian boy called the birds—chickens?"

"Yes."

"Now I know I don't want to hear it, saying pine trees sing, and telling their little children to call birds chickens. That's plain nonsense. Pine trees moan and that's the living truth. I never heard one sing."

"Sighing is a prettier word than moan."

"Well, maybe."

"I think I remember a little bit of Hiawatha."

"Say it."

"Stood the grove of singing pine tree,
And beyond them stood the forest."

"The pine trees were the forest," Thelma said. I kept on,

"You who know the haunts of nature
Love the sunshine and the meadows
Love the wind among the branches
And the rain and the snowstorm"

"We do," Thelma said, happily.

"And with dreams of visions many
Through the leafy woods, he wandered."

"We don't have squirrels and rabbits in our woods, I wonder Why?"

"Well, who needs them we have violets, don't we?"

"You know I would read that Hiawatha, but I never crack a book in summer. There's too much to do. It's against my principles too. I knew the Indians were not much, but to let their children lie, calling birds chickens. It was a big lie and not a white one either."

"Oh, Thelma, it was Longfellow who wrote about the Indians how they felt and all. They couldn't write but they had pretty thoughts about the stars and sky, the trees and the sun and the Milky Way and all."

"And letting their children tell lies. Come on, I hear Daddy's truck."

Thelma's father drove the oil truck for Gulf delivering oil to the few grocery stores or gasoline to the few who sold it for the few cars, who were not supposed to exceed the ten mile an hour speed limit at this time. In these early nineteen hundreds there were few machines as cars were called and the truck, the only one in town.

The best of his job was that he always came home for lunch, and was generous with his dimes and nickels.

I remember, I remember how my childhood fleeted by,
The Mirth of its December, the warmth of its July.
W. M. Praed

"Well, will you just listen to them today," Thelma said, next day as we came into the woods. We sat down to eat our candy and sour pickles.

"The wind is blowing hard today, but they sigh all the time, Thelma. You know that."

"Yes, but today, it's for that little baby that we carried flowers to yesterday.

Sometimes they really have things to sigh for. Like if my father, or my mother, or your father or—."

"No, Thelma! No!"

"Or your Aunt Sallie."

"Thelma, I wish you wouldn't notice."

"Who can help it, the way they do. Ye are born to die. The Bible says that. It was on our Sunday school card last Sunday."

"Well, we don't have to talk about it. Harriet was making pound cake when I left home. Come on."

"How long has Harriet worked for your Aunt Sallie?"

I thought hard and said, "Forever of course. She works for the Stoughton's too. Let's run."

I remember, I remember, where I used a swing,
And thought the air must seem as fresh
To swallows on the wing.
Thomas Hood

Later that day we were back in the woods with a picnic lunch Harriet had made us, with generous slices of pound cake.

"I guess the woods is really sad, with all the sighing, but we do have fun here. Let's play. That looks like a good bouncing tree over there."

We would pull the young trees down and sit on it, and bounce. Such fun Most of these, I think, were sweet gum trees. They have great resiliency and would bounce right back up straight again, as we jumped off.

"This woods is the nicest place in the world," I said "Of course, I'd love it if only for the violets."

"Yes, one thing our woods does have and that's violets, and not those crazy pink pipes."

"What Thelma?"

"Yes, when we went visiting Sunday. Mary Anne took me out in her woods and there they were. They looked like pink wax, pretty but scary. They were nothing to pick, just to stare at."

"Did they smell sweet?"

"Effie, how would I know? I didn't get close enough. Probably poison too, not me. I'm glad they don't grow in our woods. Glad. Glad. Glad."

Later, at high school age, I found a new friend, and in her woods saw pink pipes. Like Thelma, I didn't like them at all. Their pale pink shade was lovely, but they had no fragrance, and as Thelma had said they were—well, unearthly—was the word.

Chapter II

Our little life is but a breeze
That bends the branches of the trees.
Suspera
H. W. L.

The magic of summer, days full of fun, nights full of beauty and lovely security. The fascination of the starry sky, the Milky Way looking as if all the white flowers of earth had been thrown up into the sky to make its path. The little dipper and the big, the moon giving so much light that we could see one another's expressions as we gazed and talked, in the cool of the evening on the porch. Some nights Bill Bibbins, the hired man, and Levi, Aunt Jane's grandson would join us and sit on the edge of the porch.

The tombstones at the far side of the yard gleamed in the moonlight, and the white picket fence that enclosed the graveyard was startlingly white. Aunt Sallie was talking, what Thelma always said, sounded just like poetry.

"Yes, every experience in life needs to be shared, whether it is through words or music or painted in a picture or sewn with a needle. It is a way of reaching for immortality."

I'm sure the children sitting there didn't even know the word immortality, but they loved the sound of her voice. And as Aunt Sallie said, "In memory live all precious things." They would remember these evenings.

Leaf, bosom, blade, hill
Valley, stream, unclouded sky.
Still mingle music with my dreams,
As in the days gone by.
William Merriwell

Lots of times Thelma and I would just sit quietly in the woods and talk, tired of all play. The dignity and beauty of the towering trees was so peaceful, the coolness so refreshing.

"I'd like for things to go on as they are forever," I said, happily.

"They won't," Thelma said, darkly. "It will be different, your father will—"

"Oh no, Thelma, no!"

"Even little Thomas, my darling baby brother that I love so much, may get deathly sick, even ..."

"Thelma, let's go spend our quarter now."

A little while ago, Thelma's father had said, "There, I haven't a dime, would a quarter do?"

We both said, "Yes," at the same time.

"Have a party," he had said, "invite your friends."

On bravely through the sunshine and the showers,
Time hath his work, and we have ours.
W. Wordsworth
Never let her memory die,
Heaven is so wide and high.
M. Lavin

My Aunt Sallie was a queenly woman. She was tall, and held her head up proudly, always.

When she was very young, her father had told her, "Hold high your gallant head, because I love you."

Every day, in fact every minute of the day, was to her a challenge. Later she gave me this challenge in words. I wasn't very old when she told me that the way to live was to meet each day with a brave heart, a calm mind, and an undaunted spirit. My Aunt Sallie was my father's sister. My father, my Uncle Sam, and my Aunt Sallie were unusual people.

Later, when older, and thinking things over, I decided that it was the way they were educated, not at school but at home, by my grandfather and the current minister.

Such a wonderful store of knowledge they had, the great literature of prose and poetry, they had been taught. Astronomy, chemistry, psychology, the Bible, was instilled in their minds. Their general knowledge was boundless.

Beside factual education they had a large supply of the virtues, kindness, tolerance, courage and compassion, a love for fairness and a gift of being unafraid of life or death.

Aunt Sallie's kindness was perhaps the reason that I spent so much time with her from babyhood to little girlhood. I followed her around as she worked, and was completely absorbed in all she said or did.

My Aunt Sallie had three children; two boys who were away at college and Priscilla, who taught school and lived at home. I asked Aunt Sallie how Henry and Sterling could bear to be away, but she just said, they liked the city better, and she smiled.

I couldn't see how anyone would want to be away from here, with the tall maples, shading the yard and porch, the nice white house with green shutters, the fruit trees and strawberries.

Strange that remembrance seems to be always summer. Fragrance of flowers, blooming locust trees, and tall brown and white lilies sway in memory.

Earth is nearer to the sky
Never let her memory die.
M. Lavin

And my Aunt Sallie was a poet, though she never wrote a line. She knew the things that poets know, the woods, the fields, the name of every tree and bush and vine, all the stars by name. She knew the secret of the wind, whether it would bring rain or sunshine tomorrow, the names of the murmuring insects in the grass, and the birds flying in the air.

Her house was all a home should be, neat, cozy, livable, pretty. There was a tea set in the china closet that we used to use on rainy days that would have brought delight to an artist's soul. The striking clock with flower decorations on the glass said, beauty lives here.

An unwritten poet, who lived her lifetime without putting her lovely thoughts on paper. Not a line, but who never ceased to marvel at the hydrangeas blue and the amethyst and rose tints of nature. Pink and green were everywhere, but a blue flower was strangely rare to our sight. I wish she could have lived to have seen a pale green zinnia, a flower with green petals. Amazing!

The memory of her makes the common things, like trees, grass and flowers more beautiful to me, the milky way more white the sunshine more golden.

Because I loved Aunt Sallie so, didn't lessen my love for my mother and father. I could just think of them dying, as when Thelma mentioned it and tears would start. It was just a special love I had for her.

There's rosemary, that's for remembrance.
Shakespeare

I suppose I should tell you how my Aunt Sallie looked. I wish I did not, but could take you up the stairs at Calvary, and say, on the landing, "There, that's my Aunt Sallie in that oval frame."

The dress she had on seemed to be taffeta a lovely material, perhaps golden brown of a kind called changeable or iridescent. There is no lace collar. It is plain, but fashioned in folds and pleats, as was the style of the day. Her hands lie on her lap, and her uplifted chin give dignity and pride to the picture.

The features do not matter. Her brown hair the expressive eyes, just go to make up the whole. Her hair is pulled gently high, in a lovely past fashion.

Was she pretty?

Pretty is not the word, nor is beautiful, she was just right.

The description of the elder sister in "Snowbound" describes her perfectly. "A full rich nature, free to trust, truthful and almost sternly just, prompt to act, and make her generous thought a fact."

Once she asked me if I wanted to be great.

And I said, "Oh, yes, Aunt Sallie. Tell me how?"

And she looked at me steadily, and said, "Be kind."

I think she may have noticed perhaps, some childish unkind act of mine and this was her way of putting my mind in the right direction.

Her conversation to me was a way of inexhaustible joy, the shared laughter over nothing more than a fundamental understanding, gave me happiness each day. She lives in memory, where all true friendships glow. The past is sleeping, but yesterdays live on, like long shadows playing like light and shade over the surface of a changeable silk or sunbeams over the grass.

Chapter III

Friendship is undying constancy,
Once a friend, always a friend.
The gift of making friends is one
of life's precious attributes.
H.W. Longfellow

Most of the houses in Calvary were of the contemporary style of the period, but a few were from another generation.

Ours was one of these, and away down the road, past Mr. Jim Brink's store, and over the bridge, there was another one. Three stories high with an attic with lovely pealing gingerbread trimming and an upstairs porch.

The Fluharts home was also one of these last generation homes, with shutters and large porches. There were perhaps six in all.

This one, over the bridge, we only visited once in a long while. It had been vacant for years. We had been told that it was best not to go there, for various reasons. Tramps used it to rest in, and it could be dangerous, going without repairs for so long.

Carved over the door, neatly and deeply into the wood was its name. "Welcome Hinges." It was the only house we knew that had a name, and it thrilled us to go there.

In the closets, half on, half off, were still pasted old newspapers, telling of sales of slaves at the Countryseat of Princess Anne.

"The poor, poor people," said Thelma. "Selling them like that."

"It's all over now."

"Yes, and I'm glad of it."

"Look at all the graveyard lilies. How sweet they smell."

The place seemed to have thousands of them. Later, I learned their real name was Narcissus.

"I bet the people who lived here were happy and nice."

"I hope children lived here. The banisters are just right for sliding, I'll try it."

"Wait let's walk around a little outside."

Old rose bushes and ivy still climbed over everything.

"Thelma, what is different about this place? Something we've never thought of before."

She was quite a while, "I don't know, what?"

"No graveyard!"

"That's a fact, and all big houses have them, especially the ones with big yards."

"Maybe they didn't want one, but I think they are so nice. You can put flowers on graves every day. Imagine."

"Well," said Thelma, "if you want to be buried in that kind you had better tell somebody. You are not going to live forever. Write it down someplace."

"I'd like for my grave to be covered with violets, white and purple both and…."

"That would be pretty."

"I saw one like that, Thelma. We walk right past it when we go to town to visit my Aunt Sis."

We went into the house again. It was windy and the door was banging.

"The house is banging us a welcome."

"Yes, seems sad, the pretty door, half on, half off. I bet they had good things to eat in this house, and the pantry was full of preserves and jelly, pickles too, and pies and cakes."

"I'm starving," Thelma said suddenly.

"And pretty furniture too, mahogany."

"Ma-what?"

"Mahogany, pretty dark wood, like your piano."

"Effie."

"And looking glasses and curtains, maybe a piano here," I leaned against the wall.

As we left, Thelma said, "Don't mention that word. Six hundred dollars it cost and nobody to learn to play it, but me. It's so hard on …."

"Thomas, maybe, someday."

"He might die. Babies are dying all over. No, I'll take music lessons, maybe forever, to please people."

"You can't just take them, Thelma you have to practice every day."

"I'll do it. I'll take one a week, but I'll never go for this two a week thing. I've got my principles."

"Let's hurry!"

"Look, there's a rainbow, and we didn't even notice it had been raining."

"Oh, it is so beautiful!"

"Yeah, but pale, I think I like sunsets best."

"I like both, but the rainbow best."

"Have it your own way. We never agree."

"Sometimes we do."

"When?"

"When we're looking at the violets and liking to play in the woods."

Out of my childhood rises in my mind the recollections of many things, rather as poetic impressions, than as prosaic facts. I remember some indefinite longings, feelings of wonder at it all. Things that I could not fathom, even after explanations. I could not even interpret the explanation. Some have remained in my mind still seeking the answers.

Chapter IV

The day is done.
H. W. L.
And lend to the rhyme of the poet
The beauty of thy voice
H. W. L.

Sometimes, on a summer evening we all just sat on the porch and talked. The children always congregated at our house, for some reason.

Thelma would say. "Miss Sallie, will you tell about the Captain, who took his little girl on his boat and she got frozen to death, and so did he."

"That's the Schooner Hesperus, Thelma."

"I feel so sorry for them. She was such a pretty little thing, blue eyes, and …."

"Longfellow was a good poet," someone said.

"Yes, I remember the account of his death in the newspapers. Someone gave a blanket made of ferns and daisies. The Alcott's, I believe."

"It's a shame people have to die, who are so smart and nice," Thelma said.

"But you can find anyone you love after they are gone, in something they have loved, in poetry, in certain places, in flowers. In any shade in nature they loved, in violets, lilacs, wisteria, all flowers with this hue, if they loved them best. In any sentence the loved one spoke or wrote, when the wind blows gently or fiercely strong. In a song they've sung, a lullaby, maybe, or a fluffy dandelion, all gold, cushiony, and fragrant, in kindness, in love for one another. In beauty of the earth and sky, in the beauty of a tree, holly berries, even ….."

"In a pine cone," Thelma said suddenly.

"Yes," said Aunt Sallie dreamily, "Even in a pine cone."

"Miss Sallie, sounds like you have been talking poetry."

"No, to care for poetry does not make one a poet, but it does make one feel blessedly rich and quite indifferent to many things such as wealth, fame."

I am sincerely grateful that it was given to me from childhood, to see life from this point of view. I think that it is meant for our childhood to live forever in us, in the charm of sun and shadow, the moon, the Milky Way, the stars, all completely ours in appearance.

Sunday is the golden key that opens up the week.
Anon

Sunday was a sort of poetry. To be different minds, poetry suggests different things. To me it was the people who loved me, the blossoms, the trees, and the grass.

The Sabbath seemed to have a peculiar charm. Everyone looked and acted differently, dressed in their best for Church services and Sunday school. Clean, shining, happy and glad to spend a day of rest from work.

The graveyard, which to me was merely an extension of the yard, seemed more beautiful and peaceful as if every grave had a stone saying *At Rest.*

Quite often on Sunday afternoons, my mother and father, Aunt Sallie and me would take a walk to see my grandparents. It was probably less than a mile, cutting though the fields and woods.

I would be satisfied most Sundays just to walk around in my grandmother's garden, or in the yard playing by myself , but sometime I would ask if I could take a walk up the pavement, which was new to the corner. Here I knew a little girl my age, named Lois.

Today she was not at home, so I stood on the corner a moment looking across the street.

An enormous rose, blooming over there called me and the magnet in me took over. I knew the man's name. He was a friend of my grandfather.

I knocked on the door and when Mr. Matthews open it, I said quickly. "Mr. Matthews, will you please give me your big pink rose?"

He was very surprise.

"Just why—do you want my rose?"

"Well, because it's so magnificently beautiful!"

"Where do you learn such big words?"

I thought a second. "I read a lot, but I've heard my Aunt Sallie say that the sunset is magnificently beautiful through the trees, and...."

"Little girl, what is your name?"

"Effie, Effie Dix."

He pondered for a second. "There are just two families of Dix's. William and Samuel."

"I'm William, I mean my father is. My grandfather is Mr. Wingate Lewis. I am taking a walk from his house. We're Sunday visiting."

"Mary," he called opening the screen door. "This little girl wants me to give her our big rose."

"Well, John, I've been listening to you and if she had the nerve enough to ask you for it, give it to her; and here's some salt water taffy to go with it. We'll never eat it all ourselves."

"It is beautiful," he said, "Five inches across."

"Yes, and it called to me from across the street, like a magnet, it pulled me and I'm not supposed to cross the street. I'm just supposed to go to Lois' house. I did look up and down though."

"I hear there are six of those machines in town, now." his wife said.

"Would you like the rose with a long stem?"

"Oh, very long, it is so beautiful it deserves one."

He took out his knife, cut the rose with a half yard stem and cut the bottom thorns off.

"Thank you, kindly," I said happily. "Goodbye."

I looked up and down carefully and crossed the street quickly, and called when I got over. "Goodbye again."

"Effie," said my mother. "Where did you get that rose?"

"Mr. Matthews gave it to me."

"John Matthews gave you a rose," my grandfather said, "He never gives anybody anything. He is the closest, the—."

"Now Wingate." Grandmother touched him on the arm.

"Will wonders ever cease? But Baby, you had to cross the street, and I heard at last count there are nine machines in town and outside of town they've put signs, Do not exceed the speed limit, ten miles per hour."

"Mrs. Matthews said six, Grandfather."

"Well, thank the lord you are safe and sound."

My mother was really displeased, but my father said, "Now, Annie honey, she won't disobey again. Come on, let's get home. Sister Sallie has gone on ahead."

"I am going to give the rose to Aunt Sallie. I told Mr. Matthews she would probably measure it, but he finally said he already had, five inches. He ask me if my Aunt Sallie didn't have any roses and I said lots of them and he said doesn't Wingate Lewis have roses and I told him a whole backyard, all colors and I could take the garden scissors off the nail and cut all I wanted anytime. That's true, isn't it Grandfather?"

"As true as truth itself. What did he say to that?"

"He said, well then…."

"What did you say?"

I said, "But not this one!"

It was an enchanting walk home, through the fields and woods. Yes, Sunday was different. People were, and the out of doors was too, quiet, beautiful, fulfilling. God seemed to be closer. He was love, and was with us, as I walked ahead of my mother and father proudly and carefully carrying my pink rose.

Chapter V

On the well, just outside the kitchen door, there were two things; the bucket, with a long rope to throw down and pull up filled with water, and a basket, fills with perfect pine cones.

The wooden top of the well cover was in two parts, one half circle sliding under the other. After drawing water, as the phrase went, one pulled the half over so that leaves and such would not fall into the water.

Someone was careless once, and Kitty fell down there. Tragedy! Quickly Aunt Sallie tied the hoe to the rake and let it down. Kitty got on and was pulled up safely and wrapped in a blanket until fluffy again.

Kitty must have really learned from this bad experience, for it never happened again, though she lived to be seventeen years old.

It is about the basket of pine cones that I want to tell you.

There was a family on the other side of the woods, who had very little.

The father was said to be in the Navy. In those days, early nineteen hundreds, the Navy was reportedly composed of very rough men. It wasn't considered such an honor as now, to be a Navy man.

I understood the Calvary public opinion was that he should have stayed at home, and got a job, so that his four children could have had things.

But he didn't, and they did not have the necessary things, not even enough food.

We would miss Aunt Sallie, and we would all know where she had gone. It was to take groceries to this family and to see what they needed in the way of fuel and necessities.

Why didn't she get Bill Bibbins to take the groceries? I didn't understand either then, why she didn't take me. Now I know, she didn't want to embarrass the mother or the children. She was thoughtful, which is among the loveliest gifts from heaven.

Whether the Navy paid any maintenance for families then, I don't know, but if it was paid, it must have been an extremely small amount.

Aunt Sallie not only took plain food, but cookies, fruit and candies. Sometimes when she went to the store she would bring back two bags. One she gave to us, my brothers and me, and one she put on the cupboard shelf until she made her next trip across the woods.

The grocery had been Aunt Sallie's second husband's, but now a very nice man ran it for her on commission. About once a month the new boxes of penny candy were delivered. Something new and different every time. This time it was chocolate filled with the new peanut butter in the shape of pillows.

A few days before, Thelma and I had been in Mr. George Mason's grocery store. It was low and rambling, cool in the summer and cozy in winter, with the two big stoves he used to heat it, one up front and one in the back.

In front was the glass showcase with his penny candy. “One of that, two of those, some of them,” (Give me’s—nonexistent), “One O.K. chewing gum, a long peppermint stick.”

Also in there with the penny candy were the chocolate bars, Baker’s, Hershey’s and Lowney’s, wrapped in something called tinfoil, silver, very delicate, not like today’s.

Thelma and I bought our candy then walked back to where Mr. George was talking to Miss Lizzie Ward, Mrs., of course.

In front of the meat case there was a low table with the buckets of preserves, plum, and peach, cherry, strawberry. You bought them by the pound, in a paper tray. Good!

Today there was a new bucket and this was the conversation piece.

“George, what is it?” She said, stirring it with the paddle.

“Lizzie, that’s something new. Peanut butter.”

“Peanut butter. What’s that?”

“It’s ground up peanuts, with a little salt and peanut oil.”

“What’s that?”

“It’s something to keep it moist and fresh. First they tried melted butter, didn’t work, it turned rancid in a week.”

“Well, I never, what good is it? You can’t use it on pancakes.”

“N—ooo, maybe not, but it is good on crackers and even bread. My boy George made himself a slice of bread spread with it and a slice spread with jelly, grape I think it was. His mother said, for heaven’s sake, George, slap those two in slices together. That jelly is dripping,” so he did and began to eat it. He said, “Mom, this is the best thing I ever had to eat. She told him exaggeration is a sin,” but he said, “Mom, it’s the truth. Now he eats it that way all the time.”

“Well,” Miss Lizzie said again. “I never! Give me half a pound. I’ve got plenty of Jelly. My kids might like it too.”

Thelma and I had been listening, and Thelma said eagerly, “Mr. George, will you sell five cents worth? That’s all I got left.”

“You keep your nickel Thelma. I’ll give you and Effie some in a penny ice cream cone.”

“I’ll take it home and try the jelly business,” Thelma said.

“I’m going to eat mine plain,” I said putting my finger in and tasting.

“Imagine,” said Thelma, “Mashing up peanuts and making butter. What will they think of next?”

The next thing they thought of was Ka-Ka, a cake mix in a box. Imagine that. You only had to add milk. I remember it was bright yellow. Everyone tried it then went back to making their own.

Chapter VI

Sterling and Henry were Aunt Sallie's sons. They and their friend Archie, who all went to the same college, were on vacation now and resting in the shade of the big maple tree and their conversation was very strange to me.

They were talking of things that I didn't understand, of being Atheists. I listened for a while, and some of the words worried me. I must have become word conscious very early, probably from my first primer, with the little pictures, and the printed word beneath.

I ran into the house and upstairs, where Priscilla was sweeping and said, "Priscilla, what does Atheist mean?"

"How do you spell it?"

"I don't know, but Sterling, Henry and Archie said they were going to be …."

"Oh, that's just their college talk, acting different and smart. What it really means is a person who doesn't believe in God."

I felt pale, "Doesn't believe in God!" My world was shaking. "Everybody believes in God!"

"No, there are some people who don't, at least they say so."

"But, God made the world and everything."

"Don't you worry about it. They're only talking their talk. We'll make a cake after I dust."

"I'll dust. You can go start the cake."

"Do it well," then giving me the cloth reluctantly, "promise?"

"Oh, I will."

"I'm going to make devil's food with white icing and black walnuts. You can roll the walnuts with the rolling pin."

"I'll hurry," for the moment the world was forgotten.

I loved it when Sterling was home for the summer, for almost every day he and I went fishing. If I had been a sleepy-head, I would never have gone fishing.

My little bed was by the window and a strong summer breeze came in before the sun. I think I was a light sleeper. Anyway, as soon as I heard someone down in the summer kitchen, or Bill Bibbins at the well, I was wide awake and got quickly dressed.

The reason I went fishing was that I was up. I was there. My brothers were still asleep.

"Want to go with me, Effie?"

"Did I!"

My mother always said, "Here, take your straw hat. The sun will be very hot later."

I wore a sun-bonnet for play, but not for fishing.

Sailing, sailing, over the bounding main.
Godfrey Marks

There was not always a good breeze when we were returning from fishing. Sometimes the wind died away and the boat was just about motionless. All sailboats carried two long paddles for just this emergency, to push into what breeze there was, until a strong wind came up again. If there were two men, one pushed on each side. Though the progress was slow, it worked.

This day, returning, the wind was just about still and Sterling said, "I'll give her a push."

I picked up the long stick from the bottom of the boat, jumped up on the other side, as said, "I'll help."

In a second, I lost my balance and was overboard.

I felt my head hit the bottom of the boat as I came up, and at that second Sterling grabbed me dragged me back in the boat.

He flung me across the seat that ran across the middle and began slapping me on the back, as I sputtered and shivered.

"Oh, God, let her be all right. Oh, God, please let her be alright."

"Sterling, you're killing me, and I'm freezing, I'm not drowned!"

"Thank God. Here, get into the cabin and dry yourself. Wrap up in that old coat that's in there. Give me your clothes and I'll spread them on top of the cabin, they'll soon dry in this hot sun."

"I'm freezing," I shivered.

"Hurry, get out of those things. Here comes a breeze now."

I had just had a dress on with bloomers to match. It was the style at that time, so in less than twenty minutes both pieces were dry enough to put back on. My mother understood how I got my dress so wrinkled that day, just going fishing.

"You know, Sterling, I felt my head hit the bottom of that boat when I came up."

"Does it hurt? Here, let me look."

"No, it was only a tap. My ribbon bow was on top, sorta like a cushion."

The wind was up now and the boat was sailing smoothly, leaning over to one side. There's nothing quite so thrilling, a summer day, a good wind, a free feeling. Something no one should miss. In a short time we were at the wharf, threw back the fish we didn't want, and put the others in a basket, trout mostly, and flounder.

We walked along in the early afternoon silently. Sterling held my hand. After we got over the second hill (just large crushed piles of oyster shells over wooden planks over a ditch), I said slowly, "I'll never, never tell!"

"Well, perhaps it would be better to wait until you're an old lady and tell the tale to your grandchildren someday."

This was so farfetched that it made no sense to me, but what did make sense, I knew if we told, never again would I be Sterling's fishing companion.

"Sterling, I heard you tell Archie and Henry that you didn't believe in God, that you were going to be an agnostic, an atheist, or…."

"Effie, always remember this, everybody believes in God when they need him."

We heard wheels behind us and it was Bill Bibbins, coming back from delivering groceries.

"If Uncle Bill knew!"

"I know," I said consolingly. "I'm his pride and joy. I'm ten now, but we've decided, and I keep promises."

We got into the wagon, and Bill said, "You two really like fishing!" Sterling and I didn't feel like talking.

"What's the matter? You didn't get crab bite, or sun stroked, or anything, did you? Did the boat spring a leak?"

We were very close to Bill and he was puzzled. He shook his head and said, "Trout and flounder. I sure hope Miss Sallie makes cornbread for supper."

Chapter VII

Her speech was pleasing, her voice never to be forgotten.
Robert L. Stevenson

"This year we will leave the old lilac bush alone, for a robin has built her nest there. Do you know I saw three dandelions this morning, and it's only April the tenth? I've heard they're the first flower that the bee visits in the spring."

We would have little conversations as I helped do things.

"Aunt Sallie, I write things down, for no reason. I will just write: I love my mother, be kind, or just pretty words like shell, leaf, or flower. I like how words look."

"I do too," she said. "I also think verses from the Bible." She stopped her work and repeated,

"Forgetting things which are behind and reaching forth unto those things which are before, I press toward the mark. That is from the epistle of Paul to the Philippians, a very inspiring verse."

Remembrance is forever.
Shakespeare. King Lear Act I

It was morning of a new day. Aunt Sallie was talking but I was still sleepy and only half listening.

"Some days you will remember. Of whole years you will have only the vaguest memory, and yet certain whole days will be sharp and clear in your memory. The least little detail will be there."

This day was hot, and quivering butterfly companies looked like living crocus flowers flying around.

Each word now calls back her voice. Yes, to have been born to people of character and faith is better than wealth.

The sun shone though the maples and here at my feet was a spider's web sparkling in the still wet grass, flowers were still fresh with dew. The leaves twinkle. They were meeting a new day.

"Why did you get up so early Aunt Sallie?"

"Just to be alone a little while and think about the day. In the dawn you seem to be the only living person in the world, you face truth, and are at peace. Dawn is the newest thing to youth, after youth is gone. Youth is wonder and belief. All things seem possible at dawn. It is in itself a miracle. I will call you tomorrow, and you will understand it all better. There will be a whole day ahead, a day that never was before. We will see it begin, and be a witness to its creation."

After a storm, opalescent drops fell from the lilac.
Coleridge

The summer rain, so delightful, was sometime disastrous to both people and crops. These were sometimes ruined by the hail and wind. Once the lightning split a tree down the middle in our back yard. Everyone came to see it the next day, and during this same storm, a man, whom we all knew and loved was killed by lightning, while sitting by a window in his home.

A tragic death, one hard for children to understand, how could anyone?

The storm that bought tiny frogs down from the sky was a very severe one. By the time the storm was over they had all hopped away to the fields, but we really saw them. A spectacular phenomenon!

I believe it was Elbert Hubbard, who said that in his childhood during a storm, tiny fish rained down.

I'm sure there is a scientific explanation for this, but that is not my field.

What did other children do?
And what was childhood wanting you?
Robert L. Stevenson

Through winter snow and summer sun, the split willow basket of pine cones stood on the stationary part of the well top.

Split willow! The name always fascinated me. They were woven of a pliable wood in a checker pattern, with a strong handle, not especially beautiful, but sturdy and useful. Every family used at least one, as they were very nice for vegetable and fruit picking, and they could carry two pies or two cakes to the church social, four with napkins between. They were a fact of life, probably inexpensive too.

Ours was always piled high with perfect pine cones that Aunt Sallie loved. Every time she went through the woods she would come home with one, two, or maybe a dozen. If this many, she gathered them up in the skirt of her dress.

Aunt Sallie did not like aprons. She told me once that they were a badge of servitude. She thought as Lincoln, "I will neither a master or slave be." Aprons and Aunt Sallie were not compatible. She was of the outdoors, the woods and the fields.

The well on which the basket stood was of brick, circular. Everyone remarked at the clever style of the half circle sliding top. There was a handle to open it and to push the front one under the stationary half. Of course, the whole circle could be taken off to clean the well once a year, also to paint the circle always white. This was done while the water was very low, the last of the summer. The water was all dipped out, and how deep it looked. Away down there!

The pine cone basket was Aunt Sallie and my project together, though I never, or hardy ever put any in. I took old ones out to throw to the chickens, when the basket got too full and added fresh ones that Aunt Sallie brought every few days.

There is a time, when her pleasant trees,
I feel a free, leafy luxury.
John Keats

We were resting under the maple, Aunt Sallie and I.

"Aunt Sallie, How can you get so mad with somebody you like?"

"Thelma?"

"Yes, she wants her own way."

"Well, not only Thelma is like that, but everyone is. It's human nature to be."

"Oh, is that it."

"Someday you will have other friends. Now Thelma's your best friend, and…."

"Oh, I love her. So I'll put up with her. Seems sad Thelma will never be in my class at school. I'd like that. I wish she could be."

"Well, that is unfortunate, but her mother thought that she was doing the right thing to send her to pay school those starting years."

"But she didn't learn a thing, not even to read. She didn't even learn her A, B, Cs. I guess you can't read until you know them. Of course she does now."

"Well, maybe there will be a new way to learn to read some day. Not learning A, B, Cs first. Perhaps the way they look or sound."

"I'm glad I can read," I said complacently. "Of course, not all words," I added, "like atheist, agnostic, infidel, hypocrite, and …"

"Effie, where did you hear those words?"

"I heard Sterling, Henry and Archie talking them. I asked Priscilla. We hunted them up in the dictionary."

"Well, you should have a good vocabulary someday!"

"I don't know that one. Vocab….." I said puzzled.

"It means to know lots of words, their meanings, what part of speech they are and how to use them in sentences."

"Oh, I'd like to know every word. I love them all. Here comes Thelma."

Chapter VIII

Build these more stately mansions,
Oh my soul –
The Chambered Nautilus – O. W. Holmes

It seemed sometime, that Thelma couldn't stop talking about her Uncle Gus. I liked Uncle Gus too. He was so blithe and gay, friendly, kind, so handsome with auburn hair and brown eyes.

He was the youngest of a family of five girls, one of which was Thelma's mother. But all the spoiling in the world couldn't hurt Uncle Gus. He was a thoroughly nice person, loved by everyone. As Thelma was always saying, he had principles and stuck to them.

He had a proud, joyous walk, as if he were going places, somewhere special and he knew just where it was. Happiness and contentment lived with him. If only speaking a sort time with him, one felt his ambition, and also his concern for other people.

Thelma's Uncle Gus had graduated from Crisfield High School, then the Maryland Agricultural College (now called the University of Maryland), and now he was going to Law school in Baltimore. He did not want to be a farmer.

"Imagine Uncle Gus being a farmer. No indeed, he is going to be a Senator; as soon as he could then he's going to be Governor and live in a big mansion. I'll bet that mansion has a bigger banister than Welcome Hinges and ten times more rooms. Boy, will we have fun!"

"But Thelma, how long will that be? We might get too big. We might get boy crazy or something like that."

"Well, here's one that wants to stay young."

"Yes, young, but you know we're getting older every minute. Maybe by that time we can go to a ball and have evening dresses, I'd like lavender net."

"After the ball is over," Thelma sang happily. "That is a pretty song. We'll have the most fun. That Governor's mansion is so big, you can stay all night with me."

"I do hope your Uncle Gus does get to be a senator. He does make good speeches."

"Oh, he will. He keeps saying, I'm going to win and be the best senator Maryland ever had, I'll put more bills on the floor than ever have been before."

"On the floor," I said.

"Yes, I asked about that. It does sound crazy but he was busy talking, so …." He said something else funny too. "My hat is in the ring and I never give up."

"I'll ask Aunt Sallie about the floor and the ring."

"Yes, Effie, you do that."

Cultivate the spirit of courtesy and friendship.
Emerson

Thelma kept on talking, "Uncle Gus has such pretty thoughts. He could be a poet, if he didn't want to be a senator. He likes to talk instead of writing things down, so he won't ever be one. Senator first, then Governor, that's the way it works. Right now he's up in Baltimore studying to be a lawyer. You should see the big books he studies. You have to learn an awful lot to be a lawyer. I miss him. When he's home he reads us poetry in the evenings to rest his mind from the studying."

He said one poet said that maybe we are not here at all, but in a dream. That was the poet's, very words, "Life is a dream within a dream."

"Oh, Thelma."

"Well, suppose it's true, we're dreaming. I know you've got your locket Mr. Jordan gave you and you wear it every Sunday but…." she looked around mysteriously and clutched me by the arm. "What if what that poet said is true? Even Uncle Gus wouldn't be here at all, would he, or Mr. Jordan, ever."

"Thelma, just which poet is this that your Uncle Gus is talking about, that says such crazy things?"

"I don't know. I'll ask him."

"Wait," I said "I'll ask Aunt Sallie. She'll know."

When I explained what Thelma had been saying, Aunt Sallie said, "That would be Edgar Allen Poe."

"Was he cracked," Thelma asked?

"No, he was what is known as a genius. If he wanted to write that, it was his right."

"But, Mr. Jordan, Aunt Sallie. Thelma says if it's true, he wasn't here at all. It was one of those dreams, inside another dream."

"Nonsense," she gave my arm a tiny pinch. "Did you feel that?"

"Yes, but it didn't hurt much."

"Well, Mr. Jordan was as real as that. Did you remember to put your necklace back in its box yesterday?"

Chapter IX

God's in his heaven
All's right with the world.
Robert Browning

"Effie, will you answer me this question? Why is it that every kid in Calvary has been to stay on the lighthouse two weeks, but us? It's just as if somebody had a party, a birthday party, and we're not invited."

"Oh, Thelma, we're invited to every party."

Mr. Lum B. really Mr. Christopher Columbus Curtis kept the third out lighthouse. Two weeks he was there, every minute; and two weeks a man from Virginia was there, for the third light was very close to Virginia.

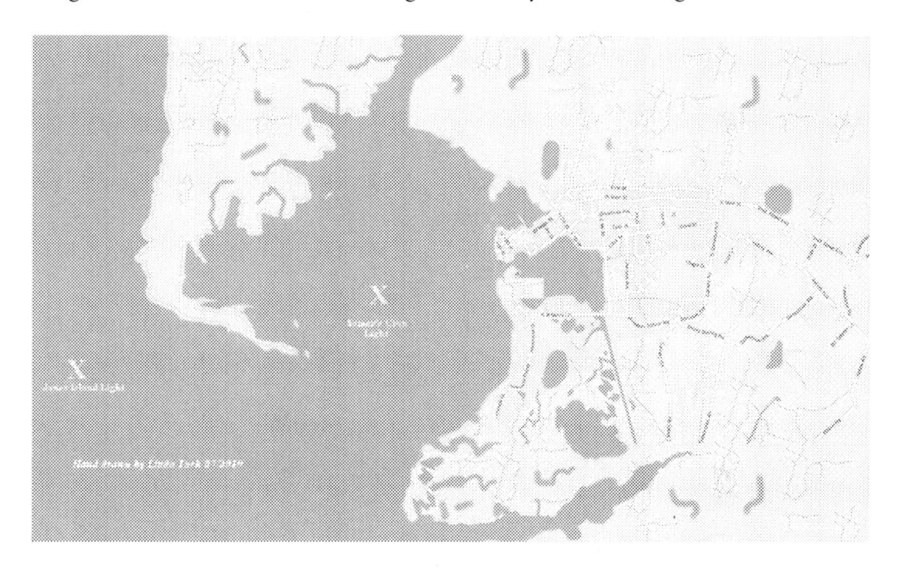

It was a very nice job, good pay, and he had it for life. Sometime he took his wife for two weeks, and at times he took one of his children and a friend or two of theirs.

Nancy was the closest to our age and was always begging us to go. Everyone reported such fun they had, fishing, swimming, helping keep things shining, playing games in the evenings.

I had asked to go dozens of times, and so had Thelma, but this pleasure we had always been refused.

"Why? Why?" said Thelma stamping her foot angrily.

"Well, I'll tell you what my father said …."

"What?" Thelma asked eagerly.

"He didn't want me to get something that I might get if I went. I was too young. It would be hard with me. He said he wanted me to be older, before I got it."

"A disease from staying on the lighthouse?"

"I don't know whether it's a disease or not, but it surely sounds like one. It's called nostalgia, and it's very bad. It's better to get whooping cough or measles, and I've never even had them."

"Somebody's crazy! A disease from all that sunshine and fresh air. It would blow the germs away. I never heard of anybody getting anything but sunburn. Nancy did have to go to the doctor for that one time, they all stayed out on the upper deck too long in their bathing suits."

"Effie, beg your mother to let you go and I'll beg harder too. It would be such fun to go together with Nancy and Louise, Roy and Joe. They say Mr. Lum B. lets everybody make fudge and taffy and help make doll house furniture."

"Grandpa says Mr. Lum B. must have the patience of Job to put up with all the kids. Course most of the time he only takes three, but maybe we could talk Louise into staying home, for he may draw the line at five."

"I can't go, Thelma," I said miserable.

"Say Effie, I wonder if it's like what Mr. Jordan had. What was that, am—."

"Amnesia, No, I'm sure it's not like that, but don't mention Mr. Jordan. Anyway, they specially don't want me to get it until I'm at least seventeen."

"Seventeen!"

"Then my father says I can cope with it. Let's not talk about it. Let's go look at Thomas. Babies are so cute. Anyway, they will never let me go. I can tell how they talk."

"Well, I'm going to keep on begging. You can give up the ship if you want to, but not me. Fudge is the best stuff, and Nancy says they make it every single night. We'll go play with Thomas for a while. He is cute, but why my mother wanted him, I'll never know, never. I like him to hold onto my finger though. Smart though and he's only three months old. Come on."

Chapter X

The groves were God's first temples.
S. Lanier

Thelma said, as we walked into the woods today, "Sometime when I walk in here, it feels like I'm walking in Church."

"I know the groves were God's first temples."

"What?"

"Jesus preached under the trees before they had churches. They called churches temples then, after they built some."

"Oh," Thelma picked up a pine cone and then threw it down.

"Not perfect?"

"No, mashed on one side. It looked perfect on the ground."

"Yes, they do some time."

There is a pleasure in the pathless woods.
Lord Byron

"I hope there's a pine woods in heaven. You know, Effie, I bet as long as we live we will never forget these woods, or the violets."

"Of course not, how could we?"

"Well," Thelma said darkly, "I asked Grandmom something about what she did when she was little, and she said, I forgot."

"Well, we won't."

"No, I think it will be stamped on our brains."

"Yes, it will be in our memory. Aunt Sallie says memory is the most beautiful part of life."

"John Williams' children will have nice memories of Aunt Sallie as good as she is to them. Everybody knows how she's so kind and good, getting them brand new clothes for school and big dolls and toy tool chests for Christmas."

"Everyone does? She doesn't know that!"

"Well, they do. Your good deeds as well as bad deeds will be found out. I heard Grandmom talking to Grandpa, and she said, "Surely goodness and mercy will follow her all the days of her life."

And Grandpap said "And she will dwell in the house of the Lord forever." They were talking about Miss Sallie. Yes, she's just plain good, and Grandpap said the best of it was that she had the constitution with the resolution."

"I think that meant she has lots of energy to do things, and enjoys doing them. Come on Thelma, let's go to Mr. George Masons, I've got a dime."

So shall the dream be
Whatever will be, will be
Today will be thine

To all eternity.
J. Bennet

A little later we are back, sitting near the pines, with a bag of penny candy and two bottles of a new kind of pop Mr. George had given us free just to try.

"Effie, just suppose that poet is right, and we are in a dream inside another dream, then we're not really here at all, are we?"

"Oh, Thelma, of course we are."

"Well, just suppose it's true, and only you and I see the violets, no one else."

"What do you mean? Of course the violets are here, and more beautiful than ever today."

"I am going to tell you something," she looked mysterious. "You remember the day that Nancy and Edith were playing with us, and Edith was trying to climb a pine tree and she fell, right into the violets? I snatched her off of them, and told her she was mashing the flowers and to get up quick. She looked down and said Thelma Coulbourne are you crazy? There's not a flower anywhere around. She looked down again real good. You are crazy, there's not a leaf here, she said. Come on Nancy, I'm not playing any longer here, jerking me off of flowers that's not there."

"Thelma, it must have been another pine..."

"No, she shook her head it was the one where they grow, and another thing. I was telling Grandmom about the beautiful violets here, and she said, Thelma, stop making things up. I've lived beside these woods for sixty-five years and I've never picked a violet there. Just suppose Effie it's true, and only you and I can see them."

"Thelma, let's just enjoy them, as we decide that first day we are so happy to find them, and let's not wonder too much. It tires me out. That Edgar Allen Poe must have had a magnificent imagination."

"Imagination! He was crazy."

"But, Thelma, he was...."

"Come on, let's go play croquet."

Chapter XI

Drifting meadows of the air, where bloom
the daisied banks of violets.
Thoreau

We were sitting on the porch in the cool of the summer evening again. Twilight had come and gone. The stars were out.

"Look at all those stars," said Thelma. "A billion and see those lightning bugs sitting on the air. There's a circle of them; and hear the crickets and the fogs. They never give up."

In the evenings some summer nights, we played what we called the poetry game. Aunt Sallie would say one line and the first child to know would say the next one or who wrote the poem.

"Maud Muller on a summer day," and Thelma would be first to say "Raked the meadow, sweet with hay."

"Woodsman, spare that tree," and as it was Buddie Widdie's favorite, he would say quickly, "touch not a single bough."

Bud Charles always answered, "The woman was old and ragged and gray," right away he would say, "and bent with the chill of a winter's day." He liked this one and could repeat all of it from memory. He probably has compassion for the old lady.

Some evenings there were as many as ten children on the porch, tired from playing games Lay-low, hide and whoop, and relaxing with the poetry game.

The school readers of the day were crammed with selections from poets, and all children knew some of them, Longfellow, Whittier, Tennyson, and William Cullen Bryant.

Darkness came on, and Thelma said, "I didn't mean for it to get this dark, I'll be afraid to go home."

"Thelma, Charles will take you on his bike," Aunt Sallie said.

"But," said Bud Charles, "the graveyards! We have to go by three of them."

"Nonsense," said Aunt Sallie. "Thelma's mother may be worrying about her. Charles, graveyards are just another piece of ground. The people are only resting there."

"To me, the graveyard is just another part of the yard." I said.

"To me, it's a graveyard," Bud Charles said, "Come on, Thel, we'll ride like the wind and coming back I'll fly."

"Buddie, don't be afraid," I said, "I do think graveyards are nice, with all those roses and lilies and the poetry on the tombstones."

"I've never stayed long enough to read things. When I cut the graveyard grass, I cut it fast, which reminds me, I did it for you last week when you went to that birthday party. Cutting the grass is one thing you're big enough to do."

"Yes, but I get tired of it. Maybe I could learn to dig potatoes."

"No," he said "You'd cut them all half in two, and I know the right way. Bill showed me. Willie can't do it right yet. He just picks them up."

Buddie Widdie said, "Effie, when you get tired of cutting, stop and come get me, and I'll finish."

"No, it's bad for your back, I'll do it."

Thelma jumped up, "Charlie, will you all shut up and ride me home. It's getting darker every second."

"Come on, Thel, get on."

We kept on a few minutes longer with the game. Under the Spreading Chestnut Tree, The Schooner Hesperus; Longfellow was the best known of all, so understandable.

Someone said, "I remember, I remember, the house where I was born." "Thomas Gray," someone said quickly. "No, Thomas Hood Gray wrote Gray's Elegy. It is said that he wrote it sitting on the steps of a church in England and looking over at the cemetery. The church is still there today, now as it was then. Perhaps some of you may make the trip across be ocean and visit the place someday."

When Aunt Sallie had told us this before, Bud Charles would say, "Across all that water. I'd be scared to death, all those big waves, maybe bigger than the ones at Ocean City."

I would tell him, "You'll be grown up then Buddie, not afraid of graveyards and oceans and snakes and….."

"It's you that's afraid of snakes, not me," he would say.

"Well, I'm not afraid of graveyards, and I never will be. I refuse to be. Those people are only resting. It's just ground like, like the sweet potato field. Anyway, they're beautiful."

"This is the last guess for tonight," Aunt Sallie looked at the sky, "Stars of a summer night."

My mother was calling me, but quickly I said over my shoulder, "Far and yon, azure deep. Longfellow."

In the distance we could hear a hay ride celebrating someone's birthday, perhaps. Hayrides were very popular. Fun!

Chapter XII

Summer afternoon - the prettiest phrase in the English language.
Henry James

We were going fishing this morning. We bought our watermelon, ten cents, and a piece of ice, to make it cold, five cents. We had our lunch that Harriet made and lemonade in a jar.

The river was full of sails. How beauty they looked from the shore. The sails seemed to be pure white in the early sun, though they were sewn together in pieces and perhaps dirty and discolored with the weather, but from a distance they looked beauty perfect and snowy white.

The lighthouse boat was the only one with a motor. During the two weeks Mr. Lum B. was at home we use that. What fun! How fast we could go, but sails were our love, bending low to one side, as we came back with more fish than anyone knew what to do with.

Today little boys are not named Christopher Columbus, Gorge Washington or Abraham Lincoln. Of course these were shortened to Lum B., Wash and Link. These men were all kind, jolly, full of love for all us children. One knows Mr. Lum B. had to love children to take as many as four for two weeks on the lighthouse. He had six or seven of his own.

That kind of lighthouse that he maintained are no more. It seems so sad. They were so beautiful, that big welcoming light, the green, red and white house out in the very deepest water, the spiral staircase going up to the top deck. It was a marvelous piece of engineering to build.

Though I never spent the two weeks there, my father did take me for a visit one time and Mr. Lum B. showed us everything. My mother did not like long sails. Just around to the Lavalettes was enough for her. This was a showplace, with pavilions and electric lights. A lovely home in its day.

The day was beautiful, the fish plentiful and in just a short time we had more than enough.

"Sterling, could we sail out to the lighthouse? Thelma is there. She finally begged hard enough."

"Well, maybe we could, there is a good breeze."

In just a little while we were there. The children were out on the lower deck, and happy to see us, but I didn't see Thelma.

"Nancy, where is Thelma?"

"Thelma, here's Mr. Sterling and Effie," she called.

In a second, Thelma was leaning over the railing, but …what a woe begone Thelma. Her eyes were swollen red with crying and she looked sick.

"Oh, Mr. Sterling, will you take me home? I'm awful sick. I've got to get home."

Sterling looked at Mr. Lum B. "Yes, Thelma doesn't feel good. I am as glad you and Effie came."

"Well, get your things, Thelma. It's getting late and we must get back."

"Can't you come in a little while, Sterling and have some coffee and..."

"You can't waste time like that," said Thelma. "It's getting awful late."

Mr. Lum B. walked down the steps with Thelma and put her in our rocking boat. Thelma's face was happy, as she said, "Thank the Lord, thank the Lord I'm going home." She took a long breath, "Anyway, I didn't stay long enough to get that disease your father talks about.

Effie, maybe you had better mind your father, for I do think I was getting something, after only one night too. I felt real bad. Awful, just awful, but I feel good now."

"You're not going to fish anymore are you Mr. Sterling? I'm dying to get home and see my darling little brother, that darling baby."

"But Thelma, you say he ties you down and..."

"That darling! Never. Effie you must have dreamed I said that. I can't wait to let him hold my finger."

"We've got a good breeze and in ten minutes we'll be in," Sterling said.

"Thank the Lord," Thelma said again.

"I don't think you should take the Lord's name in vain, Thelma. The Bible says...."

"The Bible says *Rejoice and be Happy* to, and I'm glad, glad to feel good again."

Sterling laughed. "I hope you never feel that way again, Thelma, and I hope Effie never does."

"Have you had what I had, Mr. Sterling?"

"Yes, I had a touch of it just once, and not too long ago. Let's get ship shape, here toss the rest of the watermelon over and five more minutes will do it."

We seemed to be flying. The boat was cutting swiftly through the water, making lovely foam and leaning far to one side.

Chapter XIII

"Forget thee!" Bid the forest birds
forget their sweetest tune.
John Moultre

I had been picking blackberries back of our Stell's stable, and suddenly I slipped into something crunchy, and heard a loud buzzing. I knew in a flash what had happened. I had stepped into a low built hornets' nest in the tangle of vines.

I ran toward home and all of the hornets ran after me. I saw Aunt Sallie in the yard, and screamed.

At once she knew what was happening. The black cloud behind me, determined to catch up with me, hundreds, maybe a thousand. The roar was terrific, and I was giving out.

"Lie down, lie down!" Aunt Sallie called.

Where did I get the courage to lie down? From faith in her, I'm sure. When I lay down, they lost me and scattered.

Aunt Sallie came running. I was sobbing.

"Don't cry. You're safe." She took my hand.

"Aunt Sallie, how did you know if I lay down, they would lose me?"

"I didn't. I prayed they would."

"But you didn't have time to pray!"

"I breathed a prayer."

I said thoughtfully, "It seems everybody has to believe in God."

"Yes."

"Even when we were out fishing."

"Yes," Aunt Sallie said softly. "God is a very present help in time of trouble."

"Yes, and it was in the very present that I needed Him."

The saddest words of tongue or pen,
Are these, It might have been.
J. G. Whittier

Thelma's Uncle Gus did run for Senator and won, but before he could take his place in Annapolis, he died suddenly, a great tragedy. As the hymn says, grief was wide, for he had been loved by all.

How everyone enjoyed the election campaign and his wonderful speeches. Uncle Gus was at rest. Augustus C. Ward was no more.

It was hard to console Thelma. I told her about my Uncle Sam, and how my heart was broken when he died, but she just sobbed the harder to know that I had felt what she was feeling now and said,

"Is everybody going to die and leave us?"

If Uncle Gus had lived, he would have been great, because of his inborn genius for rightness and his sensitive perception, innate tenderness and nobility of character, but now he was to be always with *the resting ones*, and his mother had planted ivy to cover his grave.

As Thelma said, "He made his speeches so pretty, so we could go to the mansion, if your father would have let you go. It wouldn't have been like the lighthouse because he would have gone too."

And she sobbed and would not be comforted.

And in short measure
Life can perfect be.
Ben Jonson

Today, Thelma and I just sat under the pines and talked.

"You know, Effie, I'd like to hear Uncle Gus' voice speak just once more before I cross the river Jordan and rest on that beautiful shore."

"Oh, Thelma no."

"I'm just talking church talk. Come to think of it, shores of rivers are not pretty."

"You're right."

"Maybe ocean shores, but not rivers. They're spongy, and full of snake holes, ugly bushes, marsh grass...."

"But maybe a heavenly shore would be different, pretty shells and flowers. There's nothing prettier than a marsh flower. Five stars they have. They are the starriest flowers and cattails are pretty so brown, maybe thick green moss, like green velvet. I wonder if what they call bull rushes in the bible are really cattails?"

"Maybe, but we'll never know."

"The dictionary may say so."

"Who'd look it up, with all the other words in the way?"

"You look in the B's. I may look sometime."

"Go ahead. I'm too sleepy to crack a book at night, much less a dictionary, an anyway it's against my principles to open one in summertime, and it's August, and my Uncle Gus always said, you must stick to your principles."

"Of course you must," I agreed. "I'll do the looking."

Chapter XIV

And all the world,
a solemn stillness holds.
Grays elegy

"Tonight," said my father, "we are going to have a treat. Sister Sallie is going to give us the Elegy,"

The twilight was deepening, as he pulled down the shades. The room was cozy with lamplight. The flowered china lamp gave a lovely light. The mantle clock tick loudly and began to strike eight. It was a nice sound, homey, comforting.

We were all so happy. There may have been worries for the grownups, but we three children were blissfully unaware of them. I knew that when Priscilla got her check, anything that I had been wanting would be mine, such as an angora hat, with a scarf, or whatever the rage at that time.

Name, her name keep memory
Glowing, like a flame.
M. Lanvin

"The curfew tolls the knell of parting day. The lowing herd winds slowly ov'r the lea."

I was dying to ask what curfew meant, but I could not - should not - must not, not now. It was amazing to us how she knew the long piece of poetry, thirty-four verses, every word.

If Thelma had been there, she would have said, "That's the reason everybody say's Miss Sallie's mind is like a steel trap."

A crazy expression, but one frequently used to describe intelligence. My father said softly, "That was splendid. It puts the question of death in such a beautiful way, unlike Shakespeare's harshness in his description in..."

"Death?" I said. "is that beautiful poem about being dead? Who died? What was the matter?"

"Later, Sweet, later Baby, you will understand the beauty of literature."

"But that was poetry."

"Yes."

This was grownup talk, but how we loved the words, and the cadence of Aunt Sallie's voice.

My mother had sat down quietly, with her sewing; and Priscilla with her papers, saying "Go ahead Mother. I'll do these later, in bed." My brothers were quiet and I was completely enthralled.(I must remember to ask Priscilla about the curfew. It tolled the knell. I'll have to ask about knell too. I know toll. The bell at church tolled, when there was a funeral.)

My brothers went up to bed. After getting a glass of water, I went upstairs too. The day was done.

Full many a flower is born to blusk unseen,
And waste its sweetness on the desert air.
Grays Elegy

I told Thelma about it the next day.

"The next time Miss Sallie reads that Elegy, I'm coming over to hear it."

"She doesn't read it. She knows it by heart."

"Imagine that. I'll be there. Is it something like Snowbound? I know what that's about. A family gets snowed in, after it snowed all day and all night. The school teacher lived with them, a man teacher, and they're sitting around the fire and taking. The cat is there and their dog and in the morning, the father says, boys! a path, a path to the barn, and they were so happy to get out in the snow and dig."

"Thelma, I didn't know you knew that piece?"

"Of course I do. Uncle Gus used to read it to rest his mind from studying."

"No, it's not like *Snowbound*. It's about death."

"Death?"

"But it's beautiful, Thelma. And all the air a solemn stillness holds. That's beautiful."

"Well, I'll be there, for I do love poetry."

"I did ask Priscilla what curfew meant."

"It means the day is over. It is still and the poet could see the darkening shadows on the landscape. Then from the distance he heard the bell. It does not ring cheerily. It tolls. It is very solemn. It is a knell for the day that has been so bright and is dying. The poet says parting day. He means departing. The mere fact that it is an unusual expression fixes it in the mind, parting, not departing. It would be difficult to forget that line after all this thinking about it, so thinking is the thing."

"I also noticed," Priscilla continued, "that Grays Elegy was written in 1757, a long time ago."

I loved Priscilla. We used to talk while she was doing her hair at night. I mentioned how Thelma had loved her Uncle Gus, and she said, "Yes, he was a rare personality, unique."

"Unique?"

"Yes, unusual. Very."

"Priscilla, do you think anyone could memorize Hiawatha?"

"Not the whole. I can't imagine anyone trying, but parts. Sometime, I will mark some passage for you."

And she did not forget.

She kept promises too.

Chapter XV

Time goes, you say, ah, no
Alas, time stays, we go
Or else were this not so
What need to chain the hours
For youth were always ours?
Time goes, you say - ah - no.
Austin Dobson

Could I believe that there was a heavenlier world than this, with fields of daisies, shadows under trees and hearts tuned to mine, that owned this heaven of love.

I couldn't even believe, that as Aunt Sallie said, "Someday, I will call and a little girl will have gone away."

The day Aunt Sallie went to rest, a little part of me went to rest too. All along the way of our life, slowly those we love and those who love us - go.

In Calvary, there is love. The heaven that lay about me is still there for me. It is in the people, the woods, the flowers, the humming birds.

She was dead. There she lay, at rest.
The solemn stillness was no marvel now.
She seemed waiting for the breath of life.
She was dead, past all love or need of it.
The garden she had tended, the eyes she had gladdened,
The quiet haunts of many a thoughtful hour,
The paths she had walked in the yesterdays could know her no more.
Dickens
Old Curiosity Shop "Death of Little Nell"

The years went by. Yes, Aunt Sallie had left us, and it was, as she said, if anyone should call, no little girl would answer. She was gone away, grownup, with children of her own.

Our sweetest songs are those
that tell of saddest thought.
Percy Byshe Shelley "To a Skylark"

In the cool of summer evening, riding with friends, I said suddenly, "Let's ride down to Calvary." I felt the magnet, pulling me there. "Sterling and his wife are there for the weekend."

They sat in the car. I went in and as usual they were glad to see me.

Harriet, now quite old, her pure white hair contrasting oddly with her kind brown face, was ironing in the summer kitchen, and she called, "Is that Miss Effie?"

"It surely is, Harriet," and I went in to say hello to her.

"Miss Effie, before you go, I want to show you something. I'll have these shirts done in a few minutes."

She came into the living room and said, "I want to show you the new rose wall paper in the parlour, and how pretty it looks with the new furniture. The roses and buds are so pretty, you can almost smell them."

We went into the parlour, and Harriet said, "I want to tell you this, because. Mr. Sterling won't, and he won't let Miss Charlotte speak of it."

She paused.

"What is it, Harriet?"

"Miss Sallie came back one night last fall."

In amazement, I turned to her, "Harriet, you're joking .... No, you're not, tell me about it."

"Well, I was ironing late and it was close to midnight. Mr. Sterling and Miss Charlotte had just turned off the radio everybody sits up late now because of the clearer music late."

This was true.

"Suddenly we heard, yoo – hoo –, yoo – hoo," just as Miss Sallie always called. Mr. Sterling jumped up and said, "That's Mom!" Then we heard the noise or pine cones being thrown on the porch from her dress skirt. Mr. Sterling pushed the porch light on quickly and there was the scattered pine cones.

Then he said, "I don't believe this - Mom - Mom."

There was no answer. "Harriet," he said to me, "Give me the broom. I'll sweep them all together. If they are here in the morning, this happened. If they're not, it didn't."

This yoo- hoo had always been her call, followed by Effie K. and always as she threw the pine cones from her dress to the porch, she would say. There! Effie K., get the basket. Throw the bottom ones away. I have to go back tomorrow and we'll fill her up again.

Aunt Sallie had said, someday Thelma will not come up the lane to play, or Bill rest under the big maple. Things would change. I would not be there.

A felling of sadness came over me, as I looked at Harriet. Her brown face wrinkled, but her body still had the same comfortable feeling, as I put my arm around her. Her face had the same kindness as when she had comforted me and helped me bear a childhood disappointment. A childish dream that didn't come true for me a long ago.

Childhood, that happy place, where one day of happiness is followed another, where kindness reigns. I didn't even know that there were unhappy children. The closest we knew to poor children were John Williams' and Aunt

Sallie kept them happy with candy and things, even dolls, for she said, the doll years were so few and had Bill put up swings for them.

Harriet and I were silent for a few seconds. There were tears in her eyes.

"Harriet, are you sure she didn't call, Effie K. Think hard."

"I'm sure Miss Effie, just yoo - hoo, two times."

"She said, some day I wouldn't be there, things would change."

"Yes," said Harriet, "she knew Effie K. had gone away."

"Thanks for telling me, Harriet."

In the light from the living room, I could see the well, but no basket of pine cones adorned its half circle.

Harriet said softly, "There were there in the morning."

The basket on the well was dust years ago. It was an Aunt Sallie and me thing, ours alone.

Harriet was saying, "Mr. Sterling had me put them under the cedar tree, by the well."

I got up quickly, "Oh, do you think they..."

"Miss Effie that tree was cut down when the sun porch was made."

"The crazy sun porch, I hate it," I said angrily. "I liked it best the way it was. I wanted to see the pine cones Aunt Sallie had brought."

"They were just ordinary pine cones, the kind your Aunt Sallie always picked up, perfect ones. There is a lot of things in this world we'll never understand and this is one of them but there they were, some large, some small, all perfect."

"Her spirit lives, Harriet. It lives in the pine cones. I remember her saying one evening to Thelma,"

"Yes, even in a pine cone. It will live forever. She wanted us to know."

"I knew you'd like to know, and the only one to tell you was me."

"Thanks, Harriet, I love you," I put my arms around her and kissed her fondly.

I never saw Harriet again. She died that winter. A good kind person, who, if there is a heaven, is there, or if there isn't, she is just resting.

Sing it in a lullaby.
Heaven is so wide and high.
M. Lanvin

The pines will always sway, the cones will fall, and the violets will bloom beneath them, redeeming the sadness of the sighing, and nice people will live on the Calvary earth, again and again.

Yes, the violets are there, darkly purple. The cushiony pine needles make a soft brown carpet, and the fragrance of it all is in the soft air.

I like to think that the same permissive angel, who gave Aunt Sallie a short leave one night to bring the pine cones, will let me and Thelma play forever in the Calvary Woods, loving the violets and not minding the sighing, at all.

For us, it could be, our Heaven.

THE END

PROFESSOR RIBEAU DECLINES THE HONOR

In the not so early 1900's, 1908 or 1909, there appeared this advertisement in the Crest Times:

Professor Ribeau. Teacher of piano, violin, harp.
Lessons - $1.00, in your home.
Call room seven, Crest Hotel,
Nine until nine,
Monday through Saturday, this week.

Call, did not mean call on the telephone. It meant come to his room and talk. Telephones were few. Doctors and undertakers, of course, had them, though very few places of business did. Why add such on expense?

Professor Ribeau walked to all of his appointments. Someone had asked him, "Why not ride a bicycle?" And he turned pale. "Never, an accident to my hands would be fatal." Cars were not even in the picture yet. One doctor, a Dr. Hall, did have one, and a very few daring younger people.

Though his lessons were expensive, his services became extremely popular. In a short time he had more pupils than any other piano teacher—so many that he could choose the location of their homes or the status of their parents. He instructed in town and out of town, Lawsonia, Calvary, Birdtown, all around.

He was - the word "portly" comes to mind - had a ruddy complexion, and brown curly hair, just beginning to thin, and dark eyes. He dressed nicely in velvet collars on suit and overcoat, brocade vest with gold watch chain across, a soft becoming hat, and gloves always. He was very quick, with a friendly smile for everyone.

My mother and a friend were sighing and talking out in the yard swing.

If one had children of music lesson taking age, the subject was sure to go like this.

"Will she be taking?" nodding at me, sitting by my mother.

"Yes. Oh, yes." My mother drew in her breach from the quick answer.

"Yes, yes indeed, just as soon as she is seven. That first year at school must be over. Seven is the perfect age to start. She is so anxious, and I can hardly wait. Some do start at six," persisted the friend.

"Yes, but it is a little early. I taught a few years before my marriage, you know, and I would say seven, from experience. Have another glass of lemonade, Dora."

I started school in September and was six in January. In June, my mother decided that though not seven, I was six and a half. School was over, and it was time to begin to take. She made arrangements with a friend; Mrs. Ethel Derling to start me at four o'clock Monday, the week after school was over.

My brother, Charles, took me into town on his wheel (bike). In my hand, I had a half dollar to pay for the lesson. My mother had paid the one dollar for the instruction book which I would get today.

"Now, Effie, pay close attention to every word and try hard."

"I will."

"And, Charles, pick her up just one half hour from the time you leave her."

"I will. I'll go to Si Layman's and eat ice cream while I wait."

"Alright. But don't overdo. Not over two cones."

We rode swiftly into town. My brother was a big boy now, twelve, and responsible for his little sister getting to her music lesson.

"It'll be nice to know how to play, Ef."

"Yes, I'll learn fast, but Buddie, you know you shouldn't call me Ef ?"

"OK, Ef . Here we are. Get off. I'll be back. You can sit on the porch and wait."

"Don't be late." I turned back to him before he got on his new bike.

"I'm afraid, Buddie, I. . ."

"Oh, go on. You want to play, don't you?"

"Y—e—s—."

"Well then."

I walked up the path. There was a bell, I turned it softly. The bell was not electric; to be pushed. You turned it as when winding a toy.

"Oh, Effie, you're right on time."

Then there was Miss Elsie. I took from her because Dot, my best friend, did. She had a unique way of keeping the lessons straight. She had a large calendar and wrote our names on the days we took. After I talked with her the first day, she wrote, EFFIE; on September 8, 1910. Her calendar had a picture of Niagara Falls in color. Beautiful!

After Miss Elsie, a new lady came to town, Miss Doffit. She gave music lessons in groups. At that time, this was a way-out idea. It cost twenty five cents, twice a week, Tuesdays and Fridays. We all sat in a circle, mostly girls, but a few boys. She was so pretty. I just looked at her - brown hair piled high in the Gibson girl fashion. Her shirtwaists were so lacy and lovely, the contrasting skirts of pale pastels, pleated in an intricate way. Her wide velvet belts with buckles of gold or silver were so beautiful. She would explain the lesson and then as she called our names, we would go to the piano with her to play. I'm afraid none of us got very far advanced, but we did love the way she taught, and her beauty was a delight to us. Miss Doffit did not stay long in our little town.

Miss Lettie was the best teacher of all. What I did learn was from her. She was kind and patient and very understanding. She said one day, "Effie, your time leaves a lot to be desired, but you play with expression."

"That's because I imagine as I play. When I play *Morning Prayer*, I see a little girl kneeling by her bed. The bed is made, and the spread is rose-color. The curtains are ruffled around the canopy bed and the windows too. Her nightgown is pale pink. Her hair is gold. And in *Falling Leaves*, I imagine them green instead of brown. The wind is blowing hard, and …."

"Well - well- do try to count as well as imagine. It's very important."

"Oh I will."

Seventeen years before 1900 in the year 1883 a wonderful, far-reaching, and lovely happening occurred (modern phrase). Etude magazine began and continued to be published by Theodore Presser, a Philadelphian, for over seventy years. Their slogan was *Music for Everybody* and that's just what it had. When I began to take lessons at seven, it was twenty- seven years old.

I'm quite sure that, at the time, more children took lessons on the organ than on the piano. Almost every family had on organ, and what beautiful music everyone enjoyed. It was such fun to pump the pedals. And the interesting stops to push in and pull out so intriguing. Tremelo is one, I remember. With some, organs, all of the stops had to be pushed in before the lid would close, but not ours. How lovely it was, with all the carving and little round places on each side to put the lamps. Gradually, organs were replaced for pianos, for the day of the music lesson was abroad.

Everyone took, and almost everyone took the Etude. As soon as one was fairly started with a new teacher, she would say, "It would be so nice if you could take the Etude. It is so helpful especially the junior page, and sometime we could use the little pieces for a lesson instead of sheet music."

I myself loved the Etude, but I did lean toward sheet music. Though I didn't know the word, sophisticated, it made me feel that way to set it up on the rack and play.

When a child played a piece exceedingly well, it was asked, "Who does she take from?"

Not, from whom does she receive musical instruction? If the answer was, "From Professor Ribeau."

"Oh, well then, of course, a whole dollar for one half hour, no wonder."

Professor Ribeau had two pupils of whom it was said he had taught them all that he knew. So he finally just gave them a long list of musical compositions to order and marked them off his list, after advising them to go to the Peabody Conservatory in Baltimore for their full course. These were Allean Tull and Richard Lee. Both had the talent to become great pianists, but alas, it also took money, and Baltimore was a strange and faraway place. Of course, we had those who had graduated from Peabody in our little town. Miss Lettie was one. But most people just took lessons to certain point.

In between teachers, my mother would implore me, "Keep your music up, darling. I do. I play every evening for us to sing. One must not miss a day. It shows."

"But - you - play."

"Playing is practicing, and practicing is playing. Surely you can see that, Effie."

Yes, my mother did play every evening. True as truth.

I begged and wouldn't give my mother any rest. "Please, let me take from Mr. Ribeau."

The reason I begged so hard was because Allean did. She lived next door, and she learned so fast and living only one field away, she was another best friend too.

Everyone said that after only one month of taking from Mr. Ribeau, one could play hymns, popular songs, and *Mendelsohn's Spring Song.* I was just dying to do all this. I had been taking from Miss Lettie for almost a year, and I was still playing only the easiest hymns, *Work For the Night is Coming, Rock of Ages, Blest Be the Tie that Binds.* Popular songs were beyond me, and *Mendelsohn's Spring Song* was beckoning from a great distance, though I loved to fiddle with it and still do.

Finally, my mother said, "Effie, go over to Allean's when Professor Ribeau comes today; and ask him to stop by on his way to town."

"I'll tell Allean to tell him."

"All right, but if you're going to take from him, you might as well tell him yourself."

"Is it alright if I tell Allean?"

"Yes, you can, if you had rather."

A knock came at the parlour door from the porch. My mother had put on a light blue house dress, and I had changed my dress for starched pink and green plaid gingham. My hair had been replaited, and a fresh pink bow tied on.

"Professor Ribeau. Come in. Have a chair and rest yourself."

It was a summer day, and I knew my mother would offer him lemonade. "Good afternoon, Mrs. Dix. I received your message from Miss Allean, a warm day for the first of June."

"Very. Professor Ribeau, I wanted to ask you if you would take Effie as a pupil this summer. Allean has done so well and...."

"Ah, Miss Allean, now, she ah...."

"Let me get you some lemonade."

After my mother left the parlour, Mr. Ribeau said, "The piano is in another room perhaps?"

"Oh no, this is the parlour. We have an organ."

"An organ? No piano in the home? Ah - ah....."

It sounded like a disgrace the way he said, "Ah..."

"My Auntie has a piano-organ. It looks like a piano. It has the same number of keys, but it is really an organ. I love to play it when I visit her on Sunday. Her name is Effie, like mine."

"Indeed !"

My mother came back with lemonade in three of our best glasses and slices of freshly made banana cake on our hand-painted rose plates, and three fringed napkins, all on our silver tray.

"You are too kind, Mrs. Dix."

"Not at all Professor Ribeau."

"This cake is glorious. Exquisite! Words fail me."

"Don't they know how to make banana cake in France, Mr. Ribeau?"

"My dear child, it has been many years since I have been in my native land, but I would say, no. No banana cake. Tarts, yes! To you, pies, I think ...."

"Have you considered my request, Professor?"

"Now, Mrs. Dix, as to that," He delicately touched the fringed napkin to his lips after finishing his lemonade.

"I am devastated, really, but I do not teach organ. You see, I have a great un-need for pupils. I am busy, very, very busy."

He got up and started for the door, but turned. "Is there a violin available, or perhaps a harp?"

My mother said proudly, "Thank you very much for stopping by." She walked over to our organ and put her hand lovingly on its dark wood. "No, the organ is our only musical instrument. Thank you again."

"If you are going directly back to town, please use the side hall door. Take the narrow path to the sweet potato field, cross it, and follow the wider path past the small dwelling you'll see, and you'll come to the main road. It will save you more than a mile."

She unhooked the screen door. "Please feel free to use our pebble path through the yard at any time. It does save steps."

Now I know that my mother understood the Professor perfectly that summer day. He was so popular that he could choose. He didn't especially want another pupil, who was not an Allean Tull, to struggle with. Oh, she understood, and he knew she did.

I hooked the screen door and stood there, looking at Mr. Ribeau through a mist as he hurried to town.

"Effie, don't cry. It isn't the end of the world, you know."

"I am not crying." I couldn't see my mother, only a blue glimmer. After all, when a dream is shattered, someone cries. No fat, bald-headed person who calls himself a professor could make me cry. Anyway, there's always Miss Lettie, and seventy-five cents for two lessons is a bargain.

"I'll give you a dollar each time we pay. You and Thelma can spend the quarter on the way."

"Why, he doesn't even know our language. A great un-need, what kind of a sentence is that?"

"Well, you see, he had to learn English. It must have been very difficult, as hard as it would be for us to learn his language."

"Well, if I ever did, I would learn the grammar and not go around making up new words."

"Mother, why do the children say, Mr. Ribeau and the grownups, Professor Ribeau?"

"Well, Effie, I …." My mother had no quick answer, but I did have one, and I said clearly looking into my mother's brown eyes, "Children are very smart people."

"Effie!"

I stopped with the plates in my hands.

"When you meet the Professor, treat him in no way but with politeness. Don't lift your chin and look beyond him."

"I'll try." At ten, my mother knew me well.

"And this is our affair, Mine, yours, and the Professor's. Remember?"

"I will remember." I added, though she didn't hear me, "Forever."

Shortly after our confrontation with Mr. Ribeau, the Etude magazine had a cover picture of a beautiful girl in an evening dress playing a harp, golden curls piled high. Oh, for that to be me, with lavender chiffon swirling at my feet, trimmed with velvet violets and satin sash. To have a harp was such an impossible dream that, I kept it to myself.

Many months of many years have been born torn off of pretty calendars, crumpled and tossed away, since Miss Elsie advised me to take the Etude. I have lots of Etudes, perhaps a hundred, for I adore them. I buy them at old book stores and antique shops. Their covers are so inspiring, their articles about the great composers, so wonderful. Lovely pieces to play, with beautiful titles, and they have the grade for each one: *Rose Petals, Grade 2, Visit of the Hummingbird, Grade 2 ½, Fairy Harp Song, Grade 3, Summer Day, Grade 4, Pastels, Grade 4 1/2.*

Difficult pieces for even the Allean Tull's and the Richard Lee's of this world.

In the evening I play. Sometimes I actually find that I can play a Grade 5 or even 6. Then I am very happy and fulfilled.

For playing is practicing and practicing is playing. My mother told me so.

THE END

REMEMBRANCE AND COMPENSATION

In childhood time, little children play
Under big old apple trees, with blossoms gay.
But years go by, and they go back and see
A weeping willow, where the apple tree used to be.

It happened to me. I went back
One sunny day in summertime.
I felt the willow - weeping, was crying with me,
And apologizing for not being my apple tree.

I didn't cry. I never cry, why cry?
But a sense of loss came over me.
For the brief happiness of childhood hours.
Following butterflies, gathering flowers.

My playmate and I, here, dreamed our dreams
Of being real mothers some far-off day.
My little girl, now, held fast my hand,
The most loved little girl in all the land.

THE END

THE CAKE WAS BANANA

March is a good name for the third month of the year. Everything is marching in, and we hope snow and cold days are going away. Here and there you may see a bird that you haven't seen since last November. They are back from their bird Shangri La.

On a low branch, still bare, you may see a blue-jay, and flying by as you admire his lovely blue and grey beauty, a red cardinal stops to rest on a living etching of a rosebush.

The little winter robins look full of purpose, not all scrooched up as if trying to hide themselves under their wings, as they have been doing. They haven't had an easy time, but they will not go.

The lily and hyacinth points are barely showing above the ground, but they are so green. Spring green!

Some morning soon, a crocus will be just ahead, as you put your foot almost down on this brave darling.

I think of Thoreau, and I trust sincerely that he rests in a valley of violets. Oh, please let all shades grow there, lavender, white, purple, purple blue, a reward for the awareness he gave us.

Yes, the last of March can be violet time, for it is the welcoming month. That strange, dim shade of pale green will be given to the trees for our joy, a gift of the springtime.

This year I had reached the age of ten in January and I was ready as everyone for the pretty days, and the warmth of sun. Of the big thrills of March coming in was to watch the men of the neighborhood plowing, getting ready to plant.

Most everyone had a garden, some small, just vegetables enough the family. Not so the neighbor who farmed the acres across the road. His crops were to sell. To whom I wondered. Perhaps he shipped them away by train, as the seafood dealers did. When he started to plow, I would go over and keep him company.

I was the only child who talked to Mr. Curtis. Of course, Mildred, his retarded daughter, really seemed to love him. He had grown up children too, three daughters and one son, Lester, surely if they did or didn't one couldn't detect it their manner. There was Edna, Emma and Gertrude who lived at home and taught school. She never married but lived a long life. She was one of those teachers unliked, but so nice at home and a real pleasure to her mother and Mildred, and patient with her father.

"Mr. Curtis, do you like to plow?"

"No."

"Looks like fun."

"Well, it's not fun. It is plain hard work. If I don't plow, I can't plant, so I plow."

"Why do you use two horses?"

"Easier on me."

"Most people use one."

"Well, they don't know. I rigged the harness up myself."

"Um, why don't you tell people?"

"Tell who?"

"Other plowers."

"Where? How?"

"You could write it down," I thought a second. "Maybe just tell them."

"Let them find out. Most people only have one horse," he slowed down. "Of course, they could hire one from me."

Mr. Curtis was ever ready to make money. "Yes, I'll tell old Mr. Nelson. He plows slow."

After the plowing, the next thing was the pulling apart of the big clods of earth. This was done with a unique device. About five or six boards were put together. Underneath there were iron spikes, some straight, some pointed, others curved this way and that.

This was hitched to the horses and driven up and down over the field tearing the sod. The blacksmiths must have been very busy people to do all the work required then. The Smithy a mighty man was he with large and sinewy hands. Yes, Longfellow, he needed them, and strength.

It looked like fun seeing Mr. Curtis bouncing over the ground. When he reached the end, I said, "Mr. Curtis can I ride on there with you?"

"No, indeed. If you got hurt, your people would blame me. Probably have me up in court."

"I wouldn't get hurt, please."

"No."

But, I wouldn't take no for an answer. I knew he would not finish this part in one day or two, maybe even three.

"Goodbye, Mr. Curtis." No answer. I called back. "Mr. Curtis, has the man come yet, who is going to live in the little house near the woods and help you this year?"

"Yes."

"Do they have children?"

"Girl baby, they're black."

"Oh, I don't care. I like colored people."

No answer. I called again. "Is the girl as big as me?"

No answer. He whipped up the horses and started another section. It did look like fun. Tomorrow was another day, and he might say, yes.

That was Monday. On Wednesday I saw he was still using the board. If it had a name I never heard it. He was over in a field near the woods. I ran across the edge of the plowed ground and finally reached him.

"Mr. Curtis, will you please let me ride on there with you? I want to so bad. I see this is the last field. Tomorrow will be too late."

He stopped the horses. "Why do you keep pestering me? The other kids around—."

"But, I like you. I like to watch you get the ground ready. Please..... please. It will seem I'm helping you."

"Get on, and hold tight to my pants leg. It's a rough ride."

I got on. "Hold on tight."

In a few minutes I was holding on to both of his pants legs, as he said, it was rough ride. He was so right.

I felt that I was loved by everyone in Calvary and I had a great love for them, with no exceptions. Yes, I'm sure the reason I felt everyone loved me was because I loved them. It was a time of love your neighbor.

Most of the people only spoke of Mr. Curtis to condemn him. They deplored his profanity toward his horses, his hired man and the weather. Yes, Mr. Curtis was disliked. He was not a mild man in the day when men were coolly affable. There were no women libbers around as such, but they knew about injustice and that he practiced this in his home.

At the Curtis home were two servants: Mag, a deaf and dumb colored woman and Annie and her little boy. Annie was said to be Spanish, a pretty woman with very curly hair, brown eyes and a glowing light brown complexion. She spoke no English, but for me she had a friendly smile and would sometimes touch my hair ribbon and say a word. It must have been a lonely life for these two, as they never went anywhere. Mag never left the place. I never even saw her in the front yard. Mrs. Curtis did send Annie on errands with a note. Perhaps down to the hired man's house or across the road to a store for a spool of cotton or something else needed.

The women around Crisfield said Mr. Curtis was carrying on slavery after it had been over forty years or more. The only evidence of ill treatment I ever did see was to Annie's little boy. He would be sitting on the edge of the back porch and Mr. Curtis would kick him off into the yard for no reason at all.

He was never hurt. The grass was thick and soft there. Annie would quickly run to pick him up or Mag would if Annie was not around. This kind of behavior was what made the neighbors hate Mr. Curtis. They really did. His actions were inconceivable to all.

There was always the question, where had Mag and Annie and the little boy come from? Some said the poorhouse. There was still one at this time and sometimes one would serve more than one county, perhaps even three.

Yes, Mag may have, but Annie, I don't think so. I think Annie was intelligent but what dark destiny had put her here? The slavery of hard work, no beauty, no contact with her own race. Why didn't Miss Gertrude try to teach her English? Why did Annie stay? A mystery in our midst, and no one liked what they didn't understand.

It was said Mr. Curtis wanted to work on Sundays! Oh, how could he? Remember the Sabbath Day and keep it holy. Didn't he read the Bible? Mrs. Curtis, who had been a preacher's daughter, Dr. Berry, drew the line.

After breakfast on Sunday she took Mr. Curtis by the arm and marched him out on the front side porch to a rocking chair, in the shade, gave him the newspaper and said, "Mr. Curtis, I will call you when dinner is ready. In a few minutes I will send Mildred out with fresh lemonade with banana slices, as you like it. Now relax. This is a day of rest."

I have said no one loved Mr. Curtis. Mrs. Curtis did and he loved her for to have influence over another, there must first be love.

"After the sun goes down today we will take a walk over our place. I will take a pie down to the hired man's family."

"Now Annie, that isn't necess—."

"And some strawberry jelly, about half a dozen glasses. I over made our winter supply."

Though Thelma was my best friend, I did play a lot with Mildred. There was something about her I learned but didn't really know it until much later.

Retarded children have no imagination. This is a sad sentence.

Thelma and I had an over-supply. When I played with Thelma, I came home refreshed and ready to do other things, but when I played a few hours with Mildred when I got home I would lie down on the sofa and sleep.

"I don't know why Effie seemed to be so tired." Mother would say to Father.

"Just over play, Annie honey, don't worry."

Mildred and I had lots of tea parties. Mrs. Curtis was very generous with tea party food making us fresh lemonade, always. When I played tea party with Thelma we always had Mrs. Brown, Mrs. Green and Sometimes Mrs. White with us. I tried this with Mildred, and it made her very unhappy. I explained that they were only make believe people and how Thelma and I talked with them about their children.

"I just want you, Effie."

I gave up. "Well, you eat Mrs. Green's cake and I'll take Mrs. Browns."

She took Mrs. Greek's cake and reached over for Mrs. Green's lemonade, and gave me Mrs. Brown's and that was the end of make believe with Mildred.

Every Sunday night almost everyone went to Church. They went to sing. Of course the long sermon must be endured, poor Mildred, poor me and all the other children. Mildred and her sister Gertrude never missed a service.

At the end of the sermon, there was another hymn or two, and then a prayer for us all. At the close of the service the hymn was one of two, always. *God be with you till we meet again* or *Stand up, stand up for Jesus.*"

We all really felt that God would be with us during the week and we knew we would stand up for Jesus.

One Sunday night after returning from Church, Mildred went into the kitchen and picked up the glass lamp, kept burning there. "Gertrude, I want to play the organ." she said. Though surprised, her sister said nothing, but in a minute she leaped to her feet.

Mildred was playing *Stand up, stand up for Jesus*, every note true and in perfect time.

Gertrude had tried to teach Mildred to play, but it had been impossible, as it had been to teach her letters or numbers or anything. Mildred was now thirteen. She was unteachable. Books were never to mean anything.

She was capable of love. She did love her family. She loved me. She loved her pets. Imagine Mildred playing a hymn.

"Play it again Mildred."

She did and again. Of course her mother was told, but no one told her father and he never knew until the night of his birthday party in August.

I continued to watch Mr. Curtis get his acres ready for planting. After the board's ugly prongs tore up the clods of earth Mr. Curtis used a huge heavy roller. This was six or seven feet long and as high as I was. It must have weighed over a ton.

Then came what was called the cultivator with more capacity for pulverizing earth. Those two horses worked hard and so did Mr. Curtis.

One day he stopped a minute and there seemed to be a smile on his face for he looked really pleasant. He said to me. "Effie, I won't be using my board again until next year."

"I know."

We looked at one another and laughed. I think this may have shown that Mr. Curtis did have a sense of humor. Only then was the hoe used. No, not yet. First the checks had to be staked and strung.

Mr. Curtis drove pointed stakes down about six at a time, three or four feet apart. Then Mr. Curtis tied twine around a stake and walking the length of the field with the ball of twine, he drove a stake and tied it securely, after he had driven one at the other end.

Sometimes he would glance back and see that the line was not straight and do it over. Under this string the row was made straight and beautiful. A small field could be put into rows without staking but not fields the size Mr. Curtis planted.

Now and only now, the seed or baby plants were put in the soil. The planting was done.

Since the coming of the tractor all this can be done with so much less labor. And time. The farmer of the days before World War I had to be what people called a worker. No one could say Mr. Curtis didn't qualify.

My mother and father and I were invited to Mr. Curtis' birthday party. It was in August. In the evening my mother called me in from play.

"Effie, put on your Children's Day dress and your pink satin sash. Bring your pink ribbons down and I will replait your hair."

The family was in the big dining room and there were roses on the table and two large banana layer cakes with slices of bananas on top and swirls of white boiled icing around them making the top like a rococo frame, beautiful. Of course that word was unknown to me. That beauty was far in my future. I loved it. Loved it then, love it now. Wonderful things can be done with boiled icing, I know, I've done them.

Mr. Curtis looked so nice in his best suit, so respectable, so handsome, and amazing. White shirt, black bow tie, gold cuff links, he reminded me of a picture of Jefferson Davis in my history book. Mr. Curtis looked like a gentleman.

During the conversation, Mrs. Curtis would say at intervals, "Where can everyone have gone tonight, Gertrude? You did give them all a cordial invitation?"

"Yes, Mama, I did. I said just what you told me to say."

"Of course you did." my father spoke. "I hear quite a few are down with summer colds. They seem to be prevalent just now."

"Yes, perhaps I don't understand. I...."

"The heat has been so oppressive these past few days," Mrs. Gunby said. "It just wears some out by the end of the day."

We had finished our cake and ice cream in the dining room, big slices, too big, and bowls of ice cream, also too big. I couldn't finish my cake, good as it was.

"Gertrude, did you light the lamps in the parlour?"

"Yes, Mama."

"Then, let's all see if it isn't a little cooler in there. The palm leaf fans may help. Mrs. Dix will you play for us? Mrs. Curtis likes music so much."

We went into the parlour. The pretty flowered china lamp was lit, and a glass one on the organ. Sitting down on the sofa and the pretty rockers, we picked up fans. I was fascinated by the organ. It was so different from any I had ever seen.

Across the top was a border of carved dark wood in an open work design, with heavy shirred lavender satin showing through. The front part had panels on each side with the same material showing and the music rack was also like this. For an added glamour, the square organ seat was of purple velvet with lavender fringe.

It seems to me when anyone wants something to be truly beautiful they use lavender. I wonder if it seems this way for other person's favorite colors.

"Please play, Mrs. Dix. Mildred, open the piano, dear." Mildred jumped up quickly, and my mother played some Stephen Foster songs from memory. Then she opened the hymn book on the organ and played a few hymns.

"Oh, thank you so much. We all enjoyed that tremendously," Mr. Curtis spoke in a disillusioned way. "Why I was talked into buying that organ...."

"Now, Mr. Curtis," his wife placed her hand on his knee.

"The most expensive one they had, and not one of my children really learned to play well. Oh, I put out the money for lessons to every teacher in town. I even ...."

"Papa," Mildred said timidly, "Would you like to hear me play?"

She sat dove at the organ, her three tiered, ruffled dress bouncing, pulled out every stop, and flipped the pages of the hymn book, said timidly.

"Stand up, stand up for Jesus.
Ye soldiers of the cross,
Lift high your royal banners
It must not suffer loss."

She played the hymn through. In the middle, Mr. Curtis Jumped up. "Anny, you didn't tell me, Anny!"

After Mildred finished, she stood up a second. "Let's all sing."

And we did, and again. We all knew the words. Then Mildred got up and went over to her father.

"Now, Papa. Aren't you glad you bought the organ?"

He put his arms around her. "Yes, Mildred. I am very glad. It was worth every penny of money."

My father got up and while shaking hands with Mr. Curtis said, "Your daughter plays beautifully. We have enjoyed the evening, and speaking for all, we hope you have many more birthdays as nice as this one has been."

We all started to leave. Mrs. Curtis got up quickly.

"Effie, don't forget your cake for tomorrow after school. Come with me. I will send the boys some and some ice cream too."

Two four layer banana cakes and four gallons of ice cream is a lot. She cut huge slices of cake, and covered them with a fringed linen napkin and went into the kitchen for some ice cream.

Annie was sitting in there in the dim light. She seemed so alone. Coming over to me she touched my pink satin sash and said a sentence.

I think she said it was pretty or maybe that I looked nice. I did have imagination.

"You can bring back the things tomorrow, Effie. Oh, yes, don't forget the ice cream." She murmured as she put more in a bowl.

"I will."

"I still don't know," she spoke softly.

I knew she was thinking of why the Jawes, the Lawsons, the Wilsons and others had not come to the party.

"Thank you, Mrs. Curtis."

"Child you are welcome. Come play with Mildred." My father took the bowl as it all was too much of an arm full for me. We went down the steps. Mr. and Mrs. Gunby had already said goodnight. My mother was talking as we walked the short distance.

"I just don't understand how can Mildred play that one hymn so perfectly?"

"Annie, there are some things about this life that we are not meant to understand."

"Every note so perfect— a miracle. It is a miracle, Mr. Dix."

"Yes, one that gave her father some happy moments and could make him a different person."

I ran ahead with the cake. Charles was asleep on the sofa and Buddie Widdie was reading an Alger book at the dining room table.

"I brought you both some cake from the party. The ice cream is….." My brother Charles was awake now.

"Cake? What kind?"

"Banana."

"Oh Boy! My favorite."

THE END

THE COURTESY PATH

Imagination, it is certainly one of those best things of life that are free, but perhaps in a category of its own.

What uses I have found for it, getting myself to sleep. Let it soar! Write perfect paragraphs, never remembered. Sometimes I do pick up a sleepy pen and write a few words, such as titles for collections of beauty, poetry I mean. *Some are Gold, The Beautiful, Sun for my Winter Snows, You Will see a Rainbow Again, Soon*; and imagination is for getting teeth filled, pains, that sort of thing.

I hope everyone has it. I do trust it is not like a sense of humor, lacking in some people.

There's a lack of imagination in most doctors, dentists and teachers to mention a few. I've known only one doctor, three teachers and not one dentist in a lifetime that had it, but let's forget these people and think of fairy tales and wonderful books that give lifetimes of pleasure.

Imagination is a big and wonderful word.

It is hard for me to imagine that the house in Calvary where I spent happy years was not always there. Once, just an empty field, not a tree even. Yes, there was one, a very old cedar in the graveyard at one side. Look carefully the tree has actually grown around one of the first headstones placed there now.

Eight years after the Civil War was over three people stood where the house now stands. My Aunt Sallie, young eighteen at the time; her father, William T. Dix and young Stouten Sterling, a fine, upstanding gentleman of twenty-three.

"Yes," my grandfather said, "this seems to be the place a nice southern exposure. You will have sun in some rooms all day long. The Riggin brothers are good carpenters and will put you up a find, custom built house. Plenty of windows in every room, wide doors, mantels in all rooms, up and down, for beauty. Front porch and side porch. It will be nice to eat meals there in the warm weather. Big summer kitchen. I'm glad the well is already here, fine tasting water. By Easter, the house should be finished." He looked across the field at a weather beaten two storey house. "I'm glad Jane's place is so close by. She will be a big help to you, Sallie, a kind and good person."

In the corner was the graveyard, fenced in white with a pretty gate. It was still there and still gleaming white in the 1920's.The old cedar, still living, my rope swing there, too.

"Let's walk over here," my grandfather said, putting his arm around his daughter's shoulder. I like to think Aunt Sallie had on a coat of a color called burgundy that day. Not dark red, not purple, just beautiful. I have seen this shade in a velvety crab apple or a plum.

"Yes, I want to see how the old cedar doing." As they walked, he continued talking. "Sallie when the house is finished and your yard made, it will be nice if you have a courtesy path through it, for I see the folks have been using this field as a short cut to the main road."

"A courtesy path! Father what a lovely idea. We will surely have one."

"They can be an ornament to a yard, and the upkeep can be made part of the day's work."

"Oh, how I love you, Father, for the beautiful thought. Our place will be as beautiful as . . ."

"As love can make it." young Stouten said.

"Yes, you'll be very happy here, so nice the business is so prosperous. You can certainly afford a nice home. The path will be an addition, with small stones and shells pressed down after a rain, about 18 inches wide and curve it at least twice and go by the near side the side steps. Plant an elm or a weeping willow. They both grow quickly. Someone may want to rest in the shade."

Our little stories, beginning with the Christmas tree quilt have very little embroidery in them, that one, none at all. Others, even *We Will Remember Him* are completely true with their tiny plots, their tiny climax and their happy or enigmatic endings.

They are just little gifts, just bits of the days and the lives of people I loved and who loved me, and Thelma, don't forget Thelma.

We will play here in these pages until they crumble to dust away.
(H.W.L.S. Children's Hour).

A few years ago Uncle Willie brought me a letter from Uncle Stoutie's brother, Henry, who said among other nice things, "And how is little Effie, a darling if ever there was one."

There's no one, or at least very few left who can ask that. I was close to 70 and he was 86 at the time. People seem not to talk that way anymore, maybe later. There is a return of all things.

The bit about my grandfather, Aunt Sallie and young Stouten was embroidery. That is what imagination is for. The business, Dix, Sterling and Co. had to be very prosperous, for it supported four families: My Uncle Sam, my father, Stouten Sterling Senior and Junior. Everyone worked with joy. A day's work was a happy thing. They shipped the seafood by train, heavily iced. Every train that pulled out of Crisfield had iced cars with Dix, Sterling and Co. painted in white on it, for at least thirty-five years. Seafood went to the Astor House, Delmonico's, to the ships at the docks ready to cross the ocean. Dix, Sterling and Co. seafood served on a ship was good reason to buy your ticket on one particular line.

When the Titanic sank, my father said. "I wouldn't be surprised some of our seafood was in her frozen lockers."

Business is such a complicated affair. There are contracts, subcontracts. Even such a perishable thing as seafood was sold and resold here and abroad.

I remember the letter paper and envelopes. Light blue linen with dark blue printing. I loved how my pencil would glide over its surface.

One time, in the second grade, Miss Ethel Johnson said, "Effie, if your father's business can have embossed paper, why can't you have a composition book?"

I said, taking them out of my desk, "Oh, I have three new ones I haven't started. I like how my pencil slides on this."

"Start a new composition book at once, and use that at home, perhaps for art."

When I came to live at Calvary, the courtesy path was many years old. So many people had saved weary steps, cutting through.

I loved the courtesy path. We were the only family in Calvary who had done or needed one. Their homes were mostly one after another along the roads, fields between, maybe gardens or sweet potato patches.

This is not to be a long story, so I will tell about just a few who used it, some daily, some now and then.

We had one Confederate veteran and one Yankee veteran. They were getting along in age, but on days like Decoration Day or the 4th of July, they marched in the parade in town and came through the yard, both going and coming back, though walking more slowly returning. I asked Mr. Nelson, if that was the uniform he fought in, and he said, "By jing, the same mess of wool and buttons, only one I ever had." He was very friendly and sat down on the side steps to talk.

I asked him if he ever saw Abraham Lincoln, but he said "No, I saw those southern mansions though, with porches on top and bottom. Sometimes, if you can believe it, there were three porches front and back, something like that one," pointing to the old Zahariah Nekon place across the field on the main road. "Yes honey, I saw mansions bigger than Asbury Church. They were mighty pretty. Some had eight columns across the front. Somebody said they were made of redwood trees brought from California around the Cape, all of them painted as white as alabaster."

"Alabaster?"

"Yes, the whitest of all white, bible white. They shone in that southern moonlight. There are pretty things all about down there. Now, Crisfield, Crisfield has the nicest people."

I said quickly, "Specially Calvary."

"You're right. This little courtesy path proves your conclusion."

"My concl—."

"Well, there comes Asa. He stopped by Miss Annie Gunby's store for a list to get for his wife. He'll probably stop to pick up a few honey pods from Aunt Jane's."

Asa was the Yankee veteran.

We waited until he got close then made room for him on the steps.

"Boy, am I tired. I rested on the steps with Jane, but it didn't help. She was working on a quilt, all roses and buds, mighty pretty. One time now if I didn't see her making one with Christmas trees all over it."

"That will be the prettiest one," I said softly, "It isn't finished yet. It takes a long time to make a quilt, years I think. I threaded the needles for her."

Asa said, "And you will have stars in your crown for doing it."

Aunt Sallie would say once in a while, "Effie, you don't have to talk to the people who use the path. They may not want to talk."

"But they do. Well, almost everybody. Sometimes Mr. Dennis ask me why I'm not in the house piecing up a quilt like the other kids."

I began to help Bill Bibbing, the hired man. I begged and begged. "Please Bill, let me cut the grass just a little bit. It looks so easy."

"You can cut a little in the graveyard. That grass is not very high and I just sharpened the grass cutter yesterday. So, I'll let you try. Soon, you'll be taking my job away from me."

"Oh Bill."

"There were only three graves at this time. A baby's grave with a beautiful three-tiered tombstone, all stone flowers, leaves and vines. Washington Tull Jr. age, one year, I learned the story of this little grave much later, years later.

There were also two other graves. One, Aunt Sallie said, was Aunt Priscilla and the other Uncle Stouten. No stones. One had a pink rose bush and one a white one where the stone would have been. They flourished and were never replaced by stones but kept neat with trimmed ivy.

"Effie, you can pick all of these roses you want. If anyone is sick, take them a large bunch." She showed me how to put pink ones in the center and the white ones around for a border, to also trim the lower thorns doing this through the summer.

The years went by and the fence was removed and the graveyard made part of the yard. The grass grows smooth now over the graves of Aunt Priscilla and Uncle Stouten but I know the very spot where the roses thrived. So many years my eager hands and Aunt Sallie's heart gladly put them there.

"Always pick buds," she would say. "Then, the next day and the next the bouquet will last. Three days it will be beautiful, thoughtfully given."

Beyond Aunt Jane's house I could see someone coming and hear the notes of a coronet. Oscar Jacker was still enjoying the parade, playing "Dixie" as he came along. He always carried his coronet in his hand, never in a case. He came jauntily across the sweet potato field from which one stepped on to the courtesy path. He changed the tune to "Marching Through Georgia". He knew I liked this.

Oscar came along happily, a real easy going sort of person. He had a continual surprised expression, definitely one of a kind. I've never met anyone who even faintly resembled him. He was called Tucker, his mother was Mrs. Morgan.

She also had young boys. Mr. Morgan went on the water. That means he owned a boat and made his living that way. Mrs. Morgan also worked, which made it necessary for her to go to town six days a week using the path every day.

One snowy time when she was hurrying home after a hard day's work. The snow was deep. She lost her way coming through Mr. Ben Somer's woods and being exhausted fell over a sharp pointed stump covered with snow and died.

How sad all felt for the family. A week or so later I was sitting in school and looked across at Willie Morgan in my class in the fifth grade and thinking how awful that he had no mother and how terrible it would be if I didn't, I began to cry and sob and put my head down in my arms.

Mrs. Lucy Scott who had no sympathy with anything or anybody asked Grace Sterling who was sitting with me to ask me what was the matter. Grace said, "She's crying because Willie Morgan has no mother, she says."

"Nonsense, I have no mother either."

At hearing this, I cried louder, but I raised my head and dried my eyes. It seems sadder for Willie not to have any than Mrs. Scott.

Willie crumpled up a piece of paper, and coming back from the waste basket stopped by me and said, "Effie, don't cry. Oscar takes real good care of us."

Some days I was too busy playing with Thelma or threading needles for

Aunt Jane to notice the people who came through. There was only one lady who, one could say, breezed along. She was always in a hurry it seemed. Miss Mary was a dressmaker and during the early nineteen hundreds they were busy people. Miss Mary does make the prettiest dresses, even my school ones I like. My mother wants them all tucks and ruffles and little ones in just the right places for people to say to me, "Mary Morgan made that dress. It has that touch."

"You're right, Miss Mary made it and five more. One of them didn't seem like there was enough material, but there was. I bet Mary could make a dress out of a bunch of handkerchiefs."

I laughed, nobody could.

"Well, if anybody could, it would be her and she would sew the style right into it."

It was true. She had that something that few have, style. Even her hats had it. If she didn't have them that way, she bent it in. It was the way she put it on. The style was in her, not in the place she had bought from the milliner in town.

One day Miss Mary breezed through the yard. I was on the porch and she came up and sat down. She picked up a magazine and began to fan herself.

"I'll get you some cool lemonade to cool you off."

She finished the glass, and as she turned to go, noticed she had on a dress made of handkerchiefs, actually red bandana handkerchiefs. She saw me staring, unbelievably.

"Yes, Effie, this dress is made of bandanas and not one was cut. Folded and stitched, yes, even the sash. How do you like my red slippers?"

"Red slippers!"

I looked at them a little sadly. One time I had wanted a pair. At that time there was no store in Crisfield with such out for merchandise, only black, white or brown. This was a daring new store run by out of town people, perhaps from Baltimore.

"Well, Effie, tell your mother I'll have your school dresses ready to fit, Wednesday. Goodbye."

"Goodbye."

A dress made of handkerchiefs! I had to run tell Thelma. My mother called from inside the house,

"Effie, stay out of sun. It's 97 degrees." Evening would come, or maybe rain and make it cool.

I went on reading and drinking my lemonade. It was a hot day. One of those ninety in the shade, people talked about. In our little town, we had very hot summers and very cold winters. Some said we might as well be in New England, as Maryland.

New England, where on earth was that? I had heard England where they had a king and queen, princes and princesses, as in fairy tales. Oh well, I would ask Aunt Sallie.

As looked up I saw Aunt Jane coming along the courtesy path. "Where are you going Aunt Jane?"

"I'm going to the store to get a little dab of that new stuff called peanut butter. I have a hankering for a different taste."

"Do you want me to go for you?"

"No, honey, my old bones need a little exercise. You can go with me, though."

We talked as we walked.

"I've heard people say, if you add a little hot water, a little butter that's melted and a grain or two of salt, it'll go twice as far."

"But," I said aghast, "it might ruin it." Little did I dream that years later I would buy sandwiches at the school lunch room for five cents made this way and never seem to get enough.

"Some people put jelly on one side of bread and peanut butter on the other and put it together. Not me, I like them separate. Thelma didn't like it that way either."

"Do tell . . ."

"We like to eat ours plain, with a spoon. We love it."

"Well, I'm going to try it, today. Maybe I had better get a pound. Levi's appetite, you know. He might like it."

"Oh, he will."

"I've got my pension check so I can and some groceries too. Maybe I'll try that Ka-ka cake in a box. You just add milk, they say."

I stopped walking.

"Aunt Jane, don't do it for you'll be throwing your money away. It isn't any good and not even pretty, too yellow in color. Thelma's mother made it and she gave it almost all to us for our tea party. We couldn't eat it, being used to good cake, we crumbled it up for the birds."

"Do tell. Honey, on your advice, I'll leave that off and get some store cakes, maybe a few chocolate marshmallow ones. Boy, they are good."

"Now you're talking." My mother deplored the use of slang and I was aware of it as I said it.

Buddie Widdie used it not at all, but Bud Charles added it to his language as he heard every new phrase. My mother said it mortified her to hear her children talk so. She also didn't want anyone to call him Charlie, or Bud Widdie, Willie. Willie was used rarely. A real puzzle, they were all around, William's that is.

After a rain, Bill, the hired man would press down new shells into the path all open side down oyster and clam. Our path was never muddy. If it was covered with snow it was the first path shoveled.

One day my father came home from town with the news that they were making concrete side-walks in town.

"Concrete! What is that?"

A Mr. A.P. Gray and Mr. Carter had the work already started. The machinery was already on the street, but what concerned us was what my father was telling Aunt Sallie.

"Sallie, I noticed there were piles of pebbles, and would you believe it, some of them had color, palest pink and lavender. I was wondering if I could ask one of the men to sell us a bag for the path. It would give added color. I will try to find time to ask tomorrow and perhaps Bill can bring them home in the wagon."

I was listening. "Pebbles, with color. How big a bag? Can I go with Bill to get them?"

"We'll see."

"Yes," my father went on, "there will be sidewalks, such a safety measure with more cars all the time and the horses still being afraid of the noise. Several people have been injured. It will look well too. I understand the pebbles are mixed with the concrete for stability."

"In other towns and cities there has been word of crumbling after a certain time. The process is not yet perfected, I infer."

My father asked Mr. Gray the next day. He explained about our path and our need, and Mr. Gray was glad to let him have two bags. They must have held a bushel each, perhaps more. I didn't get to go. We were all happy to have them.

"Billie that was a real favor. How much did he charge?"

"He wouldn't state a price, so gave him five dollars."

My ever generous father. Five dollars was a small fortune for pebbles.

"That's nice. We must use them sparingly for pebbles are not easy to acquire."

Now the path was a true line of beauty in our yard, sparkling in the sun, and gleaming in the rain.

One who used the path almost every day was Edna Tull, Mr. Washington Tull's daughter. She came through swinging her tennis racquet, going into town to play with her friends. She was going to college in Baltimore and it was mostly in the summer and saying Hi or Hay-o to her, never hello, oh no.

Soon, Edna had finished college and married. Then in a few years tragedy came. Her infant girl died and Edna died. It was a sad time in Calvary. Thelma and I went to carry flowers with our parents. Edna and her tiny baby were buried together. We two cried so much that the condolence visit was short. Everyone attended the funeral in Asbury Church, and Edna's husband, from family of means in town, meaning they were very rich, left town to become a preacher. He had already finished college. Soon the news was in the Times: Rev. Frederick Gibson has a charge in Jacksonville, Florida. He never returned to Crisfield to stay, though his mother paid long visits to him. He had been an only child.

I was resting under the elm tree, being half way through cutting the yard, when I looked up and saw Mr. Tom Coulbourne, Thelma's father coming across the sweet potato field toward the path. He drove the new oil truck for Gulf. A good job, good pay.

"There" he said, "you're surprised. My truck broke down out on the road and I took advantage of it to go home and eat lunch with Doll. I remembered Aunt Jane's honey pods and red cherries and came this way. She had two cherry pies just out of the oven, and…."

"I know. I always eat two slices. She puts tapioca in it to make them hold their shape and nutmeg to make them good."

"Good, they are! But, some Sunday afternoon I'm going to walk over here, with Doll and Thelma and eat honey pods. I wonder if Doll ever had one."

"I don't know about Miss Dollie, but Thelma says they're the best thing she ever tasted, like bananas."

"Yes some Sunday soon."

The number of Civil War veterans was not great in the whole town, but those of the Spanish War seemed to be many.

Only one, however, used our path. Mr. Moore. He had lost a leg and now had a wooden peg leg. He made his way slowly using one crutch. He would say, "Sorry, to make holes in your nice yard."

"Don't you worry about that Mr. Moore, how are you today? Surely is hot."

"Extremely, for June."

He always came through the yard after visiting some friends, and was going into town now. He lived in Lawsonia, but probably from town got a ride home.

He was a very neat person. When looking at him, I always seemed to see him in uniform, though of course he never was unless there was a parade. He had a military air about him and his injury didn't detract from it at all.

It seemed when the Spanish American veterans marched in the parades, they showed a lot of injuries, one leg gone, one arm, quite a few with eye patches.

These men were still young when I was eight or nine or more, forties maybe, early fifties, even late thirties.

Not everyone can make their personalities overcome their handicaps, but I know many who kept their presence no matter how difficult. I feel their bravery now that was only interesting, then.

Since the afternoon of our banana cake tea (lemonade of course for the beverage), with Mr. Ribeau, he came regularly through the yard.

Due to the fact that he did not teach organ, only piano, harp or violin, fate did not agree for me to be one of his pupils.

I was devastated, but I survived and began taking again from Miss Bertie, whose price, two organ lessons for seventy-five cents could not be equaled.

Disappointment is very hard to bear. I took mine extremely hard at the time. I had my heart broken with my Uncle Sam's death the year before. I forgave Miss Ethel for never sending me the red slippers she promised, with ties of ribbon to cross around my ankles. My heart broke again when Mr. Jordan had to go, and the organ never sang again. Our every evening singing was never the same again.

Disappointment seems worse than heartbreak. One knows heartbreak will be forever and ever and you live a little bit away from every day into time. Also, to be disappointed carries some resentment, also some hope. I could hope that the next summer Miss Ethel would remember to bring the red slippers. I could faintly hope that Mr. Ribeau would stop by some day and say he had decided to teach organ.

I wouldn't have left Miss Bertie, of course.

Very courteously, my mother had said, "Well, thank you, Professor Ribeau for stopping by" as she let him out the side door and told him he was welcome to use our small path at any time. This seemed to me to be doing as the Bible said, *turning the other cheek*. She explained to him that it did save over a mile to the main road.

I can hear her voice say, "Cross over the sweet potato field where the path ends, go past the small dwelling and use the added short cut…"

My mother had said, "Treat the Professor with politeness at all times."

I did, but I couldn't resist overdoing it.

I never called him Professor after that day. I left that to the grownups. I always did say, "It's a very nice day, Mr. Ribeau, I hope you are well."

"Yes, my child, my health is excellent. Goodbye for now."

"Goodbye."

I heard running steps and Levi came through the yard Aunt Jane's son's, son's, son Thelma called him. It was said that she was over one hundred years old.

"What's the matter, Levi?"

"Nothing, only I'm late. I'll lose my job at the park."

"Maybe not. It won't be dark for another half hour. You'll make it." He stopped to rest.

"I hope I do. Granny needs the money to feed us. That Civil War pension check seems smaller every month. You know what we had for supper last night?"

"No, what?"

"Oatmeal. I had three bowls, sugar but no milk. When I got home last night from dipping the ocean wave, I was weak as a kitten."

"You could have had some fried potatoes, and I know there were biscuits."

"Yeah, but Granny was asleep and I was too tired to fry potatoes or bite into a biscuit."

"You'll make it, Levi. Bye, now."

I told Aunt Sallie, "I could have let Aunt Jane have some money. When will the government ever give a larger pension? I'm sure John Roe was a fine soldier."

"Levi says the park is talking of buying an ocean wave that works with a motor, not men, and…."

"Levi needs a year round job, perhaps the lumber mill or the ice plant. I'll ask your father. He's a strong, honest, reliable boy. He really needs new clothes too."

"Yes," she looked thoughtful, "there are many problems around."

There did seem to be problems everywhere. Leila Ward with not enough money for baby food. Hattie Sterling and her mother's pension always giving out before the next check comes. Mr. Lorengo Ward, who had to have his arm taken off because a hard crab bit his hand causing blood poisoning, came through often. He talked about getting an artificial one, but the last time he came by his sleeve was still pinned up neatly with safety pins.

I wondered about this, thinking sewing would be better, and then I thought some more, and knew that way wouldn't work. He had to take his shirt off and his coat off every night. He is such a nice man, something like a poet, surely the nearest to one that we had in Calvary.

One day he came through the path in a storm and we called to him to come up on the porch until the rain stopped. It did in a short while and guess what? There was a double rainbow. He was really thrilled, and said, "Effie, do you count your rainbows?"

"Count them, Mr. Lorenzo?"

"Yes, I count mine, every year. Last year I saw nine. Two of them double like this one."

"That is a beautiful idea. I'm going start right now, two to start."

"Two to start."

How lovely it was. Why do I like pastels? How can anyone not like them who has seen a rainbow? Slowly it began to fade and soon the promise was gone. I must ask Buddie Widdie just where that is, in the Bible, I thought.

"Yes, that was the most in one year, nine. I suppose be entirely truthful I should count the two doubles as two, which narrows me down to seven. Oh, I do hope we have lots of rain this summer. Now, shall I call this one or two?"

"I suppose it's for each of us to decide. The rain seems to be over."

"Goodbye, and thanks for the shelter." Even with people's problems, it was a beautiful world.

Lucky me, I had one. Not even book ones. The glorious summer time seemed to be for just me and Thelma.

The humming birds zigzagged over the flowers. The locusts sang. Here and there a grasshopper would leap into the air, and the fireflies were just biding their time until twilight.

We were sitting on the porch in the early evening, Buddie Widdie, Bud Charles, me, Bill and Levi on the steps.

"There it goes again." said Bill. "Miss Allean is playing that fishing song."

"Fishing song?" I knew what he meant. I had heard him talk like this before.

"Yeah, the one you said the furriner made up."

"Bill, he did live across the water, but we don't call him a foreigner. We call him a genius. His name was Beethoven."

"Well, that Mr. Genus made up a pretty piece. I wish she would play it louder."

"It is not to be played loud. Moonlight Sonata is played slowly and softly. The wind needs to be just right for us to hear it at all."

I had heard Bill say before whenever he heard it, he felt like he was rocking in a boat fishing.

Aunt Sallie read to the family some evenings. Longfellow, Tennyson, Enoch Arden, Miles Standish. We loved it when the poem told a story. Once in a while she would read to me just for the sake of reading poetry. I certainly didn't understand, but the sound of the words, and my love for her made me feel happy.

"Aunt Sallie, do you think Longfellow or Emerson had a courtesy path through their yard?"

"Emerson could have, as the parsonage was set back from the road. I've read that there was a crumbling brick wall on one side of the Emerson home, and a great pear tree in the spring causing a mountain of foamy white and pink blossoms. Now on the other side, there could have been a path. Let's imagine."

"The father died when Ralph Emerson, in fact when all the boys were still young, four boys, I believe." Aunt Sallie continued, "His Aunt Mary lived with them and was a big help to their mother."

One day Aunt Mary had three apple pan dowdies, cobblers some say, she had made, and as Ralph looked at them on the window ledge, he noticed some children and their mother going by.

"Aunt Mary, may I take one of the cobblers to Mrs. Pine. They have so little."

"Master Ralph, we have so little, also."

"Yes, but we have so little in a different way. We have so little with pictures and books and flowered carpets. They have no carpets, no books, and no pictures." He lowered his voice. "Some days, they have very little to eat also. Pleases Aunt Mary?"

"Here," she covered the pan with a white napkin and tucked it around.

"You bring the napkin back folded in your pocket. Mrs. Pine can stop by with the pan tomorrow.

Now, we've pretended Ralph Waldo Emerson had a courtesy path." They both laughed.

Only one bicycle used the courtesy path. This was Mr. Chris Sterling, Christopher.

It was surprising how many were named for Columbus. Mr. Chris was one of the musical families of Sterlings. They all played instruments: two boys and two girls, Chris and Harley, Edith and Ethel. This is the Miss Ethel who was my very first music teacher.

Mr. Chris was the only one who made a living from music. He was a popular teacher. His territory was vast, all over town, every section. On a bicycle one could cover miles. There seemed to be enough pupils for every teacher. He was gay, well liked.

The town's estimated population was five thousand and with outside sections probably as many more so there was no lack of children eager to take.

Mr. Chris rode the eighteen inch path carefully. He was careful riding even out on the road. My father was this kind of cyclist too. He didn't ride a bike until well in his fifties, and it always looked as if he had never mastered the art.

"Good morning, Miss Effie, a nice day. I see you have just cut your yard."

"Yesterday, I did it in three parts."

"Ingenious! Goodbye now."

No one used the path after dark, only through the twilight. It has a dawn to dark path. No tramps, though many came to Calvary. All through the year they came by the main road.

I did like tramps. To me they were so interesting. Most always they left our house looking better than when they came. They too looked better, for Aunt Sallie kept a supply of her son's no longer used clothing for this purpose. They washed up at the well, after being given towels and soap, then a good meal. They always did some work. Most of them only wanted to work a few hours then go on. Where, I often wondered.

One day, sitting on the porch looking at a tramp doing my job for a treat for me, how that grass grew!

Thelma said, "I just wonder if Mr. Jordan ever saw a courtesy path until he came here?"

"I don't think so. He thought it was a charming idea, but you see we never knew if he grew up in a city or the country. I would say the city, for I don't think he'd ever seen a plow. Yes, he's a city person, and a book and music one. But, let's not talk about Mr. Jordan. I know the organ."

"Effie Dix, you've got tears in your eyes."

Hattie Sterling was coming quickly along the path, as I looked up from my book. She was the one person in Calvary who had a unique garden, beds of flowers in circles, stars, squares, triangles, half moons, a sight to behold.

I took Mr. Jordan to see it, after Hattie had come to see ours. He was amazed as everyone else was who has looked upon its beautiful form, or rather forms I should say.

Our garden was unique too, in a different way. Mr. Jordan called it a formal garden. Everything was very neat. The tall flowers in their places, the lower ones in theirs, and the short ones just where they graced the garden best. He, who had never seen a plow, maybe not even a seed before made a garden with Bill's help and Levi's willing hands. Thelma and I, our eager hands crumbling the earth to a fine bed of fine earth for sleeping seeds.

Did you ever see neat flowers? Perhaps the absence of weeds was a factor. Not a weed grew. If one came up overnight, it was pulled out in the morning.

"Hi, Hattie, I'll bet you have been to town to buy seeds."

"Yes, I have. You'll never believe it but they have light green zinnias. The flower part I mean. It is really green in the picture. How beautiful it will be."

I was as thrilled as Hattie.

"I must hurry home. I got a few groceries at that new store. Mother's check came yesterday. I've got to get out my pencil and budget these days."

"Budget?"

"Yes, it means divide the money into days and just use that much," she sighed. "And let me just tell you, it isn't easy. Goodbye now, Effie."

"Goodbye."

About once a month, my mother would say, "Children, tomorrow we will go visit Auntie and Aunt Sis and spend the night."

Aunt Sis was our great aunt, our grandfather's sister on my mother's side. It was spring now, late May and some pretty days were here at last. Auntie was of course Aunt Effie, my mother's sister. And she and her husband, William Blair and Annie, his daughter, were living with Aunt Sis while waiting to have a new house built.

This house, the one they built was in "The Croquet Set". It's the one where I ate lunch every three weeks unwillingly.

I liked the walk, though it took half an hour. Especially I liked walking down Cemetery Avenue, which was changed Chesapeake Avenue later, along the pavement. Yes, the sidewalks here were Avenues now.

One small grave was close by the pavement, and covered with violets. I knelt down beside it. There was no fence.

"Oh, how beautiful the little grave is," I said, patting the violets, "And it is the only one in this lot."

"Yes, its Mrs. Mallison's who lives across the street. It's very sad. She had only one boy and one girl. This is her little girl."

We walked on and were soon at Auntie's or rather Aunt Sis' house.

Buddie Widdie and Bud Charles found things to do, playing ball with the boys in a vacant lot, but for me, it was dull.

The garden here was exquisite, extremely unusual with paths and white iron lace benches and thousands of flowers, hyacinths, lilies, violets, tulips, just about to bloom or already in bloom. It was a breathtaking sight. Whenever I saw something like this, I lost my breath for a second. It just seemed too much for me.

I went in and whispered to my mother, "Can I open the gate and walk in the garden?"

She whispered in reply, "Go ask Aunt Sis?"

I went into the yard where Aunt Sis was getting something out of the spring house, and said timidly, "Aunt Sis, can I walk in your garden? It's so beautiful."

She frowned at me and said, "Yes, but don't touch one flower. Just walk down the paths."

"Can I sit on a bench?"

"Yes, but latch the gate when you come out."

My mother took advantage of being in town to go shopping and today

Auntie went with her. I was left alone with Aunt Sis. The boys would be out playing for hours and Annie, Auntie's step daughter was not at home.

I wandered around the yard and out the back gate. It was muddy there, as we had been having quite a lot of rain before the nice days came. I finally got tired and came in.

Aunt Sis, who was turning away from the stove jerked me around and said, "Look at those shoes!" She flung me into a big rocking chair by the window. "You'll sit there until your mother comes back. I'll have to clean these and polish them."

"Oh, no thank you, Aunt Sis, I can do it myself."

"Sit quietly and keep still."

I was not used to this kind of treatment and hoped my mother would return soon.

In a little while she put my shoes on the window sill for the sun to dry. I still sat there. I started to get them to put them on, but she took them away and put them back.

"I get my shoes muddy most every day." What I meant was, it was no big thing, but it was with her.

Finally, I think I must have fallen asleep. It was a long walk from Calvary. Then my mother and Auntie came back.

"Effie, why aren't you out playing? It's a glorious day."

"I am, as soon as I get my shoes on." I looked at Aunt Sis. She said nothing.

I sat at the back porch steps for a while and thought how things were. Then I went to look through the fence at the garden and smell the fragrance.

We were always glad to take this trip for less than a block away the trains came thundering in three times a day and that was besides the freight ones. This was a special treat for all three of us. When I was about six or seven these trips almost came to an end, but my mother could not stay angry, so things did get back to normal after a few weeks.

My mother loved Auntie dearly, and Auntie loved her in her own way. They were quite different. I was Auntie's namesake, although I'm quite sure in his heart my father wanted me called Sallie. They equally adored their sisters, but my mother won this one. My original birth certificate says Baby Dix, so one can see it took a while for this to be decided.

During the morning, Auntie had bought beautiful strawberries from a wagon going by. She put this quart in the middle of the dining room table on a round piece of filigree glass, first taking the reflected bouquet off and putting it on the sewing machine top.

In the afternoon, after they had returned from downtown the grownups sat in the sitting room and talked.

Yes, this was called the sitting room. The parlour (English spelling I like) was another something completely. Dark, mysterious, beautiful, filled with rare things, the like of which my eyes had never seen, gorgeous tapestries with lovely shades, shells of great proportional actually pink inside, on the mantle; among the prism candle-sticks that held many candles a gleam of sunshine came through the side of a curtain and made colors on the pretty wall paper.

Enchantment! Every single thing was more beautiful than the other. Then there was the platform rocker. How I loved it.

I said suddenly, "Can I sit in the parlour?"

Aunt Sis, surprised in her conversation, said ungraciously, "Yes, but touch nothing."

"Oh, I wouldn't."

My mother said, "Aunt, If you'd rather she didn't."

But I was halfway across the hall.

After a while I tired of rocking and looking and went back into sitting room.

"Effie, you may go out to play."

Going through the dining room, I stopped and without thinking, took a big strawberry and stood there eating it. How good. I took another and another. Then there was the question of the caps. I tossed them behind the sewing machine and went out.

I must have made ten trips in and out during the long afternoon. Going in I would eat only one for I had to hold the cap until I came out and tossed it away along with the two or three I would sample coming out.

"We will have fried chicken and biscuits and strawberry cake for supper," Auntie said. It's almost time for Annie and Mr. Blair to come home.

Soon there was the smell of vanilla in the house, the cake baking, the chicken frying. The boys came back and washed up, then sat down to look at the stereopticon card.

"Supper! Soon too," said Bud Charles.

Auntie came to the door of the sitting room, very angry.

"Annie May, Effie has eaten so many strawberries, that…."

"Effie, did you?"

"You know, of course, she did. She was the only one here. The boys just came back. Why!" Auntie's eyes flashed and she said harshly, "She is a little thie—."

My mother jumped up from the rocker, her skirt and petticoats bouncing. She always dressed nicely for these visits. Her cheeks were very pink and her brown eyes angry.

"Eff—ie," and she didn't mean me. "Don't you dare use that word in relation to my child. You have gone too far. Here children, get your things. Come, Effie." She picked up my wide straw hat with the velvet streamers and put it on my head and tied the ribbon beneath my chin. "Charles, Willie are you all ready?" She was putting her shopping packages in her basket. "We must hurry. I want to make it through the woods before dark."

Aunt Sis had come in. "Annie May, you had planned to spend the night with us. Do you have—?"

"Yes, Aunt Sis, I must go." She kissed "Goodbye now."

As we were out on the porch Auntie said, "Annie May I am sorry. It is all that I can say."

My mother looked at her steadily, tears in her eyes.

"It is not enough, Effie. Come, children."

Bud Charles said, "Ef, did you have to eat the old strawberries?" I'm hungry and the chicken smelled good. I wanted some supper."

Buddie Widdle kept still.

My mother didn't even correct Bud Charles for calling me Ef which proved how much she was not herself.

"We will have supper at home."

"But no strawberry cake," he sounded sad. "It was going to have whipped cream. It was getting cold in the spring house."

"We will have strawberry cake tomorrow with lots of strawberries." I could taste it now.

Quickly my mother turned to me. "Effie, I am not condoning the wrong you have done. I must teach you never to touch anything without asking first."

"If I had asked Auntie would have said, no, they're for the cake."

"Oh my, it's too much for me. My head aches. Here, Charles," She gave him some money, "run ahead and get a dozen cinnamon buns from Mr. Sterling's and four ice cream cones. We will be sitting on the steps of my old house. You can go, Willie, if you want to go."

She cut across two streets. Locust and Pine and walked a little way up Main St. to my grandfather Wingate's old home, which he had sold when he built the one on Somerset Ave. It was right next to Emmanuel Church. "I'm sure the people won't care. Let's rest until the boys get here."

As soon as we sat down, the door opened and a very pretty woman came out.

"Hello," she said in a friendly way. "I'm Rosa Ralph. My husband has just opened a men's clothing store in town."

"How nice, I do hope the business does well. My husband is in the seafood business, and this is my daughter, Effie. I'm Mrs. Dix."

"I'm glad to know you both."

"Here come my boys, William and Charles. We'll be getting along. Thank you for your kindness. I was quite tired and this is my old home. I and my three sisters were born here. I always loved the trees. Goodbye."

"Mrs. Dix, I love the trees, too."

My mother decided that I could not go to see Thelma for ten whole days. Thelma could come to see me, but for me, no woods, no violets, no bouncing on trees. Ten days! Forever!

Auntie did redeem herself with me, for loving and admiring something that was a part of my happiness.

I told her a short time after, without my mother making me, that I was sorry about the strawberry cake.

"Effie," she asked curiously, "what did you do with the caps?"

"I dropped them behind the sewing machine." Even my mother never knew that.

The work went on of making sidewalks. After Main Street, there was Cemetery Ave. and then they began on Somerset Ave.

This was where my grandfather's home was. The person to whom the property belonged had to pay a charge for the pavement in front of his house to the town, so much a foot, maybe.

When the sidewalk was finished, as the men were putting their equipment away, my grandfather noticed two bags leaning against his hedge, "Here boys (men really) you've left these."

"Oh they're pebbles."

"Pebbles? Mr. Carter came up. "Everything ship shape here?"

"The truck's gone and didn't pick up these bags Mr. Carter. I know someone who could use those. Could I buy them from you?"

"Mr. Lewis, you can have them as a gift. You see, it's my money that buys everything. Until we give the city the bill everything belongs to Carter and Gray. As nice as your daughter has been to us all summer, bringing us lemonade and crullers (doughnuts) on those hot days, it's the least we can do."

"Well, thank you very much." Grandpa Wingate knew how happy the gift would make me.

Yes, they were the same kind of pink, lavender, white and some with a touch of blue. Oh, happiness was pebbles for the courtesy path, and guess what Bill did?

He was supposed to be a dumb hired man with no education. I don't think Bill could even write his name, perhaps not even the ability to learn to write. Nobody knew because he was never given the opportunity to show his abilities. Who knows what artistic heights he could have attained if given the chance.

He took the trowel and dug a two inch line all along the path on both sides. Then we filled it with the pebbles. It was so beautiful.

"Oh, Bill, it's the prettiest path in the world. I'm sure it was the only one of its kind.

On Sundays, sometimes Auntie and her husband and his daughter Annie, and Aunt Sis would come to see us. They came in a hired carriage, which Uncle William drove. A two seated one, of course. The afternoon was spent in conversation on the porch and in the parlour. They stayed for supper.

"Come, Effie. Let's take a walk on the path." Auntie beckoned to me.

"We can't walk together. It's a one person path."

"I know that."

We walked over to it and admired the pebbles.

"It is beautiful, Auntie. In the sun they sparkle, and in the rain they gleam too."

"Yes, sheer beauty. Whose idea was the pebbles on both sides?"

"Bill's"

Aunt Sallie walked over to us. She did not work on Sundays, just reading and conversation.

"Effie, it would be nice if you picked a small bouquet for the supper table."

After the goodbyes had been said, I was sitting on the porch with my mother. The carriage was out on the road now. The Sunday visit was over.

"I don't think Aunt Sis likes me. She isn't kind when you take us to visit. Do you know, I've never gathered a flower from her garden, nor sat in the parlour with the shades up. One day the sun came in a crack at the side of a window and made a rainbow colors on the wall. I have never seen them more clearly."

"She gives you gold pieces on your birthday and Easter and Christmas just as she does the boys."

"Yes, but that is only money. It isn't really anything like letting me pick flowers or put the shades up. That would make me happy, money doesn't, only the spending kind, pennies, nickels, and dimes. They do. Gold is for banks. I don't want gold pieces."

"Effie, there will be lots of prisms to make rainbows for you and gardens with flowers to gather. Let's be kind to Aunt Sis. Do you think she is pretty?"

I thought for a second. "I think she would be if she didn't frown so much."

"Aunt Sis was considered a true beauty, which perhaps lead to the tragedy she suffered."

"Tragedy?"

"When Aunt Sis, Narcissa Lewis she was then, was seventeen she was extremely beautiful. She went for a summer visit to relations in the city and while there fell in love and came home with her husband. He was very young also. Her father gave her the house she still lives in for a wedding present. For a while they were happy, but he was only twenty and wild. He became what was called in those days, a drunkard. Time went by and a baby girl was born to Aunt Sis. She adored the baby. One snowy night the father came home drunk and threw the tiny baby infant out into the snow.

She finally got the baby in, but in a few days the baby died with pneumonia. Aunt Sis was very ill for a long time. She divorced that husband and years later she remarried, a fine man, and became happy again. They had no children. She could never forget the baby and grieved for her. Perhaps, though she doesn't realize it, some of the bitterness lingers on and finds release in being unkind to you. Next time I will take you shopping with me."

The happy years went by. More and more people acquired first horses, then carriages, and then the cars, machines everyone called them, more every year. They even put up signs. "Do not exceed the speed limit - 10 miles per hour. Actually seems unbelievable now.

The courtesy path was used less and less and one sad spring day in 1919, when Bill was doing the plowing, Aunt Sallie said, "Bill, the path is no longer used enough to justify our keeping it up, so, before you put the plough away, you can…."

"Miss Sallie, why don't you and Effie go and…" He didn't know what to say but he knew how we felt.

"Yes, we will go pick some pear blossoms for a bouquet," an unheard of thing. To pick the blossoms for they made the pears. We had loved the path so long.

Bill planted grass seed, and in the summer the path was pale green grass. The next summer it was a darker shade but still discernable. The next, it merged with the yard and was no more.

It is back there with the dear things beyond recall. My children never saw the courtesy path, and will hardly believe that it was so. They must use their imagination.

THE END

THE ROBIN STAYED FOR CHRISTMAS

A Story for a Little Girl - *The Robin*
Goodbye, goodbye, to summer
For summer's nearly done.
The garden smiling faintly
Cool breezes in the sun;
Our thrushes now are silent,
Our swallows flown away.
But robins here in coat of brown

Robin, oh robin dear
Robin sings so sweetly
In the falling of the year.

The fireside for the cricket
When trembling night winds whistle
And moan around the house
The branches plumed with snow.
Alas, in winter dead and dark
Where can poor robin go?

Robin, Oh, robin dear
And a crumb of bread for robin
His little heart to cheer.
William Allingham

Another summer time was stored in memory. September, with its new school beginning, was behind me. October's bright blue weather with its beautiful days, its goldenrod and bright leaves and its chrysanthemums was gone, and now it was November.

Each morning was a little colder than the one before, and just yesterday, my father had called me to see the wild geese flying swiftly and low overhead to a warmer climate than ours. Their clear honk, honk, honk was a farewell of sadness, as if they didn't really want to go. We watched them every year and I always felt this way.

Of course, everyone talked the birds flying south when the cold days came, but as there were birds around all winter, hundreds of snow birds, the others were hardly missed, and this talk just fell on my ears, as phrases do meaning nothing.

When a child lives in the country, birds are a big part of their days. My playmate Thelma, would say,

"Listen to that Bob White."

His call came clear from his perch, on the locust blossom laden tree, *Bob White, Bob White*, so unbelievably like a human voice. In the evening we listened to the cry of the *whip-por-will*, the lovely low and high notes, making music in the twilight.

"Now who named him that, I would like to know?" Thelma would ask. "He needs a prettier name to match his song."

We would listen to the woodpecker, pecking away so loudly in the maple tree.

"Effie, listen to him peck. He will wear his beak out. Do you know what he does with those little chips?"

"No."

"You don't see any falling on the grass, do you?"

"No."

"And I know why. Grandpop told me. He uses every little chip for his nest. He really does, and that's the blessed truth." she said.

We loved the little birds, the tiny sparrows, the robins. There was even an owl who came to sit in the maple, after dark, and sat there, saying *tuu-hoo, tu-hoo.*

The adorable little humming birds, we loved and felt sorry because he could only hum his little summery tune.

"Well, anyway," said Thelma, "he's the cutest one of all. Bless his little heart."

One autumn, we began to live in a new house. Living in a new house is a nice experience. One walks all over and looks at the wallpaper on the walls, so fresh and flowery and beautiful, runs up to the attic and looks into all of the closets.

My mother's organ was in its place in the parlour. The center table, with its carved legs, which ended in glass balls, encased in metal filigree had our picture album on it, and the centerpiece of linen, embroidered with violets and green leaves in crewel work, looked so pretty to me, as I hadn't seen it in a long time. Our pretty rocking chairs of wicker were there, our pictures on the wall, and our books in the bookcase.

All over the house were the things that I remembered from babyhood. I was too young to realize that they had been stored away. I was so happy always, and far too unthinking to conceive the true fact, that it hadn't been easy for my mother, with three children, not to be in her own home, with her own things.

The trend at this time was for mothers to have jobs, the weeks before Christmas. My mother had never had one, but she wanted to try.

Now, when I came home from school, my mother was not there. Though I knew she wouldn't be. I was supposed to go in, get something to eat and wait for her. I didn't go at all. I threw my books down on the grass, and would call, Mother, Mother, and then I would kick the screen door, until I was tired out, and fell down on the grass and cried.

Mr. and Mrs. Earnest Gunby lived next door to us. Mrs. Gunby's name was Annie Laurie. The only Annie Laurie, I ever heard about, but the song one. Imagine.

Everyone called her Miss Annie. They had no children. They were not so very young, but neither were they old.

As I lay there sobbing, and getting my sleeve wetter and wetter, I heard Miss Annie say, "Effie, will you come over and help me pick some flowers? Run around to the front door."

It was the beginning of a beautiful time. It was a happy winter, for I had found two grown up friends.

Miss Annie talked with my mother, and asked her to let me come to her house from school every day, so that I wouldn't be lonely the two hours before my mother got home.

Mr. Earnest and Miss Annie were two of the kindest persons that I have ever known. As Emerson has said, "Kindness is a great power in the world. Power itself has not one half the might of gentleness."

These two had the kindness of true sympathy, of thoughtful help. They were so happy to have a child around and made me so welcome. Miss Annie would say,

"Effie, I'm going to make a pie for supper. Would you like to cut up the apples, and squeeze the lemons?" (We squeezed lemon juice over the apple slices so that they would not darken, while waiting to be put in the pie.)

"You can make a little one for yourself."

Sometimes we made cake biscuits, and always miniatures for me.

It was all such fun. Some days I would do my lessons at the big kitchen table, so that I would have my evenings free for other things. It was her idea. All of Miss Annie's ideas were good ones. Some people are like that.

Miss Annie had been born in Norway. Her maiden name was Annie Laurie Nordstrom. When she was a little girl she was adopted by a Miss Carrie Gunby a rich lady who had never married. When Miss Carrie died, she left her all of her money, two stores, and the large house. Mr. Earnest was a nephew of Miss Carrie, her favorite.

Mr. Earnest and Miss Annie didn't marry until late in life and after Miss Carrie was no longer there.

It was hard to understand why Miss Annie was adopted as she had her own mother who was still living in Norway. Perhaps here is an untold story. Her mother came to visit one time and could speak no English, and to me she seemed so strange. I had never before seen anyone from a foreign country. She had a friendly smile, and Miss Annie had the same blue eyes and golden brown hair, as her mother.

Mr. Earnest loved birds. He had a large shelf fixed outside the kitchen window, and every day he would put cereal flakes and bits of apple on it to entice the birds, and how they came, hungry and chirping. He also put bits of material on the shelf and short lengths of wool yarn and small sticks to help with their nest building.

Around the window he had put wire and attached little fat glass bottles, which he filled with sugar water for them. In summer the morning glories twined themselves around the wire, and it was a pretty sight of flowers, birds and butterflies. The birds were so cute, putting their little beaks down in the brim filled bottles to drink. There was always a pan of fresh water on the shelf. I took over the job of keeping it filled.

Mr. Earnest liked to tell me about the different kinds of birds. I loved the tiny sparrows, so quick and sure as they pecked away at the corn flakes or grape nuts.

There were two kinds of robins. Both were close to the same size, but they were different. One had a yellowish red breast and brown tail feathers, and the other was a darker brown, almost black, with its breast a very dark red, with really black tail feathers. This one was rare and he told me it was called a European robin. I loved them all.

One day we were at the window, when a fat little robin flew down.

"Well, I suppose most of the birds have flown south by now," said Miss Annie.

"Not the robin," Mr. Earnest said. "If we treat him real good, maybe he will stay for Christmas."

As I looked up I saw Mr. Earnest wink at Miss Annie, and he put his arm around me and said, "Yes, Effie, you must go to the store and get a box of currants. That may keep him here." He laughed as he gave me a quarter and I was off to the grocery store in a flash.

Christmas was coming. It was hard to wait for all the days to go by. They went so s-l-o-w.

My big brother had a job after school, and was buying presents each week and putting them in the closet, still wrapped in the paper.

He seemed so happy, and went around whistling, and talking of Santa Claus. He showed the things to my brother Willie, and I could hear them say,

"Won't she be happy? How about that!" I assumed it was something for my mother.

The next day, Miss Annie said to me so happily, "We are going to have a Christmas tree. Isn't that wonderful? I have never had one, but this year I am going to borrow a little girl, and have a tree and presents, and.... Yes, I asked your mother." She hugged me close.

"For Christmas afternoon, maybe about four o'clock, not Christmas morning, that belongs to your family. Maybe three thirty. I will ask Mildred too. Oh, it will be such fun" she said dreamily. "A tree, a little girl, and presents, oh lots of presents."

Mildred lived across the road. She was older than I was, but she had never been to school. When she was small, she had fallen into the water, and wasn't rescued quickly enough, so people said. She was very nice, and I played with her quite a lot, as my mother said it was a kind thing to do, but I did it for fun. I liked her.

"Yes, Mildred will have presents and a stocking filled to the top. Oh, what a happy time we will all have."

And we did.

Christmas morning, I awoke to riches, a Christmas to be remembered forever. All the packages that Buddie Charles had put in the closet were for me. All but the Alger books which were for Buddie Widdie.

Yes, that was the year of the little punch bowl, and cups. They cost fifty cents, from the newly opened five and ten cent store. This was an unheard of, kind of store. And the little butter dish and cream pitcher and sugar dish that matched the punch bowl, all packed in their box of excelsior. A yard swing for my dolls. A doll house, with everything, dolls and dolls, books and books, toys, puzzles, bright wool sweaters, mittens and such things. A gold signet ring with E.K.D. entwined in a lovely fashion. A luxury gifts for both boys and girls. Probably one of the reasons, my mother craved a job, when she was not the working out of the home type.

Christmas is an hour, the first hour of Christmas day morning. The first magic sixty minutes. We wait a year for one hour and it is always worth the waiting.

This year was destined to contain a double Christmas, double enchantment. How fortunate could a child be?

My mother said, "Effie, it is almost three-thirty. Mr. Earnest and Miss Annie will be waiting for you. Be careful going up and down the steps. Your father brushed the snow off, but they are slippery."

The steps had been a gift of thoughtfulness and love. I have said that all of Miss Anne's ideas were good ones. She had hired a carpenter to make steps on each side of the fence so that I wouldn't have to walk all the way around the road. I could be at their home quickly. Up the steps, fling my leg over, and down the steps and a short run to their kitchen door. The grownups used them too.

I slipped on the third step to the bottom, and fell in the deep soft snow. It was only fun to fall down.

In the large kitchen, they were all waiting for me. Mr. Earnest, Miss Annie, Mildred and her sister, Miss Gertrude, and Mr. Earnest sisters, who were spending Christmas day, Miss Alda and Miss Leila.

"Now we can see our tree," Miss Annie said, "Come on, everyone," and she flung the door to the dining room wide. Though hardly anyone had electric lights at the time, this house did, for Miss Carrie had spared no expense here. As she opened the door, she had pressed the switch and the crystal chandelier blazed, its prisms sparkling in the light. This one thing in itself was a wonder for me, and thrilled me with its beauty.

The round dining room table had been moved over in front of the large, lace curtained windows, and on a red cloth, trimmed with white ball fringe fell to the floor.

In the middle of the table was the darling Christmas tree, barely four feet high, but what a dream of a tree. The ornaments were all scaled to the size of the tree, and the tinsel was put on in scallops, and with small white angels clasping the scallops to the branches. Miss Annie had made the angels herself with white crepe paper and tinsel. Around the edge of the table was a white picket fence, with a gate; white paper made the yard, and it was so pretty with tiny animals and a looking glass lake with ducks. The tree didn't have lights, but it needed none. It was perfect as it stood, beautiful and complete.

"Our first Christmas Tree," said Miss Annie, happily, "and Earnest made the fence so nicely."

"It's the prettiest tree I ever did see," said Mildred.

As for me, I was speechless at the moment. Finally, I said, "Yes." but so low no one heard me.

"Are you all disappointed that it wasn't a big tree? Are you, Effie?"

"Oh, no. I love it small. It is so different and so pretty."

"And now the presents," said Mr. Earnest.

We hadn't noticed the presents until now. At the fireplace mantle were hung two stockings, filled to the top, one for Mildred, and one for me. The presents were piled at each end of the mantle on the floor, one pile for me, and one for Mildred.

"Come girls, open your presents."

A doll, which was a Mamy doll, like Aunt Jemima with a bandana on her head, like the one on the pancake box still and when turned over, was a lady doll, fascinating. Books, games, a paint set, a sweater, a tea set, a sewing box, a white angora hat with a scarf to match. The sewing box had a doll and doll clothes all cut out to be made for her.

Well, that wasn't all, but you get the idea. I was overwhelmed. Here was another Christmas, all in one day.

"Thank you Mr. Earnest and Miss Annie. I like everything and I just love the little tree."

Mildred's face was happy too, as she held her presents; those Miss Annie had put in a large box for her to carry home.

"Effie, will need something to put her things in. Here," Miss Annie picked up the wood basket in front of the fireplace, flung the chips on the fire, and said, "This will do fine."

So I piled all of my treasures in the basket and Mr. Earnest put on his overshoes and his coat and cap and carried it to the steps for me. After I had flung my leg over, he gave it to me.

"Effie, this has been a very happy Christmas for my Annie Laurie, and for me. Thanks for letting us borrow you. Goodnight child."

It was twilight now, and the lamps were lit at our house.

"I've had such a happy time," I said, as I took my second Christmas out of the basket and put them under my tree.

Suddenly I went into the kitchen and said happily, "Father, the Robin stayed for Christmas. I saw him, as I went over the fence. I was so glad."

My father smiled. "Of course," he said. That wasn't the note of delight I expected and stopped still, and instead of going back to my things, I turned to my father again.

"Why do you say, of course, like that, father?"

"Think, Sweet, you are not thinking. The robin always stays. Like the sunshine, the clouds, the rain. We may not see them each, every day, but they stay. Remember the little verse you used to say."

The north wind shall flow
And we shall have snow
What will poor robin do then?

He will fly to the barn
To keep himself warm,
And hide himself under his wing. Poor thing.

"Oh," I said, "that was why Mr. Earnest winked at Miss Annie, when he said he hoped the robin would stay for Christmas. He said, if we treated him very good, and gave him lots of sugar water and suet and apples and currants, he might stay." I laughed, "Yes, and there's lots of currants for him, plenty for all winter."

I like to think that because of me, something wonderful happened to another little girl before another Christmas came. Mr. Earnest and Miss Annie adopted a little girl. Her name was Ethel. She couldn't have been given to nicer people. She was a lucky little girl.

The little tree lives in memory of a perfect Christmas day. I think of it as Wordsworth did the daffodils. "The picture comes back again and again," and brings to my mind a feeling of happiness.

THE END

A FAIRY, TINY AS A MOUSE

A fairy, tiny as a mouse
Once lived inside a toadstool house
Though it was pretty as could be
Close by a mossy maple tree.
Alas, alack as stories say
She was unhappy anyway.

She let her little fire go out
And she sat down by the hearth to pout.
She said, "I'm tired of looking neat and fine
And seeing that my crown's a shine."
So she jumped up from her pout
And slammed the door as she went out.

The night was very dark and blue
And the wind kept saying "woooo, woooo."
She whispered "Witches they're about,
Because tonight is Halloween
Oh, I must run and not be seen.
They would change me into something big
Perhaps an ugly grunting pig.

She crept right in a hollow tree
And found a witch as small as she.
She was inside a witch's room,
She saw a pot, a cat, a broom,
And she thought her little heart beat fast.
She stopped and stood aghast.

For though it seemed hard to believe
The witch was crying in her sleeve.
Then looking up the witch said, "Ho!"
A fairy of all things that grow.
Oh, I'm tired of going around and bumping my head,
At hours when I should be in bed.

I'm tired of all this witchery.
So the fairy said, "I know, I have a house
It's bright and new
And just big enough for two."
And so the witch forgot to weep
And both of them went home to sleep.

They live there still and some fall night
Perhaps you'll see their tiny light
Deep in the dew and dark and grass
And you will know the fairy tiny as a mouse
And the witch as small as ever she,
Home lit their fire to make their tea.

THE END

JUST FOR YOU

I do believe that God above
Picked you out for me to love.
He picked you out from all the rest,
Because he knew I loved you best.

I once had a heart so brave and true
But now it has gone from me to you
So treat it kind as I have done,
For now you have two and I have none.

If I get to heaven before you are there,
I'll paint your face on the golden stair.
I'll paint it so all the angels can see
Exactly what you mean to me.

And if you're not there on Judgment day
I'll know you went the other way
So I'll give the angels back their halos and wings to show you what I'd do for you.
I'd go down those stairs dear, just to be with you.

THE END

MRS. PUSSINS

Once there was an old lady cat, and her name was Mrs. Pussins. Now Mrs. Pussins had three children, Tommy and the twins. Mrs. Pussins loved the twins dearly, but Tommy was her pride and joy because he looked so much like his dear father, and for this reason she sang him to sleep every night while the twins took their candles and went to bed.

Now one day Mrs. Pussins had to go to the market to get some fish for dinner and she said to the twins, "Take good care of Tommy," and they promised her they would.

After Mrs. Pussins left, they put on Tommy's little blue snow suit and buttoned every white button neatly. They put on his cap and tied it beneath his chin, put on his mittens and his boots to keep his feet warm. It was a cold day though sunshiny, so they started for their walk. Now Jack and Polly Somers wee swinging on their gate, and do you know what they did?

They tied a string to a tin can and tied the other end to little baby kitty-puss Tommy's tail. The twins couldn't get it off and Tommy kept crying, "Take it off, take it off!"

After a while they got him home and called the doctor. The doctor cut the string, and bandaged up his tail real neatly and gave him little pills to take every hour by the clock. By this time Mrs. Pussins was home and the doctor advised her to move out of that neighborhood as quickly as possible for he didn't know that Jack and Polly Somers could be such bad children.

So bright and early in the morning before anyone else was awake they started for the country. They found a little house and moved right in. Tall flowers grew by the little house and there were white ruffey puffey curtains at the windows.

Here Mrs. Pussins and the twins and baby kitty-puss Tommy lived in happiness forever after.

THE END

CURLS, BEFORE PERMANENTS

Twilight, and Sallie nestled close
Mother make curls for tomorrow
So, taking the shining strands of gold
She wound them on rags and tied to hold.

Hair twisted up in rag curls
Promise, of beauty to be
Fresh little faces, eyes of blue
Tomorrow a halo of curls for you.

THE END

THE MAGIC DOLL

Once upon a time, there was a little girl and her name was "Jennie", just like yours. On Sunday morning, her mother got her all ready for Sunday school and told her to sit on the front steps until she finished dressing. This morning her mother was slow getting ready, so Jennie got up and walked around the house, picking a flower here and there. She wandered out the back gate and into the woods as she kept on picking a violet here and a violet there.

All at once, she looked around and realized that she was lost. She began to cry, sat down on a large stone, and sobbed,

"Oh, I'm lost and I don't know how to get back."

Just then she heard a sweet voice say, "What is the matter little girl, why are you crying?"

Though Jennie didn't know it this lovely person was a fairy. She was dressed all in pale shimmering blue and silver, and in her hand was a fairy's wand and on her head was a crown of pearls and diamonds, shinning in the sun that made lacework through the tees, she was standing right in a sunbeam.

"I'm lost," sobbed Jennie, "I'm lost and I want to go home." And she cried and cried.

"Now dear," said the fairy, "If you will do me one little favor, I will see that you get home and a present too. Under that stone on which you are sitting there are steps which go down and at the bottom is a little room. In the little room is a golden chest, and on top of it is one green stone. Pick it up to bring to me and then open the chest, lift the present out and it will be your very own."

So she waved the stone away after Jennie got up and there were the stairs going down. She went down picked up the green stone put it in her pinafore pocket, then opened the chest. Inside there was a large doll, all gold, her dress was gold, her hair was gold, her high heel slippers and her stockings were all gold.

She drew in her breath at all the beauty and lifted her up in her arms, closed the lid and went back up the stairs. "Did you bring the green stone?" asked the fairy.

"Yes, here it is," Jennie said taking it out of her pocket.

"Now," said the fairy, "the golden doll is a magic doll, and whenever you want anything all you have to do is hold her tight and wish, and right away the wish comes true."

"Oh," said Jennie, "I wish I was home sitting on my front steps." And right away she was.

Her mother called, "I'm almost ready."

But first Jennie went up to her room and put the golden doll away and forever after when she wanted something very bad, she held the magic doll close to her heart and said,

"I wish,"

and

the

wish

came

true.

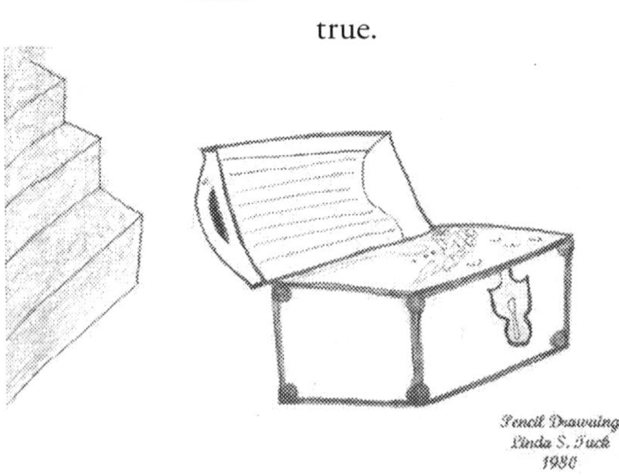

THE END

THE LITTLE DOG WHO COULD SAY MAMA

One there was a little girl and her name was Anne. She had a big mother dog and the mother dog had some puppies, four. Three of them were fluffy and white but the other one was little and skinny and brown with spots.

Now Anne loved the three pretty ones and cuddled them all the day while the little brown one just stood there with his head on one side and wished. He wished for love and cuddling and that made him have a lonesome feeling.

When Anne brought the big bowls of oyster soup made with butter and milk and some little squares of beefsteak and melted cheese he just took a little taste but he couldn't eat. He thought to himself, "Nobody loves me even my mother probably wishes that I was white and fluffy."

So he decided to run away! He ran and he ran and he ran down the road until finally he got so tired, he stopped running and began to walk, slowly.. slowly..slowly. He was so hungry now. His little appetite was saying, "I want to eat, I want to eat."

He came to a trash pile and he scratched around and he scratched around until he found a little piece of dried up sausage. It didn't taste good so he scratched around some more. He found a little round piece of something and he bit into it. It wasn't too hard so he swallowed it whole. He was so hungry.

Do you know what that was? A "Mama" box out of an old doll baby.

Now he was really tired and homesick too. He longed for his mother. He wanted to get close to her and snuggle. He was sure now that she loved him, and he felt sure Anne loved him too.

So he started back. He ran and ran and he ran, after a while he slowed down and walked slowly...slowly...slowly. Then he ran some more and got home just as Anne was bringing out supper. Oyster soup, little squares of beefsteak, melted cheese. He ate and ate and ate it tasted so good. He was in such a hurry that he dropped a little square of beefsteak out of his mouth and as he leaned over to pick it up he said, "Mama, Mama."

Anne ran to him and picked him up and held him close to her heart. "Oh, darling I didn't know you could talk. I love you, I love you."

It was music to his little ears. So she went in and got him extra milk, extra melted cheese, and four more little squares of beefsteak. Ever after this, he was happy, for everyone loved him and he loved every one.

THE END

HENRY PUTS HIS TOYS AWAY

June l, Henry is 8

Flowers of the fields with petals thin
Lilies that neither toil or spin
And tuft of wayside weed.
Tales of a Wayside
Henry Wadsworth Longfellow

The small group walked slowly in the Sunday morning sunshine to the Meeting House, all dressed in their best. There had been talk of rain earlier and the children's father had asked his son Stephen to check the Almanac. He always left early to see that the Meeting House was in order for the service. Stephen finally found the Almanac, on the sofa where Ann had been doing her copying, and her papers were still inside. She had been trying to draw the small pictures of birds, fish and small animals.

The Almanac said for Portland, Maine, the day would be bright and sunny, with temperature at noon, ninety degrees, so someone's forecast of rain had been untrue.

Chorus of Birds
Pandora
Henry Walworth Longfellow
Every flutter of the wings
Every note of song we sing
Every murmur, everywhere
Is of love and love alone.

The mother and children walked on, Stephen 10, Henry 8, Elizabeth 6 and Ann 5. Baby Alexander was home with Mammy Sue.

They were hurrying now, a little for the bell was going to ring soon. The birds sang their songs of love from the fields and trees, this beautiful Sabbath morning.

They passed a field, tangled with daisies and purple clover, and Henry stopped to pick a few to add to the little bunch of flowers that he was carrying. He had picked them in his grandmother's garden while waiting for his mother to finish the conversation and resume their walk. He had a spray of clematis, two white lilies, a spray of bridal wreath, and some small white roses.

"Now children, sit very quietly in the Meeting. Refrain from reading the hymn book, and Stephen, do not keep turning around looking for your friends. Sit still, look straight at the preacher and listen to the words of wisdom."

"Does he know more than father?" asked Ann.

"Of course not," Elizabeth, called Betsey, answered, "How could he?"

"Mother," Stephen said. "Are you going to let Henry take that bunch of weeds into church?"

"Be quiet, Stephen, I will attend to Henry. Daisies and clover are flower weeds and very beautiful, just as the buttercups and bluebells and wild violets are." Mother said.

"I like the Goldenrod in autumn," Stephen replied, "Is that a flower weed too? Is Honeysuckle a flower? Henry is getting some of that now."

"Yes, Stephen, that is so," Mother said, "Honeysuckle is a lovely wild vine and I wouldn't degrade it by calling it a weed. There is pink Honeysuckle as well as white. It grew around our porch when I was a little girl, and my mother said it was a reason for being glad that we were living. Perhaps Henry—," she paused and then continued dreamily, "It grew so thickly that the birds made their nests there and sang their lullabies. The baby birds were so precious."

Henry came running to catch up, holding tightly to his small bouquet.

Now they entered a small stretch of woodland and all were grateful for the shade. Henry took the advantage of this to gather some short fronds of lacy woods fern to put on the outside of his bouquet, like a frame and held it in front of himself to admire the look of greenness in contrast with the flower colors.

They had almost reached the Meeting House now and as they entered the grounds and looked up, the small building looked so pretty. It was painted white and the many small panes of glass that made the large windows sparkled in the sunshine. The last note of the first bell was in the air. In five minutes it would ring again.

The Meeting House was in a grove of trees. At one side were the graves of Portland citizens, resting for eternity.

"Henry dear," Mother said "I don t think it is the correct thing for a little boy to take flowers into the church, maybe...."

Henry put the bouquet to his nose and inhaled deeply, and then withdrew a long stemmed daisy. "I will tie them together with this daisy stem, and—," He said

"Yes," Mother said. "You can make a double tie. Daisy stems are very strong."

"Mother," he said. "Will you wait here in the shade, I will hurry."

Henry walked to a little grave with a small headstone. He parted the ivy on the small grave and put his flowers between the leaves. He started to turn away then knelt down to rearrange the flowers so that the small white Roses were in the center. He patted them softly and went back to the group in the shade of an elm tree.

His mother put her hand ever so lightly on his curly chestnut hair, "That was very kind of you, Henry," she said.

"Mother," Henry said, "Her name was Baby Bessie, and she was one."

"Yes dear, she is with the angels. Come on, let's not be late," Mother said.

Childhood is the bough, where slumbered
Buds and blossoms many numbered.
Maidenhood
Henry Wadsworth Longfellow

August 1, Henry is 9

And the song from beginning to end
I found again in the heart of a friend.
The Arrow and the Song
Henry Wadsworth Longfellow

After supper was over and before the reading hour came on, it was the children's way to sit on the porch steps and discuss things that concerned them. Betsey and Ann put in their little opinions with the boys.

One question they pondered was - If you had to give up everything else on earth and could have only one thing, which would you choose?

"I'll be first tonight," Stephen said. "My friends, I would die without them."

Henry thought for a second, "Mother."

"Betsey?" Stephen questioned.

"I don't know," she said. "Why do you ask such bad questions, Stephen? It isn't fair."

When Stephen pointed at Ann, she said, "I suppose my dolls."

"Oh well," Stephen said. "That wasn't much fun anyway. Here's another. Name four people outside our own family that you like the best?"

"The best of all? I only have two best friends. May and Lucy Courtney." said Betsey.

"I like my four dolls best. May and Lucy are Betsey's friends," said Ann who looked ready to cry.

"That's six Ann," Stephen said "Well, Henry?"

"You haven't named yours yet, Stephen," Henry said.

"Oh, I like Tom the very best, then Jack and Vance, and I like Mr. Bowers, the blacksmith. He is a very nice man, always has time to talk and he lets me do things around his forge. He lets me blow the bellows to start the fire again." Stephen said

Henry had been thinking, and now he had them ready when Stephen pointed to him this time. "I like Ben Black, because he is my best friend. We watch the ships come in together and we fish from the bank and then I like Joe Brown. He is my second best friend and I like Aunt Flossie and Uncle Joe."

All the children looked at Henry and there was a short astounded silence.

"But Henry," said Betsy. "All your friends are colored people!"

"I know," he conceded happily. "They are the nicest. That is why I like them best."

Aunt Flossie does make good gingerbread and Uncle Joe can whittle anything, Stephen mused thoughtfully.

"Children," their mother called, "The day is ending and Father is ready to read now."

Then, when tranquil evening throws twilight shades above you,
think on those who love you
To Ianthe
Henry Wadsworth Longfellow

October 1, Henry is still 9

Burn, Oh evening hearth and Waken
Pleasant visions of old.
Though the house by wind is shaken
Safe keep this room of gold.
The Bridge of Cloud
Henry Wadsworth Longfellow

It was Sunday evening. The family had just finished singing hymns, with Mother playing the piano and Father, the flute.

Stephen was now hitting one key after another and saying, "I wish I could play like Mother. I think I will ask her to teach me. It's so nice we have a piano. When we got this one, Father said it was the first one in Portland."

"The very first," questioned Betsey?

"That's what I said," Stephen replied "now there are—."

Henry spoke suddenly, "I will ask Father to teach me the flute. It sings so, like birds."

"Stephen," Mother called, "close the piano gently. I am ready to go to the meeting now. Father left a few minutes ago."

She came into the room quickly and looked expectantly at the children.

"Do you have your verses ready? I hope they are new ones. Repetition shows a lack of interest and also inconsideration to the ones who are listening each week. Come, time and tide, you know."

"Yes, Mother," Stephen smiled. "we know, they wait for no one."

There was a short session before the regular service for the young people. It was held in a small room and one of the Fathers took charge each Sunday evening. The service started with a hymn and this evening it was "Safely through another week, God has brought us on our way."

Mr. Vance explained that it had been written by a minister, the Reverend John Newton in 1779. They all sang the hymn, but at other times it was read. Tonight Mr. Vance chose to read it, all verses.

Henry liked the last words. "Day of all the week the best, Emblem of eternal rest."

"Now we will have our verses."

"Stephen?"

Stephen rose quickly, "Jesus wept."

"Yes." said Mr. Vance.

"Henry?"

"God is love."

"Yes, we all see the manifestations of his love all around us. Thank you, Henry."

A few more boys and girls were called upon. Mr. Vance said a short prayer, a short benediction and the meeting was over.

"Stephen?"

"Yes, Mr. Vance."

"I would like a word with you and Henry."

The other children went out to the adult meeting, and Mr. Vance, holding up a book asked quietly, "Stephen, what is this book I hold in my hands?"

"The Bible, sir."

"Yes, and it is a very large book, isn't it?"

"Yes Sir."

"Now there are lots or Chapters in this Bible and in every one a considerable number of verses. Stephen, don't you think you could find one a little longer for us next Sunday, and Henry it would be nice to lengthen yours somewhat."

"Yes Sir."

"Go into the meeting now boys and may God bless you always."

Safely through another week the family lived and the next Sunday evening, all were again at the Meeting House. The weather was pleasant, and the day had gone by so fast. Meeting was about to begin.

Another man, Mr. John Price was leading tonight, but Mr. Vance was present. He loved all children, but unfortunately he had none of his own.

The hymn which everyone joined in singing was, *Come thou Almighty King, Help us Thy name to sing.*

"This hymn," Mr. Price said, "was written by Reverend Charles Wesley in 1757."

Everyone knew this one and sang loudly all the way to the closing Amen.

"Now we will have our verses," he said.

Most of the young people took great pride in their selections, and it was a pleasure to hear them. It was not easy to learn a long verse, with all their studies and chores to be during the week, but most succeeded very well.

"Now, Henry, What do you have for us?"

"A word fitly spoken is like apples of gold in a setting of silver, Proverbs 25th Chapter, 11th verse."

"Stephen?"

All week Stephen had been studying a long verse but at the calling of has name, it left his mind completely. The truth was, he had not learned it well enough, or maybe too well. That will happen sometime.

So, he rose slowly and said. "God is love."

"Yes, that is one of the most beautiful in the Bible. Let us pray."

Lives of great men all remind us
We can make our lives sublime.
Psalm of life
Henry Wadsworth Longfellow

April, Henry is 10

Between the dark and the daylight
When the night is beginning to lower
Comes a pause in the day's occupation
That is known as the Children's hour.
The Children's Hour
Henry Wadsworth Longfellow

Early in the evenings, shortly after supper and before the children were tired from the days study, play and chores, there was a reading in the sitting room.

This room was a very pleasant place. A red carpet, with a geometric pattern in darker red and shades of blue, green, brown and gold covered the floor. The furniture was heavy mahogany and well polished, the sofa was so comfortable, and the back so beautifully carved, and covered with gold velvet gave the charm of antique grace to the room. The wing chairs by the lit fireplace made it all so homey. A loved and used room.

There was an air of lovely reserve about this room, of gentle living and happiness. Quite a few pictures adorned the walls and a great number of books filled the bookcases.

On the mantle were candlesticks of silver, a large pink shell, and of course the clock, which musically struck the hours and half hours. At each end of the mantle was a sandstone vase filled with trailing ivy. It was one of little Betsey's chores to keep this ivy fresh.

The children's Father came in quietly and said good evening to the boys and girls. He was tall with a courtly manner of moving and speaking. He received respect from all and gave respect to all family, friends, servants, and children. A handsome gentleman, whose good looks the boys of the family inherited. The girls resembled their mother, brown hair, shading to gold and brown eyes.

Now both brown eyes and blue looked expectantly at their father, as he began to read. The children's hour closed both a poem and now it was that time, and Father closed the book and recited from memory.

"Look to this day," he began,

"For it is life, the very life of life

In its brief course, lie all the verities and realities of your existence

The bliss of growth

The glory of action

The splendor of beauty.

For yesterday is but a dream and tomorrow is only a vision

But today, well lived, will make every yesterday a dream or happiness, and every tomorrow a dream of hope

Look well, therefore, to this day.

Such is the Salutation to the dawn."

"That was written by the Indian dramatist Kalidasa a very long time ago. Now, can anyone tell me the meaning of this poem? Betsey stop tickling your sister. Stephen?"

"I'm afraid not, Father. Perhaps if you read it over again." he said.

"Henry?"

"Yes sir," Henry spoke, "It says, do your best, your very best and do it every day."

"That is correct." Father replied.

The children left the room, and the mother said softly, "Stephen, dear, don't you sometimes think that your reading matter is a little too deep for childish minds. Salutation to the Dawn is a bit scholarly. Perhaps some well chosen stories or poems that tell a story."

"I will next time to please you Zilpah," he said. "I will choose differently for tomorrow evening. But, don't you think Henry did get the meaning quite well, in his summing up of *The Salutation*. I am very proud of him."

"Yes, I do," she said meditatively, "I think we will always be proud of Henry, but I worry about him a little too."

"Why?" he asked surprised.

"Well," she said, "Yesterday he told me that a boy had made fun of his name."

"Of Henry?"

"No, the Longfellow part. The boy said it reminded him of something one wears in the wintertime. You'll laugh Stephen, I did myself. I told Henry that to just gallantly lift his head high and walk on was best."

Then Stephen said, "Mother, I'm afraid you don't understand. Boys who tease won't let you walk on. They hit you and you have to fight. Did Henry fight the boy," Stephen asked?

"Not really," she said. "The boy hit Henry and Henry hit the boy, but it ended there. Henry said it was of no consequence. I asked Henry later what was the boy's last name, and he said it was Green."

"Oh well," said the Father "Henry was right, it was of no consequence."

"Come out on the porch, Zilpah, and let's look at the stars."

July, Henry is still 10

The Hanging of the Crane
Henry Wordsworth Longfellow
Upon the polished silver shone
The evening lamp, but more divine
The light of love shines over all
Of love that says, not mine and thine
But ours, for ours thine and mine.

After the children had gone to bed that evening, the mother came down into the sitting room. The Father looked up and closed the book that he had been reading.

When Henry's mother entered a room, one was aware of a true stateliness, an aristocratic presence. This was wholly independent of education or riches. It was an inborn love of the rightness of being here on earth and being happy about it. Her brown eyes had a clear intelligent expression and the golden brown hair combined to make a beautiful woman.

Stephen looked at her with love. He knew Zilpah wished to speak of something. They were together in mind and heart.

"What is it, Zilpah?"

"Stephen, I think Henry is different from the other children. He—."

"Yes. Dear?"

"Tonight he told me that he would hate to die and leave all the words."

"Words?"

"Yes, the beautiful words, he said, home, mother, heaven, meadow, tree, shell, flower all the words."

"We have read to the children a lot, Zilpah, perhaps we…."

Zilpah said sitting down, dreamily, on the gold sofa, "I think Henry will be a weaver."

Her husband turned from mending the fire in extreme surprise. "A weaver, dear?"

"Yes, a weaver of words. A weaver of dreams, you might say. I feel that Henry will be eminent and the world will know that he has lived."

"That will be very gratifying, Zilpah. Did you fill the gray cat's milk saucer? She seems to have a strong appetite just now, without waiting for an answer, he went to do the chore himself."

Henry's mother sat by the fireplace, dreaming. She said softly to herself. "My little Henry."

See the fire is burning low
Dusky red the embers glow

Sang the blackened tongs a tune
Learned in some forgotten June
The Wind in the Chimney
Henry Wadsworth Longfellow

Another August, Henry is 11

Stars of a summer night
Far in yon azure deep.
The Spanish Student
Henry Wadsworth Longfellow

The long hot summer day was deepening into twilight. Baby Alexander, Betsey and Ann had been put to bed, and Stephen and Henry were sitting on the top porch step, with the basket of kittens beside them. The gray mother cat sat on the bottom step, enjoying a moment's reprieve from the demands of motherhood.

"Which one do you like the best," Henry asked of Stephen?

"I like them all. Too bad they have to live in the barn."

"Well, we couldn't have them in our house, and I think they like the barn alright."

The boy's father came out and sat down in a rocking chair. "The day is done, boys. How pleasant it is this evening. Zilpah, come rest a while. The twilight is so beautiful."

"What have you boys been conversing about?"

"The kittens, but before that about what we want to be when we grow up. I shall be a lawyer, but Henry doesn't know yet." spoke Stephen.

"There's plenty of time. Oh, there come the stars," Father said, "Look boys, Zilpah!"

They looked up and the stars seemed to be appearing one by one, here, there, directly overhead and suddenly the whole sky was starlet.

"Stars of a summer evening." Henry looked at his mother as she spoke.

"Mother, sometimes when you say things, it sounds like poetry, instead of words." Henry said.

"Poetry is words. Henry."

"Henry," Stephen slapped him on the back knocking him off the steps. "You could be a poet," he laughed loudly. "Maybe you're a poet and don't know it. Maybe I'm one myself. I can rhyme, star with far."

Henry answered, thoughtfully. "Perhaps, I"

"Imagine," interrupted Stephen, "Hen will be a poet, Shades of Shakespeare!"

"Now Stephen," Father spoke "Henry is your brother's name."

Father got up and looked again at the sky. "Yes, Zilpah, that was a lovely line, stars of a summer night, as beautiful as the sky above us."

The calm majestic presence of the night.
Hymn to the Night

Henry Wadsworth Longfellow
Take this lesson to the heart
That is best, which lies nearest
Shape from that, they work of art.
Gaspar Becura
Henry Walworth Longfellow

After the boys were in bed, their mother went in to say goodnight.

"Mother, do you think Henry could ever be a poet, a real one?"

"He could perhaps be one, Stephen. He loves beauty and he loves words."

Henry was listening. "There are plenty of words. Perhaps I shall try tomorrow. And the words are all your very own, everyone of them. Until the day I die." Henry marveled sleepily.

"Yes," Mother said, "they are all yours, forever Henry. Goodnight boys."

Before she left the room, she opened a drawer and put a sheaf of white paper on the table, with the inkwell and pen beside it.

The summer breeze blew the sheer curtains inward and the light from the stars and moonlight made a huge Jewel of the cut glass inkwell.

In the morning, it was the first thing Henry saw when he awakened.

A youthe was there of quiet ways
A student of old books and ways
And yet a friend of solitude.
Tales of a Wayside Inn
Henry Walworth Longfellow

End of a summer, Henry is almost 12

How beautiful is the rain
After the dust and heat.
Rain in Summer
Henry Wadsworth Longfellow
The rain, the welcome rain.
Henry Wadsworth Longfellow

It was raining, and the children were enjoying it in their own way.

Betsey and Ann were playing in the attic. Alexander's mammy took him off for a nap. Stephen had some of his friends up in the barn loft.

Henry was almost twelve. Just a few more months now, and he had decided to put his toys away. He wrapped his tin soldiers carefully and put them in a box. The books of childhood he piled on the closet shelf in his room, and his drum he wrapped securely in paper, and was putting it on the top shelf when it fell and the reverberation soundly loudly in the room.

Oh, I do hope I haven't disturbed Mother and the baby, he thought. He picked up the drum and pushed it away back in his closet on the floor in the darkness. He had loved his drum. His Father had brought it to him as a present when he had returned from a trip. Henry was eight then, and there had also been a Bible with his name in gold, a second gift. Ann and Betsey he brought dolls. He had forgotten what Stephen and Alexander's presents were, perhaps books. His Father brought lots of books for presents.

I know Sammy will love the drum best. Henry's little brother was only five days old, so the toys would have to wait quite a while, before being played with again.

Tis the heaven of flowers you see there
All the wild flowers of the forest
All the lilies of the prairie
When on earth they fade and perish
Blossom in that heaven above us.
Hiawatha
Henry Wadsworth Longfellow

Henry went quietly into his mother's room and looked at the sleeping baby by her side, so tiny, his little brother.

"Well, Henry," Mother spoke softly, "what have you been doing this rainy afternoon?

"I have been looking out the window at the rain. The wind has almost torn the ivy off of the stone wall, but how beautiful and green everything looks. Some people say the rain makes them sad but to me, it is as lovely as the sunshine." Mother's voice went on low and pleasant. She smiled at Henry. "Perhaps those people have heard the saying, into each life some rain must fall. All days can't be beautiful and sunny and we wouldn't want life that way. Contrast makes beauty."

"Mother?"

"Yes, Henry."

"Mother, I put all my toys away today to keep for Sammy."

"Samuel, Dear. You know our rule about shortening given names."

"But, Mother, we do all call Elizabeth, Betsey."

"I know, your Father, conceded that. She is such a dear little girl, and she has all her grown up life to be Elizabeth, but for our boys, it is more manly to use the full name. You really wouldn't like to be called Hen, or Harry would you?"

Henry laughed with his mother. "No, Mother I would not like that, or for Stephen to be called Steve or Alexander, Alec."

Henry walked over to one of the large windows. The rain seemed to be clearing and a radiance was over everything.

"Mother, is there always a rainbow after rain?"

"Not always, Henry, only sometimes."

"Yes, Mother, I've put them all away for Samuel, for Alexander has lots of toys and a new drum, so he doesn't need them. I put my books away for him too."

"That is very kind of you, Henry. My wish is that Samuel will be as kind a boy as his brother Henry."

Henry looked out the window again. The rain was still falling, but gently and the radiance remained. It was on the rose garden now.

"Mother, just as soon as the rain is over, I am going to pick you and Samuel a big bunch of roses."

Suddenly he turned to his mother, his face alight.

"Mother, there's a rainbow, no," he said unbelieving, "there are two rainbows over the gardens."

"Yes, sometimes that is the way, double beauty, double promise."

"The colors are fading now, paler, very pale, but still so beautiful. Oh, how lovely it was."

"Henry, there is a beautiful Indian legend about the rainbow. They believed that when the flowers on earth fade and perish they blossom again in the heavens above, and that is why the colors or the rainbow are so lovely."

"That is a nice legend, Mother. I will go and pick the roses now."

Henry's mother held her new baby close to her heart, but the name she whispered was very softly – Henry, Henry Wadsworth Longfellow.

Yes, the book will look very nice, gold on blue. When the Father, Stephen, came in a few minutes later, and saw Zilpah and the baby were sleeping, he noticed the look of love and contentment on her face.

Yes, the new baby has made Zilpah very happy and more beautiful than ever, he thought. He tiptoed softly out of the room and noiselessly closed the door.

THE END

****

Henry was always one of Effie's favorites...